Don't be fooled again

Lessons in the good, bad and
unpredictable behaviour of global finance

Meyrick Chapman

 Prentice Hall
FINANCIAL TIMES

An imprint of Pearson Education

London ∎ New York ∎ San Francisco ∎ Toronto ∎ Sydney ∎ Tokyo ∎ Singapore
Hong Kong ∎ Cape Town ∎ Madrid ∎ Paris ∎ Milan ∎ Munich ∎ Amsterdam

PEARSON EDUCATION LIMITED

Edinburgh Gate
Harlow CM20 2JE
Tel: +44 (0)1279 623623
Fax: +44 (0)1279 431059
Website: www.pearsoned.co.uk

First published in Great Britain in 2010

ISBN: 978 0 273 372789 7

British Library Cataloguing-in-Publication Data
A catalogue record for this book is available from the British Library

Library of Congress Cataloging-in-Publication Data
A catalog record for this book is available from the Library of Congress

10 9 8 7 6 5 4 3 2 1
14 13 12 11 10

Set by 3 in 9.5pt Melior
Printed and bound in Great Britain by Ashford Colour Press Ltd, Gosport, Hants

The publisher's policy is to use paper manufactured from sustainable forests.

In memory of Derek Townsend: 1935–2008

'…a quiet life stimulates the creative mind.' Albert Einstein

Contents

Acknowledgements / xiii

1 Introduction / 1

Crises – not all bad / 4

We must have missed something / 6

The never-ending crisis / 12

2 Common features of financial crises, and why we don't see them coming / 15

The broad background / 16

Financial deregulation: doors to opportunity and distress / 18

The magic trick of money / 21

Confusion at the heart of money / 24

The special privileges of banks / 26

Litany of attempts to solve a perennial problem / 28

Asset prices and credit / 29

What were we thinking? / 30

Confused investment and channel capacity / 32

Keep it down! / 32

The basis of market economics: an ability to agree terms / 33

From auction to liquid marketplace / 34

Highly liquid markets create their own money / 35

Technology and the emergence of new value / 35

Logistics and statistics: twins from the same parent / 36

More potential participants increases the market price of an

   asset / 37

Time and investment / 38

Conservative investors: the perfect bubble-blowers / 39

Not exactly classical / 41

The propagation of market crises, even with no prospect of
   default / 42

Why we do not see financial crises coming? / 44

3 Did the Asian crisis teach us nothing? / 46

Asian crisis: first of the globalised era / 47

Wounded Tiger: Thailand and the crisis of 1997–98 / 48

Hedge funds strike it rich / 53

A profound effect on Chinese policy / 55

Aftermath in property: ruin, folly and delusion / 56

Lessons for China / 57

The International Monetary Fund responds / 59

Initial response: support at a price / 60

Sell high, buy other countries low / 61

The aftermath, and what we should have learned / 62

America benefits, but does it learn? / 63

4 Loving the dollar: lessons from the greatest ever
   flood of capital / 68

The shock appearance of money / 70

A trillion-dollar proof against the capitalists / 72

Foreign civil servants oust private investment / 73

The poor lend money to the wealthiest / 74

The unbalanced globe / 76

Crowding out the usual crowd / 78

The slow flow from Japan / 81

'Housewives of Tokyo' disrupt international finance / 82

The 'search for yield' drives Japanese banks abroad / 84

An early global tremor / 85

Japan's capital exports: still more to come / 86

Echoes of Japan in the West / 86

The euro: an exercise in imbalance / 87

Convergence creates its own challenges / 88

Opportunity for second-rate banks / 90

The global meaning of money / 91

5 How central banks lost their grip / 96

Japan's lost decade: a prelude to international disorder / 97

The origins of the Japanese banking crisis / 99

Influence of 'globalisation' on Japan's economy / 99

The Asian crisis, bail-out and a regional disaster / 101

Belated regulation: worse than nothing / 102

Quantitative easing, its wider effect and the flow of
    money / 103

The Fed and the bail-out of Long Term Capital
    Management / 105

LTCM: birth and growth / 106

'Convergence': politics and profit / 107

Beginning of the end / 108

The Fed saves the world / 110

The Greenspan put / 111

Greenspan and dot-com / 113

Greenspan confuses progress with irrationality / 114

A law for financial expansion / 115

Greenspan jumps on the Exuberance Express / 116

Y2K: the crash of optimism version 1.0 / 116

Downturn in the new century / 118

ILoveYou: a new disease / 118

The focus switches / 119

September 2001 / 119

Japan's dark presence / 120

The liquidity generator unleashed / 121

Long-term faith in an American future / 124

In Europe: equal rates for unequal countries / 125

Follow the Fed / 125

Local imbalances / 126

Collusion in liquidity / 127

6 Going fishing: lessons of financial innovation / 128

Why innovation is needed / 129

The dangers of uncritical acceptance of orthodoxy / 131

The risk revolution: innovation for all / 132

Efficiency or avoidance? / 133

Why derivatives are so important / 134

Merton and 'convergence' / 136

Swapping efficiency / 138

Bringing liquidity to the illiquid / 139

What can go wrong? / 140

Lower cost, higher competition / 143

The star innovation of avoidance was securitisation / 144

The downside to securitisation / 147

Staggering growth rates / 148

Working ever faster / 149

The shadow banking system, distorted money and SIVs / 150

Computers change everything / 153

What's the future of financial innovation? / 154

7 In God We Trust: banks and their errors / 157

The bill so far / 158

Tensions arise / 159

Originate and distribute becomes 'originate and hoard' / 160

An era of free money / 162

Why mortgages? / 164

The Great Moderation / 169

We're losing money, buy more bonds! / 170

Originate and distribute, the case of UBS / 171

Subprime securities as 'central bank money' / 173

How to place 'value at risk' / 176

High pay policies / 178

Banks writedowns are loss of Western wealth / 180

8 De-rated: how ratings agencies and regulations failed / 182

Rating agencies: uncontrolled private regulation / 183

Basel I and II: regulatory innovation / 192

The problem with regulations / 195

9 The politics of housing / 198

An unproductive asset / 198

A unique housing model, with familiar results / 199

The politics of home ownership / 200

Clinton's third way: social inclusion and market economics / 202

The overlap of politics and bankers / 204

Beyond domestic politics / 208

A change of politics; a change of subprime / 209

European political distortions in lending / 213

Eurocrats and euro-lending / 215

The politics of tax / 217

Is it the same everywhere? Why some countries boom / 218

But why housing? / 220

Blinded by ratings / 222

The conspiracy of housing finance / 222

10 Why it's not all bad: the costs and benefits of financial crises / 225

The unsustainable has run its course / 229

Dear old Stockholm – and Helsinki / 229

They run, chanting revolution / 231

Not so relaxed: recovery in Thailand / 235

Japan: what recovery? / 238

Where's the good in bubbles and busts? / 240

A complex of crises: 1970 to 2009 / 245

The internet: too early to tell / 248

11 What lessons for the future? / 250

Whose reserves are they anyway? / 253

The future of America / 253

A long-term faith in the new / 255

A never-ending crisis / 257

Challenges to central banks and exporters / 258

A new role for hedge funds / 260

What kind of regulatory change? / 262

Too many crises and yet not enough / 264

Index / 273

Acknowledgements

IF THERE IS GOOD TO COME out of a financial crisis then for me
the tremendous support and assistance I have received in this
project from many people must be counted. The most important
are those closest to me, without whom I would never have begun,
let alone finish what must have been for them an interminable
intrusion.

At the end of 2007 I said to Louise, my wife, I wanted to write a
book about the financial crisis. She was, I thought, surprisingly
enthusiastic. Eighteen months later I am very thankful for that first
encouragement. If Louise ever regretted the suggestion, she did a
good job hiding her regret and remained steadfastly enthusiastic;
reading sections and adding comments throughout the process.
The greatest thanks therefore go to Louise. And for Elliot and
Millie who now have their father to talk to again.

Steve Diggle and I worried together about the excessive risk being
taken in the financial markets from 2005 onwards. Steve went on
to make significant profits for his investors on the back of his
concerns. I would like to thank him for his friendship over the
years and his contribution to my understanding of finance over
nearly twenty years.

I am grateful to UBS AG on two counts; for allowing me to write at
all, an endeavour without any obvious direct benefit for them, and
for the tremendous opportunity it has given me to converse with
some of the best brains in finance. I could not have begun the book
without numerous conversations with colleagues. I would like in
particular to thank Amit Kara and George Magnus for their patient
attentiveness. Their knowledge on the highways – and byways – of
finance was invaluable and their wisdom an inspiration. Both are
economists of the first order and are colleagues I am glad also to
call friends. I am grateful too to Sunil Kapadia whose grasp of

monetary theory will remain way in advance of my own and who offered many interesting and useful leads on the subject.

My daily conversations with Andrew Rowan were also essential to my thoughts: his scientific acuity combined with common sense provided a necessary foil to some of the more harebrained ideas I came up with. Andrew was unfortunate enough to occupy the desk next to me at UBS and so was unable to escape the stream of questions as often as he would wish. It was a trial he bore with the utmost patience and good humour.

I would like also to acknowledge the comments and conversations with others at UBS: Andrew Dennis, David Coombs, Rob Pearson, Andrew MacKenzie, Ruary Neill, Andrew Stuart; and Arnaud Gorge, for his unfailing interest. Also I would like to thank those now no longer at UBS: James Aitken, Richard Ratcliffe, Chris Morrissey. Also Antonio Giampaolo and Karim Abboud, whose first-hand counterparty experience of LTCM was profound. I would also like to thank my friends in the Boys Book Club for listening attentively and offering characteristically well-reasoned and thoughtful insights.

I owe a debt to Mark Pelham and to Ben Sills for encouragement and advice from professional writers and editors and also for Mark's assistance in locating publishers. Finally, and importantly, thanks to my editor at Pearson, Chris Cudmore, for his guidance and for his professional and good-humoured insight.

Introduction

The move of the populations of China and India from poverty to middle-class prosperity should be the great historic achievement of the century.

Freeman Dyson

On first reading you may think there are two problems with this book. First, most people already think they know why the financial crisis happened – it was the bankers. Second, this book itself is written by a banker, and so tainted with the self-interest of the guilty. Let me see if I can overcome both problems.

For most people it is obvious that the important answer to the crisis can be found in the greed and risk that characterised Western banks, particularly those in America and Britain. High risk and greed together created the toxic balance sheets that disrupted the system. Many say that the sooner we limit the possibility of both greed and risk, the better it will be for everyone.

The combination of risk and greed might have been toxic, but I think it is wrong to assume this is a sufficient answer to the problems we have experienced, and the difficulties we continue to face. This may have something to do with my career as a banker, but I think it is more than that. Greed is almost certainly a constant and while some may disagree, I assume the bankers of the past decade were no more greedy than the bankers of earlier generations. There were a lot of them, and they were well paid, but they were not extraordinary. The risk which from September 2008 overwhelmed the financial system of most developed countries, on the other hand, certainly was extraordinary. It is this extraordinary risk which is the defining feature of the crisis, not the greed. Grasping the defining features of how that risk arose is essential to understanding the crisis. Without understanding, there can be no coherent response.

> it is this extraordinary risk which is the defining feature of the crisis, not the greed

I do not deny that incentives worked to encourage the greed, and that there may be useful changes to be made in that area to limit future damage. Largely, but not completely, I leave analysis of the role of bankers to someone else, not because banks are unimportant, but because the story is bigger than banks and bigger than bankers.

The focus of this book is on the areas that I am at least partially qualified to discuss: international capital flows, interest rates and derivatives. I have worked for investment banks for almost twenty-five years. For the first twelve years I mainly worked as a trader and for the remaining years as an investment analyst. This book provides an insider's understanding of what was going on in the financial globe in the past decade or so that led to the current problems. If nothing else, there should be something worth listening to from people who were there, even if it is just a record.

But this book aims at more than simply a record. I have first-hand experience of several of the important episodes that led to the crisis, and that appear in this book. These include the Asian crisis, the demise of Long Term Capital Management (LTCM), the dot-com bust and the extraordinary monetary easing that followed. I also saw at close quarters the effects of the financial crisis on my own bank. Throughout, I have seen the massive flows of foreign capital into the US and other countries such as UK and Spain that directly contributed to the later problems. I have near experience of the mortgage and credit derivative boom that turned into crash. I would not say I am unique, but I have a certain, perhaps slightly frayed, perspective. Chapter by chapter, the book will show how we were led into being 'fooled again', just as others were in the Asian crisis, the bursting bubble in Japan and the demise of Long Term Capital Management.

Don't be fooled again came about as I began to look for an explanation of how the crisis emerged. I had two reasons for wanting to understand. I worked in the European bank that had lost more than any other – UBS – and had lost a modest amount of money myself. I had an incentive to explain to myself how the collapse happened. In the light of my experience, blaming banks alone did not make sense. Banks reveal a set of preferences that society has chosen, they cannot construct an entire social system alone. The problem was always bigger than banks, whatever their shortcomings.

Of course, it is no good writing about the crisis unless there is something useful or interesting to say that has not been said elsewhere. Many of the explanations for the crisis seem deficient. They failed to consider the wider global origins of our financial problems, and they fail also to discuss the technical and social character of both the boom and the bust, plus the role of regulators. Many of these issues remain taboo and so most of the solutions currently proposed are framed without a broad understanding of the nature of the problem they seek to address. If the analysis is deficient, it is almost certain the remedy also will be deficient. That will be bad for everyone in the long run.

Then there was also the fact that the near-collapse of Western finance (in which my own company was to play a significant bit-part) was easily the most important historical event of which I had personal experience. It was a kind of duty to try to capture, and correct, a point of view about the forces at work that would contribute to a broader understanding than the one that had become popular.

the crisis had its origin not in finance per se, but in global capital flows

From the start, I knew the crisis had its origin not in finance per se, but in global capital flows. Although some banks and some countries were affected worse than others, the global background, while not ignored, seemed to me to be considered much less deeply than it should by commentators. Key themes were missing. For instance, the present crisis seemed (to me) directly linked to problems that began around 1990, and progressed through Japan, Asia, Russia, dot-com, mortgage lending and then the global economy. It has engulfed developed and emerging economies. Why was this? How could there be such a long line of financial crises and did they have a common cause, or evident links between them? If this had been with us for so long, how was it we had missed this till we were ourselves engulfed? That is the theme of this book.

The theme I detect behind the crisis is globalisation in various forms. The tools that created the crisis were more specific; technological prowess, the ascendency of the US, mistakes by central banks and regulators, and a misunderstanding about the limitations of investment.

Of course it is a cautionary tale, but it is not a tale with a neat ending. There are more beneficial aspects of modern life that seem to have contributed to the crisis than we could usefully dispense with. Along the way, I will consider the possibility that there may be some good from the current distress. The suggestion that something beneficial can come from a crisis probably needs more explanation.

Crises – not all bad

Crises are different. Something extraordinary happens. The dates and even individual days of crises are lodged in the public mind – September 11, for instance. Universally, crises in the English language are remembered as bad.

Yet, the word 'crisis' has less dramatic origins. The English word derives from the ancient Greek κρινω meaning to judge, to separate, or to choose. A crisis is a 'decision-time', a fork in the road, a time to follow a new path. While there is no such thing as a 'good crisis' in English, in the original Greek the word could suggest qualities such as awareness of errors and a determination to change; meanings that could be neutral, and perhaps positive. Crises are not separate from everyday life after all, but are an outgrowth from everyday life that is itself evolving, sometimes abruptly. Crises represent an extreme form of everyday change. I certainly see the current financial crisis as an outgrowth of the way the world has been put together over the past twenty years or so; it was in a sense always likely, if not inevitable, and the form it took was decided by specific events.

> ## the credit crunch has affected more countries and many more people than the Wall Street Crash of 1929

The credit crunch has affected more countries and many more people than the Wall Street Crash of 1929 ever did. The speed of the economic decline has taken almost everyone by surprise, even those who foresaw problems ahead. Yet this is a symptom of how our modern world works. The passage of time may reveal that what was thought of as so disastrous was later interpreted as an aspect of some other development, possibly even leading to, or stemming from, generally positive developments. There seem to me to be some aspects to the current financial crisis that may be so interpreted. A secondary purpose of this book is to estimate the scale and implications of the crisis, including possible benefits that have emerged from crises in the past.

What might these benefits be? Often the recovery from a financial crisis, which might have destroyed old ways, has, over time, delivered new and better ways of doing things. The last financial crisis in Europe occurred in Scandinavia in 1989/91. At the time it was thought to have brought only destruction, yet that crisis was responsible for the rise of Scandinavia as a world force in mobile telephony and software. It changed the way Finland in particular worked, and increased the self-confidence of the Finnish people to unforseen levels. The forces behind the changes in Finland are still active. The networked world we now inhabit throws up opportunities for experimentation over a vast number of products. Just about all of what we consume is translated into information value of some sort. The spread of information processing is far from over and the opportunities that grow with it are just as far from over. The long-term effects of the Scandinavian financial crisis therefore changed some things to the good. We should not deny that disruption can lead to future benefits.

The most important cause of the 2007 crash was the long-running financing imbalances in the world, between exporting countries and those that consumed, particularly between the US and China. Benefits will certainly flow in the short term from the world adjusting to a better balance of trade. The imbalance will probably not survive, in its previous form. A move to a balance in trade should be viewed as a benefit compared with what went before. Such a balance may also provide new opportunities for both emerging and developed worlds.

Nor should we dismiss the idea that the calamity that has befallen the West might have been an accompaniment to some broader, positive trend. It is always easier to discern bad things as being separate from good, but life may be more complex than that. There may be benefits stemming from the same forces that helped shape the deep recession we are suffering; the 'dark side' we all wish would go away may be a consequence of other, brighter aspects of modern life. It may not be possible to gain from one without suffering from the other. The suffering will pass, leaving the benefits that preceded and succeed it. Radical change is often associated with radical disruption. Radical disruption is exactly true of the technological benefits we take for granted, yet which are a key component of the crisis.

We must have missed something

J. K. Galbraith, who wrote perhaps the most well-known explanation of the 1929 Wall Street Crash, blamed excessive speculation for the boom, and the bust of 1929:

> 'The collapse of the stock market in the autumn of 1929 was implicit in the speculation that went before. The only question concerning that speculation was how long it would last. Sometime, sooner or later, confidence in the short-run reality of

increasing common stock values would weaken. When this happened, some people would sell, and this would destroy the reality of increasing values... There would be a rush, pell-mell to unload. This was the way past speculative orgies had ended. It was the way the end came in 1929. It is the way speculation will end in the future.'[1]

the crisis was a morality tale about how little humans learn

Was the current crisis really all about speculation? Was it really about the repeat of some formula for disaster that cannot be escaped? Pessimists say that nothing changes and that we are destined to repeat mistakes. The crisis was a morality tale about how little humans learn. There is certainly a link between the crises that have dogged the past twenty years of global finance, but each has its peculiarities. Some of the causes are common, some are unique. I want to tease out both common and unique.

Another one of Galbraith's sayings was that finance 'hails the invention of the wheel over and over again, often in a slightly more unstable version'. I disagree; the results of the present crisis were a combination of particular events that, under a slightly different configuration, might have progressed without disruption perhaps for many more years. The fact that these events led to failure was due not to the lack of learning but to the unique circumstances of international capital flows in the late twentieth and early twenty-first centuries. I am not engaged in a defence of bankers, but the crisis is a geo-political event, involving technological change and changing power in the world. Although I do not aim to delve too deeply into the politics, it, too, is an undercurrent that informs much of the story.

Unfortunately, even important members of the Western establishment still seem keen to retreat into an explanation of 'greed and risk'. Perhaps the wider implications are uncomfortable for them. But if we only look at the obvious, at most we'll only get half the story and therefore half the understanding. For example

---

1 Kenneth Galbraith, *The Great Crash*, 1959.

the French and German governments want to pin blame on a group of investors who they think epitomise 'greed and risk': hedge funds. The regulations put forward in the European Union are a deliberate attack on these investors. Yet, hedge funds had no role in the creation of this particular crisis. What is the logic of a regulatory response that seeks to regulate behaviour that was not at fault? This is not just missing the point, it is a deliberate misrepresentation of the truth.

Even top regulators shirk a wider story in favour of the simple explanation of greed. Mervyn King, the governor of the Bank of England, blamed the 2008 collapse on 'hubris and excessive lending'.[2] As the man nominally in charge of UK bank lending during the period he identifies with 'hubris and excessive lending', he begs a question of himself: 'Why did you allow such a situation to develop?' But his unsatisfactory explanation is not alone and some variation on King's theme is accepted by many others.

Galbraith at least had the grace to admit 'We do not know why a great speculative orgy occurred in 1928 and 1929', and suggested that the explanation for the crash was unknown. Better to start with an admission of ignorance, than to start with a mistaken analysis.

Explanations of crises have become more adventurous since Galbraith published his book. Robert J. Shiller published *Irrational Exuberance* just before the stock market bubble burst in 2000. He warned of over-extended stock prices and railed against the lack of fundamental value in the prices of many stocks. His warnings were followed by the dot-com crash. Partly as the result of this book, Shiller acquired the reputation of a financial sage, a role he was to reprise during the US housing crash of 2007–09, which he predicted. The high reputation is entirely deserved for a man who had predicted the collapse of not just one bubble, but two.

Shiller was not the only writer to predict disaster, but he was among the most convincing in explaining how it emerged. He lists

2 Mervyn King before Treasury Select Committee, 30 April 2008.

twelve factors that 'make up the skin of the bubble, if you will'. These were 'factors that have had an effect on the market that is not warranted by rational analysis of economic fundamentals'; in other words, his reasons why the public were so blinded by circumstances that they failed to see an obvious economic incongruity in shares prices.

So, to Schiller's list: arrival of the internet; triumphalism at the victory of capitalism; cultural changes that favoured business success – or the appearance thereof; a Republican Congress in the US and capital gains tax cuts; the post-war baby boom and its investment effects on the market; an expansion of business reporting in the media; increasing optimism by analysts; an expansion of defined contribution pension plans; growth of mutual funds; the decline of inflation; an expansion of turnover (liquidity) of stock trading; a rise in gambling opportunities.

> ## to Shiller, the public could not see disaster coming because they were dazzled by other events

To Shiller, the public could not see disaster coming because they were dazzled by other events. The list reflected his belief that investors had lost their focus on long-term stock earnings. There is no doubt to me that most if not all of the factors Shiller listed played an important role in sustaining the dot-com bubble.

To me, Shiller's list could be distilled into three items: American dominance; the entry of new investors; and the effects of new technology. In many cases, the first and the last effects were largely synonymous. The internet was, after all, an American invention and the US drove its massive growth in the late 1980s; globalisation and its effects on growth and inflation were intimately linked to the triumph of America and the fall of communism in the late 1980s. Globalisation itself depended on newly expanded communication networks. From these two major effects (internet and globalisation) stemmed interest in business, expanded liquidity, increased optimism of analysts, the growth in mutual funds, a change in cultural attitudes towards business. These forces too are my starting point for the current crisis.

The effect of 'green' investors runs as a thread through Schiller's book. Whether it was individual banks, traders convinced about the safety of their high-yielding debt investments, reserve managers and Japanese households who did not know, or did not care, about the effect they had on the investment landscape, or the entry of vast numbers of the general public attracted by the rewards of market gains, new entrants were a force to be reckoned with. The problem with investment information is that, unlike medical or engineering information, the more people who know it the less valuable it becomes. The greater the involvement, therefore, the more devalued the quality of information on which investment decisions are made.

Not surprisingly, then, financial disruption often seems to coincide with an information revolution that increases the reach and accessibility of information previously available only to a few. New technology or new methods of production excite investors and bring new products. For a while, the world looks permanently different, then a collapse occurs and the speculative excess is revealed. This is something that has been noted many times by economists, including Shiller. Technological change and stock market bubbles seem inextricably linked. The inherent instability in financial markets can be tipped into boom and bust by technological change.

In many cases, however, the world we glimpse during the boom is genuinely different. The crisis is, in some ways, a rite of passage into a different way of interacting and a different world, although with some constants.

To make this easier to grasp I divided the themes that we'll be looking at into four areas. These are:

▌ The constants. Disruption may be inevitable from the way we understand and use money. Financial crises may be inevitable, not through greed or fraud or mistakes that can be curbed, but through the nature of the way we interact with money itself. At the same time money is both debt and a medium of exchange. The results of an unbalanced interaction of the two ways of using money are always alike: illiquidity, insolvency, recapitalisation, government guarantees and economic contraction. The emphasis in the past thirty years has been to promote money as a medium of exchange in the form of increased transactions. The downside has been at the expense of money as debt.

▌ Crises. Crises may emerge from new features in an economy. If symptoms are alike, the causes are also often associated with long-term developments that stand as benefits to society. The current financial crisis seems related to our technological innovations, particularly in computing and telecommunications.

> ▌ consider the entire period from 1990 until 2008 as one large financial crisis associated with globalisation

▌ Technologies. The new technological features ran in parallel with an unprecedented opening up of the global economy. The trade/finance arrangements of Asia, primarily China and Japan, and America led directly to crisis. It is sensible, as I said, to consider the entire period from 1990 until 2008 as one large financial crisis associated with globalisation – a crisis that began in Japan and spread through the world via South-East Asia and the dot-com boom. Eventually it emerged in both America and Europe. It may be in the process of returning to its origin in Japan.

▌ Disruption may be positive. Just because something is uncomfortable or disruptive may not mean it does not have long-term benefits. In one later chapter I look at some of the good as well as bad results of past crises. What looks like a disaster for the US now may be proof of its continued economic dynamism and leadership – though that will only become apparent on a recovery and may not occur for several years. On the other hand, if other countries fail to learn the lessons of this episode and do not work to avoid disruption it could limit their own prosperity.

The never-ending crisis

Since 1990, a long-running financial crisis has rolled uninterrupted around the globe, beginning in Japan and spreading initially to the rest of Asia, then into the US and Europe. In time, the series of crises will be seen as running in parallel to the unprecedented opening up of the global economy – undoubtedly a positive development in itself. Europe even had a succession of currency crises in the early 1990s, which could have been included under the heading of globalisation, but were omitted for the sake of brevity. In Asia, the collapse of the 'Tiger' economies of Thailand, Indonesia and Malaysia grew from the interaction of their economies with global capital. There have been at least three financial crises in the US over the past decade or so which had origins in similar opening of the globe; the collapse of Long Term Capital Management, the dot-com bust and the credit crunch. Each one contained similar features and causes. It is possible to view the past ten years as a recurrence of one single financial crisis with roots in the expansion of world trade. All of these episodes are considered in this book.

The capacity for calculation, the speed of transaction and the transparency of prices that accompanied globalisation have radically changed the operation of banks and their customers – and also contributed to the way the crisis unfolded. Global capital flows, cross-border lending, electronic trading platforms, online mortgage applications, financial spread betting, derivative use and structured products all grew massively, driven by information technology. Changes have brought down costs and increased speed. Yet, these changes in many ways ran ahead of the investment opportunities the West had to offer the rest of the world. The dominance of the dollar that characterised the past twenty years had an inbuilt flaw. While most assumed the architecture of global finance could accept the many millions of extra participants with their many millions of extra dollars, the system was not able to deal with the vast amounts of money directed back to America alone. There are many opportunities for investment and some are located in the developed world, but most are in emerging economies. The diversion of colossal quantities of cash from reserve managers in emerging economies into developed countries was not just a contributor to the crisis, it was an unethical diversion of resources from those who needed them. Moral questions run through the present crisis, but perhaps not quite in the way many have appreciated.

While globalisation may be new, it is not the first time technology has delivered financial disruption. Improvements in communication in both the mid-nineteenth and early twentieth centuries were also associated with financial disruption across many nations. Communications as the harbinger of crisis is not new. Once again, the novelty today is the scale, which is nevertheless entirely in keeping with the global reach of communications technology.

Communications technologies are 'socially constructed institutions, just as are governments, educational systems, family structures, self-help and charitable organisations.'[3] The major change that communications have brought is to include many more participants in a system from which they had been excluded.

Enthusiasts would say both trade and communications have created a whole new world to develop and explore. But, there are actually too few appropriate investment opportunities. There was an incentive to invest, and an increase in investment from capital flows, but little expansion in the right opportunities. When a product is in demand but unable to be supplied, a good capitalist system will create it. The extra investment needed an investment, and in US and European housing bonds and credit derivatives it received its investment opportunity. Unfortunately, the opportunities were frequently flawed, even from their very design.

unfortunately, the opportunities were frequently flawed, even from their very design

The lessons I want to draw from our troubles are not the didactic, school-masterly lessons of the moralist. They are, instead, the lessons of the unintended consequence; an altogether more

3 Carla G. Surratt, *The Internet and Social Change*, 2001, McFarland.

unsettling and less confident sort of lesson. What may in all other respects appear to be a great enhancement to the human condition – the entry of the emerging economies into the developed world – had a cost attached that neither developed nor emerging worlds anticipated. There are also lessons in the singlemindedness of our central banks, which blinded them to serious, and obvious, distortions in the financial system. And lessons too for regulators who encouraged the structures of international finance to evolve in such a way that damage was so pervasive. Yet, the lessons are unfortunately unique and probably not transferable, or even relevant for the next great boom and bust. It is possible that the great series of financial crises the world has experienced since 1990 is far from over. After all, we have not yet discovered the limits of communication. There is no reason why we should not be 'fooled again'.

Common features of financial crises, and why we don't see them coming

'Tis surprising to see how rapidly a panic will sometimes run through a country. All nations and ages have been subject to them.
Tom Paine, *The American Crisis*, 1776

Some features are common to every financial crisis. They appear so often they have come to define financial crises everywhere. Every crisis suffers withdrawal of credit, sudden falls in asset prices, requests for assistance from the central bank, or government, and funding problems. Inevitably, early symptoms of widespread losses among banks lead to later and profound effects on the wider economy. Bankruptcies and unemployment rise, spending and investment fall. These symptoms were present in the US and Europe in 2008. They appeared in Japan too in the mid-1990s, in Thailand in 1997, in the Nordic banking crisis in 1991. They were present in the aftermath of the Great Crash in 1929 and in the great banking crises of the nineteenth century.

The symptoms are seemingly common but symptoms are not causes. Too much debt is commonly blamed as the cause, with not enough concern for how it would be repaid. Debt played a part in the Great Crash of 1929, which was blamed on stock trading on borrowed funds, and excessive consumer debt. Japan's banks failed because of their vast debts. The credit crunch that followed was blamed on mortgages, and the borrowing that permeated the economies of Europe and the US. Debt is definitely important.

If cause and symptoms are similar for all crises why don't we do something about them, and why don't we see them coming? Why can't we fix the rules of finance in the same way we have fixed the rules of engineering?

Surely it would be worth the effort? Perhaps we could avoid these problems with a more hands-on approach. In the 1950s, restrictions meant it was hard to get a mortgage, but there were no financial crises. There were few financial crises between 1933 and the mid-1970s because of the strict rules in place. Would it not be better to return to the certainty of the arrangements that were in place then; perhaps with the confidence of gold backing currencies?

A return to the simpler life may be appealing. And this crisis has caused so much disruption that an increase in regulation is a certainty. Yet, going back to the past is out of the question. There are good reasons we left behind the arrangements of those days, mostly because the economic costs were unpalatable. However, surely it is possible, in highly developed societies, to eliminate financial crises, something we associate with 'primitive' nineteenth century capitalism. We must be able to craft a set of rules to prevent the sort of problems we normally associate with a Dickens story, or with the dissolute 1920s.

It may not be possible to fix the problem, or even define it properly, until we look in the right place. Debt is important. Borrowing and greed might have led us astray, but borrowing and greed are constants; they do not explain why the crisis emerged when it did. We have to ask a great deal more than who lent the money and who profited from that system. We need to know a lot more about money itself. In particular, we need to know what is meant by money.

The broad background

I believe the path to financial disaster was laid by one positive development, one distortion and one perennial problem.

The positive development was the vast expansion of trade and finance that occurred after the end of the Cold War, and the accompanying advance in communications technology. The decline of the Soviet empire and the fall of the Berlin Wall marked a definitive end to the prescribed rules that dominated both West and East and allowed an inclusive future to be planned for both sides. The benefits have been huge; in living standards for East and West, in international trade and communications. Most dramatically, China entered the world economy.

> these benefits were accompanied and made possible by the expansion of advanced communications

These benefits were accompanied and made possible by the expansion of advanced communications. Technological developments made communication improvements possible and also were a precondition for financial innovations, some of which helped create problems later. There is something different about 'the way we live now' and there is no way back to the more restricted world we have left.

The distortion was created by the trade and investment policies of emerging economies. In the ten years to 2007 they bought far more dollar assets than could be sensibly invested, even in an economy as large as that of the US. The dollars entering the US economy forced interest rates lower and pushed lending into dangerous areas, often encouraged by political policy and the structure of incentives at banks.

The perennial problem is a lack of clarity about money. A financial crisis often seems better described as a re-definition of money; what was thought of as an accepted medium of exchange and unit of account is abruptly rejected. A banking crisis shifts normal money – the medium of exchange – from the paper promises banks pass between themselves into central bank money, the most trustworthy, basic currency, and limited currency allowed within an economy. Banks' paper promises become worthless.

In this chapter I look at the factors that lead to crises, not just the current one, but almost all other financial crises. These include deregulation of financial markets, the number of investors entering the markets, financial liquidity, and misunderstanding about the nature of money itself. I will explain how money and liquidity can suddenly disappear.

Financial deregulation: doors to opportunity and distress

A precondition for every bank crisis, it seems, is financial deregulation. The loosening of banking rules and competition in the provision of credit drive banks to seek new borrowers and investors. Entrants compete, and new methods of competition are found. Old relationships break down, and new ones tend to be based on cost advantages, leading to decisions based on short-term considerations. Lending mistakes are made, debts cannot be repaid and a crisis emerges. Financial deregulation occurred before the Japanese boom, the Thai boom of the early 1990s, the Nordic boom of the late 1980s. Looser bank regulation preceded crises in mid-nineteenth century England and also preceded the Great Crash of 1929.

This is not to say that deregulation needs to lead to problems. Deregulation is often needed, and even when it leads to problems it may not be advisable to go into reverse. The primary purpose of banks is to create credit, which then becomes money, but only as long as there is confidence about future repayments.

Looser rules, paradoxically, are often associated with greater confidence about the future. The growing dependence on future claims leads to a dangerous imbalance, greater dependence on future repayments. A threshold is then exceeded, or a panic triggered, which exposes the fragility of the system.

The period since 1979 has seen a historic rise in commitment to deregulation of financial services in almost every country. It has been associated with higher economic growth, better living standards, progress. Beginning in the early 1970s, deregulation permeated the banking industry in the US and Britain, before fanning out across the globe. Deregulation affected everyone who used a bank. The public saw changes to bank opening hours, what products were provided, the range of mortgages, the level of share commissions and who was able to deal in stock markets. Between banks themselves the changes were deeper; competition opened up across the globe with constant pressure to ensure the fastest transaction, at the lowest cost, for the greatest profit. It is said that old bankers did not worry about profit; they only worried about their balance sheet. That is clearly not true, but it is true that deregulation changed the focus of banking, with greater emphasis on immediate profit, fees and what we might call 'transactional finance' over traditional credit. Above all, deregulation pitted securities solutions (markets) against relationship solutions (loans).

deregulation pitted securities solutions (markets) against relationship solutions (loans)

Deregulation has led to immense improvements in service, as well as stronger world growth throughout the past thirty years. It is by no means a bad idea. It has allowed more businesses to grow, more borrowers to invest, and it can be argued that without financial deregulation the Soviet Union might not have conceded defeat to capitalism so soon. It is possible that without the faith in market solutions that deregulation implied China might never have emerged as the economic power it has become.

There is no doubt that the deregulated financial marketplace, taken for granted for so long, now seems fragile. Yet it was, in many ways, success that led to the current problems and what financial markets, and banks, regard as success is also the source of fragility. There have been tangible benefits, but they come with a terrible cost. Even people who believe in the benefits cannot escape this failure. Nor can they escape the financial hardship that failure brought.

It is not as if we have not had regulations to prevent the sort of systemic crisis we have just experienced. Financial regulation has been present, and active, throughout the past thirty years. This crisis arose not from lack of regulation, but from the ease with which regulation was circumvented, the inappropriate way it was applied and the willingness to promote economic growth at almost any cost. It came from a collective blindness of banks – which do not set out to bankrupt themselves. Yet, though it may be hard to accept, the current generation of bankers is no more avaricious than its predecessors. Nor do bankers have a monopoly on greed. Deregulation might have been a factor, but it is almost impossible to imagine reinstating comprehensive controls on credit.

At least everyone agrees the problem originated in banks, and that banks should be the focus of reform. Lack of control, unconstrained pursuit of short-term profit, unsafe risk controls; these must be fixed. Yes, banks were at fault, but perhaps there were other factors that are less easily tackled.

After the event, some return of regulation is inevitable. Yet, with signs that most regulation will seek to avoid the prescriptive strictures used in the 1950s and 1960s, modern regulators and politicians seem agreed on the benefits of deregulation, as well as the dangers. Unfortunately, it also suggests those governing banking do not see more regulation as part of the problem.

Re-introducing old-style regulation certainly would limit economic growth. It would also undermine the struggle for advancement that millions of people in Eastern Europe – and elsewhere – have undergone. Would they agree to such limits? I think not. And what would re-regulation mean about the freedom to fail, which is at the heart of success? Financial deregulation may be a factor in financial crisis but we should think hard before committing to unwinding the process.

The truth is that finance is bigger than banking; finance is as big as an economy and today's economy is global. Although banks create the credit and gain the profits they cannot act alone in the construction of a crisis. Among more thoughtful commentators, there is agreement that global imbalances – particularly the large current account surpluses and deficits – and mistakes of central banks also had a big part to play.

Yet I think we need to look for a deeper understanding of the origin of crises, at the configuration of debt and, more especially, the definition of money itself. Globalisation and its role in the current crisis will follow in later chapters but here the concern should be for money because underlying all crises, including the current one, there's always a problem with money.

The magic trick of money

Economics is dogged by a profound lack of understanding of money. Money is a problem even to those who spend their entire life manipulating and studying it, such as central banks. This is odd; money seems such a basic component of economies that it should be clear what money means, and how it functions. Yet money is a blind spot for almost everyone; experts and laypeople alike.

Disputes about money are always implicit but, thankfully, are only rarely brought into the open. When they do appear, it is invariably bad news. Just as it is invariably bad news when we notice the plumbing, so the basic connections of our money systems are better hidden than exposed to scrutiny, but a crisis forces us to question these most basic operations. An understanding of a financial crisis therefore depends on an understanding of the nature of money itself, including its origins.

> part of the difficulty lies with an apparent magic trick

Part of the difficulty lies with an apparent magic trick. In the past money was 'backed' by holdings of gold, or silver. When there was wholesale belief in this backing then money at least appeared to have some foundation. But those days are gone. Now, everyone uses 'fiat money'. The magic trick is that these pieces of paper are accepted as tokens for payment, without any notion of independent worth or convertibility.

If a government is trusted to honour its own debts in paper money (and can persuade its citizens to honour theirs the same way) there is really no need for any convertibility. Convertibility into gold or silver was a trick anyway. Widespread use of gold would lead to inconvenient transfers of wealth from one place to another. Sooner or later, paper money, at least in the form of gold receipts for gold, would probably replace gold. And if there was trust in the 'repayer of last resort' in the system (usually the government), why bother with gold at all? It is an obvious question that did not get an answer until 1971, when the US abandoned gold and floated the dollar. From that time on, gold lost its role as the reference for money, and paper alone took over; fiat money, controlled by a central bank.

In fact, gold was almost always largely irrelevant for the prime function of money; debt. Money (in the forms of cash, deposit and credit) is an expression of the balance sheet of the economy; for every debt there is an asset. Banknotes are simply a means of recognising the interest or principal of a debt (for a borrower) and the income and future repayment for the lender. There is no need for gold in this system at all.

Apart from a small amount of the money in circulation that is the responsibility of the central bank (notes and coins and central bank reserves), all the money is effectively just a declaration by the state, individuals and companies of their debts, or their recognition of someone else's debts. As long as the legitimacy of the state continues unchallenged, its debts will circulate as money. The creditworthiness of others allows their debts to circulate as money too.

This is the magic trick of money; to persuade every individual and every business that a core set of debts backed by the power of the state (the notes and coins and central bank reserves) can provide enough confidence to support a much more extensive network of claims and liabilities. This can happen because the final settlement of debts with the state (taxes) can be made in the same currency, which translates the private circulating money into the stuff we recognise as money. Crises arise either because the sanctity of central bank money itself is compromised, or, more likely, the wider, private debts in circulation cannot be settled in central bank money. Our own crisis emerged when private money was unable to be settled in central bank money.

It is a cliché that business is about trust; in fact, money itself is all about trust and the disturbance of trust is the main cause of crises, particularly the trust in private debt settlement. Banks support the system of trust, through creating most of the debts that circulate as money. This is not money in your pocket, but money in banks' balance sheets, credit, transfers; anything, in fact, except what is needed to pay taxes. Banks accomplish this trick either by acting as an exchange through which borrowers can find lenders at the same time, or, more often, through simply creating an entry into their balance sheet to represent a debt, or a deposit that needs to be matched later. The displacement of borrowers and lenders is the critical act of trust that a bank must conduct, and which it must protect at all costs if it is to remain a viable business. Without it, depositors flee, and the bank collapses. This relationship is the key to understanding how financial crises arise.

Most countries ensure that banks can fulfil this task by demanding they hold a fraction of their deposits as reserves at the central bank – hence the term 'fractional banking'. The holding of reserves was designed to ensure depositors were protected in case of a sudden withdrawal from the banking system (hence the term reserves), but also as a protection against the capital position of the banks, for the amount of reserves is directly related to the amount of credit created. It is also an important link between private money and central bank money.

> the reserve system is described in terms of protection for users of banks. This is misleading

The reserve system is described in terms of protection for users of banks. This is misleading. Reserves are unlikely to be released to assist depositors. If a bank was so weak as to call on its reserves, it would be unlikely to survive anyway. The true function of reserves is rather more subtle. Rather than thinking of reserves as bank assets, they are actually central bank liabilities that banks are required to hold to ensure a direct link between the wider private money used in the economy, and the central bank money at the heart of the system.

Reserve money is not ordinary money; central banks almost always ensure there is enough of this special money available to satisfy their banking system. These are not reserves in the sense of 'reserve troops', to be committed to the fight in an emergency. These are reserves in the sense that they are reserved from the rest of the monetary system. It is the other money, created and controlled by the commercial banks, which constitutes money as far as most businesses and banks are concerned.

It is true that without reserves and the trust in the state money that they represent, a mortgage would probably never be considered as money, and would therefore not be granted. With these reserves, the wages I receive, the business I conduct, and the taxes I pay are measured in a common, accepted unit and my mortgage can be accepted as money, along with other debts.

Commercial banks are the hub through which these present and future claims are matched; they are a marketplace of transactions, or a clearing house. There are many banks around the world each attempting to put its own assets and liabilities to the best use, so the banking system is really a large marketplace, settling different forms of obligations. The distinction between central bank money and private money tells us about a weak point in financial systems but it does not tell us how that weak point leads to boom, and collapse. To look at that we need to examine more closely the confusion in the role of money as a medium of exchange, and its role as a circulating debt.

Confusion at the heart of money

Carl Menger, an economist from the nineteenth century, suggested money itself grew out of the marketplace. Menger thought that in a 'natural state' buyers and sellers were generally wary, and unwilling to agree terms. Barter meant transactions were difficult. Exchanging goods usually meant one side ended up with something it might not immediately need. To compensate, one side would demand more of the unwanted goods in return for its offering.

Menger suggested that if just a few traders recognised a medium of exchange it would help both buyer and seller settle on a middle price, and in the process raise the value of the selling price and reduce the price for the buyer. What that medium was, was not important. Once identified, any medium would be quickly acknowledged as helpful to both buyer and seller.

Menger's explanation has nothing to say about money as debt, yet it is clearly a compelling explanation. If money is only a mechanism by which goods are exchanged at a single time, there is no need for credit, just a medium of exchange. Menger's ideas belong to what is known as the neo-classical economic view of money. They remain useful because, as I shall show, they seem to match well the behaviour of investors in a market, where the concept of debt is often alien. They are not a full description of money, as anyone will recognise, but they offer a good explanation of how markets evolve to ensure the maximum number of transactions. Of course, transactional finance, the provision of credit through transactions in a market, has risen to great importance. But the reconciliation of money as credit and money as a medium of exchange remains unresolved. It certainly seems a common cause of financial problems.

default, or the fear of default, is often the most powerful cause of crises

Obviously, with no concept of debt in Menger's theory, there is no room for default. Yet default, or the fear of default, is often the most powerful cause of crises. Even so, in Menger's world it was still possible for a financial crisis to occur without any default whatsoever. We will come back to this point. Not everyone agreed with Menger. The economist Maynard Keynes differed in that he saw the basis of money as a system of debt and repayment.

Human transactions have always taken place based on credit, and the record of debt has been the most common form of money through history. Clay tablets indicating debts circulated as money in ancient times and, most importantly, were used to pay taxes. Medieval Europe, too, had little use for coins or notes in everyday transactions. Coins were generally of a higher denomination than most transactions, so other means were needed to settle transactions and debts fulfilled this role. Britain used a system of 'tally sticks' to denote debts till the early nineteenth century. It suggests Menger's exclusion of debt in explaining money was wrong, or at least incomplete.

Credit – or debt – was an important starting point for many, and perhaps even all, transactions.

Why this concentration on debt as money? Well, financial crises are invariably explained as the result of too much debt. If so, it is as well to bear in mind that the transactions of the entire monetary system are, in fact, based on debt.

The special privileges of banks

If money is composed of debts that circulate and is also a medium of exchange for transactions, then it is natural for banks to create as much money as is required by borrowers and to transact as much as possible. The loans can be created simply from a book entry, an expansion of bank balance sheets. To get away with this, of course, banks need particular privileges. The most important is that banking as an industry is supported by the state. This is so even if banks are private companies. This makes them very different to manufacturers, or retailers. Usually this guarantee is invisible. In a crisis it is required. Although other businesses can go bankrupt, it is essential that important banks remain in business. Citizens may not like this, but that is the price of continuing credit.

Of course, if banks create the money by a book entry system, then they have to be sure that repayment of the debt occurs. Credit is therefore bounded by the ability of an individual, or a company, and ultimately a society, to repay the loan from future wealth. If that future wealth looks unlikely to occur, the debt is worth less than it would otherwise be, even if it is repaid, because the chance of default is higher. No amount of transactions will change that.

This creates a paradox; lending helps lift growth, and therefore future wealth, but lending depends on achieving that future growth. High lending can provide the means to satisfy its repayment, but withdrawal of lending will create the certainty of default. The balance between the future wealth and future default is fine, and despite the limited number of financial crises, it is common for expectations to remain unfulfilled. It is said that only 10 per cent of new businesses succeed. How extraordinary then that there are not more financial crises?

Dependence on future wealth may explain why property booms seem so often to precede crises. It is not that lending against property is inherently riskier than lending against any other investment, but that property does not add to the total future wealth of society. A boom in property may actually undermine the creation of real wealth. That is not to say returns in property cannot exist, but overall wealth creation in society is limited, or non-existent.

Miscalculations of future wealth can also occur from population changes (part of the reason for the Japanese banking problems), from technology, from bad data, and from poor control by a central bank. The privileges of banks – ultimately the support of the state – need to be balanced by a special responsibility to assess accurately the future wealth of lending; in particular, that enough earnings are created to pay off the debt. In all the crises I have mentioned, and probably in all crises, doubt about the ability to pay was the trigger to question the basis of other claims.

Overoptimistic assumptions are a common way to miscalculate future wealth and the process of deregulation and the entry of foreign lenders is often a factor. We have already looked at the effect of deregulation. In fact, a common feature of financial crises since 1970, including the current one, has been the inflow of foreign money into a country. This happened in Thailand in 1997 and in Mexico (twice) and in the currency crises of Eastern Europe in 1996. It happened in Scandinavia in the 1980s. And it happened in Spain, the UK, Ireland and the US from 2001 until 2007.

a common feature of financial crises since 1970 … has been the inflow of foreign money

Governments or their agencies – such as central banks – try to protect against miscalculation by demanding that banks hold a portion of capital against their loans, or bond holdings. This also acts as a brake on over-enthusiastic lending.

Litany of attempts to solve a perennial problem

Now, if the natural role of banks is to create credit then it is in their interest to evade capital requirement rules. The Basel capital adequacy rules are the latest in a long line of limits placed on banks that seem to have failed to achieve what they set out to do because of this contradiction.

Regulatory failure is common. In nineteenth century Britain, similar attempts at limiting the creation of credit also failed. Then, a group calling itself 'the Currency School' believed that strict control over the amount of money in circulation and backed by gold would limit inflation and the creation of credit. It was therefore seen as a panacea for crises. The theory won over the government and in 1844, prime minister Robert Peel introduced the Bank Charter Act, which restricted the issue of banknotes by private banks and gave exclusive note-issuing rights to the Bank of England, with all notes to be backed 100 per cent by gold.[1]

The illusion that this arrangement would protect the system from crises was maintained only as long as there were no unforeseen demands on the system. Stresses, of course, duly appeared and inevitably revealed that credit had continued to expand despite the tight controls on money supply and the requirement for notes to be backed by gold. Notes and gold, it was shown, were simply irrelevant to credit creation. The exposure of the illusion occurred not just once, but three times, in 1847, 1857 and 1866, and was accompanied by banking crises. Every time there was a crisis, the system designed to avoid a crisis was shown to have failed, and in every case the solution to the crisis involved suspension of the Bank Charter Act. This was a humiliation for the Currency School but it also showed that it is almost impossible to limit the creation of credit by officially declaring a set meaning of money. Money is more than the stuff that rolls off the government printing press and

1 *Manias, Panics and Crashes*, Charles P. Kindleberger, Third edition, 1996 Wiley.

certainly more than paper backed by gold. Money is the belief that someone else will pay you back. It was a lesson that monetarists in the 1980s also failed to learn when they tried reliably to measure money and similarly failed.

This mysterious power of money – and credit – to expand and contract has been noted by observers for hundreds of years. John Stuart Mill wrote: 'The purchasing power of an individual at any moment is not measured by the money actually in his pocket, whether we mean by money the metals, or include the banknotes. It consists, first, of all the money in his possession; secondly, of the money at his banker's and all the other money due him and payable on demand; thirdly of whatever credit he happens to possess.'[2] This includes current, and most importantly, future credit.

Mills meant that money is really a merger of money as a means to assist transactions (as Menger described), and money as a system of debts (as Keynes believed). The imaginary wealth of John Stuart Mill includes both, and a market-driven economy also requires both. Economists call this 'stock' of money and 'velocity' of money, but they rarely know what stock they are measuring or what the speed limit of the velocity should be. The trouble arises when the velocity becomes confused with the stock.

Asset prices and credit

As we saw earlier, uncertainty about the future ability to pay undermines creditworthiness. In a market this is the same as saying creditworthiness is equivalent to the expected future value of an asset. Lending grows as long as the future value of an asset is expected to be higher. A financial crisis emerges when we discover a rise in asset prices is not sustainable, or that the future ability to pay for that asset is impaired. A financial crisis does not need a rise in defaults, just a fear that they may arise in the future.

Credit based on market values is inherently unstable because expectations of the future change all the time. This instability is

2 J. S. Mill in *Westminster Review* 41 (1844): 590–1, quoted in Kindleberger, *Manias, Panics and Crashes*, p. 49.

usually manageable. What can make the system dangerously prone to booms and busts is the introduction of some novel or outside influence – gold from a colony, a new technology or new financing product. Versions of this instability caused by outside or new influences occurred in Thailand in 1990s, in Japan in the 1980s, in the dot-com boom. It also occurred in the 1920s with the introduction of instalment plans for such consumer goods as cars, radios and houses (mortgages) and the buying of shares on margin. It occurred in the past decade, perhaps more than ever, with the imbalance in international capital flows, the introduction of new investors and the increased speed of transactions.

What were we thinking?

Instability can mean the entire environment changes abruptly. Because the banking system is largely based on private debt, a threat to one set of debt can undermine trust in others. A willingness to offer loans, which looked perfectly reasonable at the time, can look unreasonable later. After a crisis, balance sheets suggest these banks were hiding something; surely they cannot have thought that such an asset could have been worth that much? Were all these banks and companies cheating? Or were the auditors asleep?

> the more frequent reason is that the nature of money itself changed

In some cases the auditors have been found wanting. But the more frequent reason is that the nature of money itself changed before and after the crisis. I have already said that money is a debt based on a future return. Money changes in a crisis because expectations of the future changed. How can this happen?

A financial crisis occurs when previously acceptable terms in transactions suddenly become unacceptable. The descriptions of financial crises by those experiencing the panic are remarkably similar in different eras. There seems to be a sudden lack of money, which creates complete panic, and bewilderment. In 1825, at the onset of an earlier crisis, *The Times* reported the 'impossibility of producing any money at all'. This is the defining feature of all financial crises; money that was previously present disappears. The moment of crisis is defined by this vanishing act.

Central banks are called on to provide large amounts of cash to replace the money that has disappeared. To do so requires the central banks themselves to expand their balance sheets, as those in the private sector shrink. One form of money that has become unacceptable is replaced with a form of money that is still acceptable.

On 9 August 2007, at the onset of the credit crunch, the European Central Bank (ECB) provided €95 billion to the commercial banking system, which had found it was dangerously close to failing its obligations. This was by far the most the ECB had provided in a single day. It did so, not by gathering deposits from concerned citizens, but by simply making an entry into its accounts, just as commercial banks do. The ECB created more 'central bank' money to replace the private sector money that had somehow gone missing. Other central banks followed the ECB. It is a standard and necessary response from central banks, to stop the panic from spreading.

Unfortunately, the addition of central bank money rarely makes the money that vanished reappear. Rather, with uncertainty over at least some private sector debts, there is a much greater appetite for state assets, as the ultimate form of money. Government bonds rise in price, cash is sought and private sector liquidity seems to evaporate. This is because bank liabilities remained denominated in central bank money, while the assets – which had previously been equal to the liabilities – were effectively devalued when the wider definition of money, the money created by private banks, became less valuable. A gap opened between the two sorts of money. The money that most banks depend upon had disappeared.

So, now Mr Menger's idea of money as a medium of exchange reappears, and interacts dangerously with the idea of money as debt. Menger said money was a system that grew up naturally to aid transactions. The defining moment of crisis is an inability to transact because there is no longer agreement about the medium of exchange, about what is meant by 'money'.

Confused investment and channel capacity

The separation of one sort of acceptable money (central bank money) from other, no longer acceptable sorts of money (everything else) in a crisis is merely an extreme version of a difference that always existed. But during a crisis an abnormally large number of transactions are found to be no longer able to be settled. The transactions become invalid.

A valid transaction is one that behaves as expected when it is agreed. Validity certainly does not guarantee a profit, just expected behaviour. If I buy a car and it performs the function I expected, the transaction is valid, even if I may have bought the car more cheaply elsewhere later. If the car turns out to be a 'lemon' the transaction is invalid, no matter what price I paid for the car. A market transaction is valid if the price I pay is a fair price compared with the performance of the asset. In our financial crisis an entire economy found out, almost instantly, that it had bought a lemon.

During a very active market – a market dominated by Menger's transactional money – the value of an asset may appear to be higher than during less active times simply because there are always willing buyers and sellers. This can give a false impression about the underlying value. Too many transactions can give a false sense of value. In fact, the higher the number of transactions about a certain threshold, the greater the number of errors made, or lemons sold.

Keep it down!

Everybody has experienced a similar problem in a crowded party. The competing chatter of party-goers leads to misunderstanding. The messages are sent, but they are not correctly received. At successful parties, there is a balance between the right number of guests and the space in which the party takes place. Similar effects take place in markets (and banking). The economy profits from the right number of transactions. Too few investors make transactions hard to negotiate, and investment suffers. An increase in the number of investors increases transactions and the productive capacity of the economy. Too many, and investment is overvalued and ultimately invalid.

More is not always better. Benefits are not unlimited. There is a point when transactions reach a level beyond which the number of errors grows. Communications engineers call it 'exceeding channel capacity'.

there is … an inherent contradiction in the way people treat a medium of exchange

There is, unfortunately, an inherent contradiction in the way people treat a medium of exchange. The greater the exchangeability, the more readily an asset is accepted as money. It is easy, therefore, to confuse liquidity with monetary value. When markets involve financial assets, the dislocation between money as a transaction and money as a form of debt has serious repercussions. It is also a dislocation that can continue for a long time without repercussion, maintaining or increasing the value of assets while their true creditworthiness has fallen. Thus liquidity of an asset can actually harm its value even more catastrophically when the dislocation is revealed.

The disappearance of money in a crisis, then, is really a sudden inability to transact. Bankers say there was 'no liquidity' in the market. Money that had been available immediately before the crisis disappears. It disappears because the transactional value of the asset has disappeared.

The basis of market economics: an ability to agree terms

The relationship between money, liquidity and the value of an asset was vital to Menger's idea of money as an aid to transactions, as we saw earlier. And it is still highly relevant.

A single transaction is merely an independent event and is usually of limited interest to investors, who seek both returns and capital security. No-one will buy an investment they think they will be unable to sell in the future. The best form of security is one that trades in a market with a constant stream of prices to reassure holders their investments are always transferable. Above most other considerations, investors seek liquidity.

While there is frequently a balance between liquidity and returns, often investors will choose liquidity over returns, unless they are so sure of liquidity that they can concentrate only on returns. Unfortunately, guaranteed liquidity means the asset must also reflect cash-like characteristics, which means it pays only cash-like returns, which are low.

From auction to liquid marketplace

Markets have always introduced rules to improve liquidity specifically to attract investors who value this feature. In 1807 the London Stock Exchange introduced rules that only those whose principal business was stock broking or stock jobbing were allowed to enter. If application to join the exchange was rejected it often reflected not the character of the failed applicant, but the dedication to a sole purpose expected by the exchange.[3]

More important than restriction on people is the restriction of product specification. The commodity markets of the Chicago Board of Trade greatly increased their turnover (which is another word for liquidity) in the mid-nineteenth century simply by standardising contracts, which meant buyers and sellers could concentrate on price.

Restrictions on both participant and specification were important financial innovations, but technology has made some restrictions redundant. In the past twenty years, vast numbers of people have been introduced to financial markets. Restriction on participation was more or less rejected. There is no need for restriction if everyone wants to trade, as long as they share basic agreed rules.

3 R. C. Mitchie, *The London Stock Exchange*, 1999, Oxford University Press.

And most people, in most Western countries, did share the same rules; the rule of market prices, the belief that the market could provide the greatest good for the greatest number. Yet, expanded participation comes with a high price, and has undoubtedly been instrumental in creating the current crisis.

Highly liquid markets create their own money

Users value cash for its stability. Unlike cash, there is usually no such thing as a 'stable' market value. As more participants join, the variation in prices from one transaction to the next will tend to decline. In the parlance of markets themselves, the 'bid–offer spread' narrows as the liquidity rises.

When liquidity dominates one market, it tends to spread to others, partly because more adventurous investors get tired of the lower returns that accompany higher liquidity. Increases in participation tend to smooth price changes, and link the value of one market to another. Participation itself, not just buying, will therefore raise the value of a product traded in a market, simply because its price is a reliable indicator of where it can be sold.

Technology and the emergence of new value

The introduction of new methods of communication has always added more potential participants to markets and a common thread to many financial crises is the arrival of new investors, higher liquidity. The introduction of radio, telephone and the car preceded and directly assisted the stock bubble of the late 1920s. The boom in railway shares in the 1840s was linked to enthusiasm for the new mode of transport, and also increased the number of participants in markets.

The past twenty years has far outstripped previous communication revolutions, and enmeshed global investors for the first time in a worldwide marketplace. We should not be surprised by any accompanying massive increase in market liquidity.

And while the world has been linking itself together through communications and trade, financial markets have undergone a comparable radical change, with huge effects on the way that financial products were valued, and treated.

'Logistics and statistics': twins from the same parent

Changes in communications, the expansion of global trade and the increase in financial innovations are different sides of the one revolution; the communications revolution.

The revolution in communications fed global trade expansion. Shipping containers would never have moved so easily without logistics management, which depends on computers and international communications. And accompanying the containers came trade finance, foreign exchange, funding, cash management, port facilities, equipment, desks, employees, distribution, profit, recycled surpluses and foreign reserves.

> a financial market is an exchange of information about the cost of money

Communications have always been the most highly valued part of the global economy. A financial market is an exchange of information about the cost of money, and liquidity in financial markets is directly linked to the ability to communicate easily between buyer and seller.

The inverse is also true: the transport and communication system is effectively a market for information, which can be expressed financially. The more developed the marketplace for goods and services, the closer to a money market it becomes and the more advanced its requirement for communications.

Growth of both trade and investment has been accompanied by a capability to fashion new means of investment, and processes, from options to trade processing, relying on the same technology that improved communications and liquidity. Increased trade, communications and financial innovation all depended on computer technology. The parent, if you like, of logistics and statistics, of trade, transport and financial innovation was information technology.

Modern communications not only opened the door to greater global trade but also to increased ways of packaging investments and risk. Neither necessarily expanded investment opportunities. The ability to deploy capital increased as information links improved. Yet real investment opportunities have not kept pace, at least not in the West. Without productive investment outlets, bubbles are blown and busts follow.

The integration of countries into the world economy and the world financial network has frequently caused problems; opening the financial sector to unrestrained foreign investment in Sweden, Finland, Mexico, Thailand and America has led to problems. I highlighted at the beginning of this chapter that the trade flows acted as one of the main causes of the crisis along with deregulation. Often over-investment was indistinguishable from competition created by deregulation, which is why deregulation is blamed for causing crises. In many cases, it was the heightened liquidity, not competition per se that caused the crisis. Globalisation increased market liquidity; particularly in the reserve currency of dollars.

More potential participants increase the market price of an asset

The higher the liquidity of an asset, the more that asset is bestowed with the attributes of cash, in a way that Menger would have recognised. A highly liquid investment, such as a Treasury Bill issued by the US government, is more-or-less interchangeable with cash. Less liquid assets, such as houses, or individual loans to companies or individuals, do not so easily acquire the attributes of cash. Treasury Bills offer particularly low interest rates because they are tantamount to cash. Cash held at a central bank by the banking system in some cases pays no interest, and notes and coins, the most liquid form of money for most individuals, of course, pay no interest. A lower return is offered for the privilege of liquidity and because of the way a liquid asset acquires its cash-like attributes, a liquid asset will take on more and more characteristics of cash. This can have profound effect on the way an economy works. The liquid marketplace can add to the effective money supply for an economy simply through high confidence in the ability to transact.

Time and investment

Keynes[4] seems to have agreed, albeit indirectly: 'The rate of interest is the reward for parting with liquidity for a specified period. For the rate of interest is, in itself, nothing more than the inverse proportion between a sum of money and what can be obtained for parting with control over the money in exchange for a debt for a stated period of time.'

There is, in theory, a way to work out exactly the additional liquidity required to reduce a return of an asset down to the level of cash. In the case of a Treasury Bill, the answer is obvious, 'not very much'. In the case of a bushel of barley or a loan on a house the answer is a 'great deal more liquidity'. If the number of transactions can be confidently predicted, then this additional liquidity will certainly add to the value of the commodity, whether it is barley or a mortgage.

It is obvious that if an asset becomes so liquid that its returns fall towards the level of cash, then a rise in the cost of cash by the central bank will make the asset look less attractive. Sure enough, interest rate rises have often proved to be the pin that pricks the bubble.

In 1865, a few months before a major crisis, the Bank of England tried to halt the growth in liquidity by raising the discount rate from 3 per cent to 7 per cent. It was the last straw for the discount house of Overend, Gurney & Co and the ensuing chaos brought down many other investment houses. Many of the failures of 1865 were financing international trade – facilitators of the first globalisation. A rate rise by Germany's Bundesbank was blamed

---

4 John Maynard Keynes, *The General Theory of Employment, Interest and Money*, 1936, p. 136.

for triggering the 1987 stock market crash, and the BoJ pricked the Japanese bubble in 1989. The US Federal Reserve raised rates before the 1929 Crash. The Fed had also been raising rates ahead of the latest financial crisis.

But sometimes, the actions of central banks have no effect if market activity is really excited. Since June 2004, the Fed Reserve had been raising rates steadily for two and a half years before the subprime crisis erupted in November 2006. It took another nine months before the fury of the credit crunch arrived in August 2007.

Why did it take so long this time for the bubble to burst? For there is no doubt that if it had burst earlier, it would have been less devastating.

> the most important central bank in the world had ceded control of monetary policy

The answer is that the most important central bank in the world had ceded control of monetary policy. Years of very low rates had already added overwhelming liquidity in 'over-crowded' financial markets, so raising interest rates initially made no difference. The US central bank had competition in setting important interest rates from the most conservative investors in the world, reserve managers.

Conservative investors: the perfect bubble-blowers

What are reserves, and why does their management matter? Reserves are the stock of foreign holdings held by a country to protect itself against a run on its currency or a severe disruption to its currency. Reserves are certainly required for any currency that is pegged to the dollar, or any other reserve currency, to ensure the official rate is maintained. Rising reserves is a natural result of keeping a currency at a lower rate than its market value wishes, because a government or central bank will have to sell the currency – and therefore accumulate foreign currency – to maintain the rate it wishes to hold. All countries maintain some reserves; in the decade following the Asian crisis, the accumulation of reserves had been enormous, especially among China and oil-exporting countries.

Foreign reserve managers have always been motivated by capital preservation, not profits, and foreign reserves during the past decade swelled to many times their previous level. Their investment strategies invariably valued liquidity over almost any other consideration. It is said markets are driven by fear and greed. The motivations of reserve managers are a perfect example of how the conditions for a financial crisis may be created not by greed, but by fear. They are not alone; many, if not most, investors will choose liquidity (cash-like safety) over returns. It is a policy that fails to recognise that even in the most highly traded markets, a debt is created to match the investment, and that concern for liquidity can render prudent lending irrelevant.

The dollar as the world's main reserve currency is the most important store of cash value – and therefore the most liquid instrument in the world. Reserve managers sought that liquidity over returns.

If investment opportunities are scarce, as they obviously were in the US between 2005 and 2007, why do more investors keep coming? We are taught that investors should choose investments that offer the greatest expected return for a given level of risk. If investors based their choice entirely on liquidity they would choose the lowest return, no matter what the risk.

Even the dollar is a finite resource, with finite investment opportunities. Too much investment in Treasury Bills and agency bonds by reserve managers displaced other investors into other markets. The crowding out forced investors into buying bonds that turned sour and financial innovations we would have been better off without. The crowding out occurred for so long, and to such an extent, that there really was no other place to invest except either to double up bets on existing trades, or simply to pretend that a poor investment was really a good one. Subprime lending was certainly a colossal mistake by bankers, but if you are told by a rating agency that it is rated as AAA and there are no other opportunities, it makes some sense. Similar 'crowding out' behaviour of investors was evident in the 1920s with the spectacular growth of investment trusts, which often invested in shares in a leveraged way, and competed to push up share prices.

Economists suggest this shows investors are ignoring fundamentals. That depends on how the fundamentals stack up but it also assumes rational behaviour by investors. Reserve managers are not rational because they make no balance of returns against liquidity; they choose liquidity first every time. If they control enough assets, therefore, reserve managers are the perfect bubble-blowers.

Not exactly classical

Highly liquid financial markets are a bit like a dress from a top designer; clients will buy the product whatever it looks like, because they trust the implicit value.

The popularity of many goods depends on their function as a demonstration of a value by proxy, so why should financial products be different? Luxury handbags, fashion, popular music and design depend on the informational message of the transaction itself, the reference to how much it cost, rather than its functional value.

There is an economic term to describe a product whose demand increases with a rise in price. It is called a 'Veblen good'. Economic demand and supply curves tell us demand should fall whenever prices rise, and yet we know that some products show that demand will rise with price.

The behaviour of a Veblen good resembles the way that highly liquid financial markets attract investors even though they usually produce the lowest returns. Veblen goods signal a proximity to cash. The price of a Rolls–Royce is dependent on the communication it represents; its price has lost dependence on supply and demand. Liquid markets too can signal the nearness of cash; unlike expensive cars, they always advertise the price.

There are other features of financial markets that are not present in classical economic models. Strong and persistent price trends are one such unexpected feature. In times of high liquidity, information that conflicts with the dominant trend may be ignored, often for an extended period, sometimes for years.

The propagation of market crises, even with no prospect of default

Classical economics says that both rises and falls in markets are caused by changes to supply or demand or to a change in the discounted future cash flow of the security, or impairment in the ability to repay borrowings. Concern about the discounted cash flow assumptions motivated Shiller to warn about the dot-com boom in 2000. Both are important. Yet, both still depend on future willingness to agree terms, both are dependent on liquidity.

Let us be very clear; the state of high liquidity does not cause a market rise in price because of independent demand for the product or instrument itself. High liquidity causes a market to rise in price because it endows the underlying instrument with cash-like attributes. In this way, bubbles may arise in markets simply through an increase in the number of potential participants – possible future buyers.

> bubbles may arise in markets simply through an increase in the number of potential participants

This is a radical notion. It means financial crises could emerge even in a world in which there is no prospect of default at all. All that is required is for liquidity to be removed – for instance, for a large investor to decide to transfer investments to another currency to invest elsewhere. The resulting disturbance may drive some investors to return to real cash, the ultimate store of liquidity, the high-powered stuff issued by central banks. The liquidity process that drove the market higher can then act in reverse. The removal of one large investor prompts others to seek safety in holding central bank cash, and refusing to deal with other market participants. The market reverts to a state of primitive transactions, prices collapse. The money literally disappears, which results in a financial crisis.

This may then lead to default by borrowers who are unable to roll over their finances, but these defaults would be consequence, not a cause, of a crisis. When a crisis emerges, many of the worst effects stem from relatively trivial changes in liquidity. The subprime market was dangerous but always small compared with the size of the US economy, and for months the problems in that market were known without any systemic implications. The final straw was the announcement that some hedge funds had lost money in subprime. These funds were not large, in the scheme of things. But the announcement caused a catastrophic collapse in liquidity.

Of course, loss of confidence in subprime was itself caused by the dramatic rise in defaults; the origins were fundamental. But rising defaults had been known about since at least late 2006 and did not cause a crisis. The underlying cause of the crisis was bad debts. But the denial of problems that encouraged dangerous debt to continue to be accumulated was caused by the confusion over the role of money as debt, and money as transaction.

In some cases central banks encouraged this confusion by accepting mortgage-backed securities. Some banks actually sold Japanese government bonds and bought mortgage-backed securities because they thought the mortgages were less risky than Japanese government debt. Central banks were complicit in encouraging the acceptance of transactional money that was ultimately compromised by the debts that lay behind it.

During credit booms banks will accept almost any asset in lieu of cash, as long as they know it will be accepted by others. The value is measured in units of state money. But once that magic is removed, there is almost no way to bring back the earlier value. A crisis increases the value of state money at the expense of private assets which sets off an escalation in loss of confidence in other assets. If the crisis is not halted by massive central intervention, it can lead to an exponential decay in liquidity and the breakdown of the financial system.

Why we do not see financial crises coming?

We do not see financial crises coming because the foundations of catastrophe also offer social improvement. Extra credit increases confidence in the future; money originally gave society time for advancing education, medicine, recreation and travel, and architecture. Extra credit seems to offer more of all these things.

The opening of the world through communications and trade was a good example of this wider social improvement – for many within Europe and the US as well as outside. The spread of communications, the increase in the provision of information, is also an indisputable benefit, along with the trade it brought. Information is deemed to be good, per se. No sensible – liberal – person would permit a reduction in information flow. The higher transactions and greater liquidity that follow wider participation allow a greater range of activities to be provided and funded for all members of society, at lower cost and with less effort. There is a vested interest in maintaining and furthering the information flow.

Improved communications is a short-hand for political freedom, increased personal liberty or rising health and living standards.

The past decade (or more) added, through increased transactions, to the money stock of the US and Europe. The basis of the West's confidence about the future was thought to be secure, because the currencies of the developed world were run by central banks we thought were steeped in caution.

What we didn't realise was the victory of the Cold War and the opening of the West to emerging markets had enriched us, literally, through the creation of our own reward. When we stopped believing, that reward vanished. The groundwork for the bust is laid, if you like, by us printing our own promissory notes and transacting for so long that our credit seems secure. The downfall came when the validity of the printing press was questioned. We are left with the notes and the promises, but not the capability to pay because the money is no longer there.

the notion that the money has just gone for good is alien

We do not see financial crises coming because we learn that only conjurors make money disappear, and then only for fun. The notion that the money has just gone for good is alien. It was there, and we made commitments based on it. The Romantic poet Coleridge wrote: 'It sometimes happens that we are punished for our faults, in the causation of which these faults had no share; and this I have always felt the severest punishment.'[5] Through innovation, increased transactions, investor behaviour and deregulation we have seen the stages that cause liquidity to disappear. When liquidity – and therefore money – disappears there is a feeling of injustice by all who depended on its ability to pay, both borrowers and lenders. The lenders feel cheated, the borrowers feel tricked.

---

5 S. T. Coleridge, *Biographia Literaria*, Chapter XXIV, 1817.

Did the Asian crisis teach us nothing?

A tiger's meat is edible.

Sila Khoamchai, *The Path of the Tiger*
(tr. Marcel Barang, 1994)

In the past ten years, global flows of capital have had many effects on the world's finances and without doubt they helped create the credit bubble of 2005–07. The movement of money affected emerging Asia's trade and reserves policies, influenced Japan's export of capital and led to pressure for regional convergence within the European single currency. All three capital flows promoted huge cross-border lending with little regard for the wider consequences. In the end, the world was not enough for the flows, and resulted in huge misallocation of resources in destination countries. Along the way was not one financial crisis but a series, in Japan, Asia, America and Europe.

The causes of the current financial crisis have tended to focus on the errors of bankers, and global flows of capital have barely figured in the public debate. Yet these flows are as important an influence, and probably more so, in causing the crisis than the decisions of Western bankers. The public disgust at lavish reward should not distract from the wider geo-political background to the crisis. This chapter attempts to redress that imbalance.

> the public disgust at lavish reward should not distract from the wider geo-political background

Asia's crisis: first of the globalised era

The Asian crisis of 1997–98 is in many ways the most important precursor to the current crisis. Devaluation and the subsequent depression of countries across South-East Asia that occurred during the crisis also had long-term effects on Chinese economic policy. In particular, the damage inflicted on countries such as Thailand and Indonesia coloured how China viewed both foreign investment and the dollar. Because of policies adopted in the aftermath of the crisis, some Western countries would suffer a similar fate as the one that befell Thailand and the other Asian Tigers.

At the time, the lesson learned by Asia was to adhere more closely to the US currency. It was a policy that required a growing stock of dollar reserves. China especially expanded its reserves and re-invested into 'safe', low-yielding assets such as Treasury bonds, and increasingly the agency bonds of the Federal National Mortgage Association ('Fannie Mae') and the Federal Home Loan Mortgage Corporation ('Freddie Mac') – lending vast sums to the US in the process. As we now know, the policy was much less safe than was assumed at the time. Over the next ten years, this course of action led to distortions in investment in America and contributed to the expansion of credit: this found an outlet in subprime mortgage lending and related structured investments leading to the credit crisis. Asian foreign exchange policies, later followed by oil producers in the Middle East and Russia, have an important responsibility for the vast misallocation of capital in the US.

Nor was the export of capital limited to emerging economies. Japan followed similar policies in response to the bursting of its 'bubble economy', providing a steady flow of low-cost funding for all manner of investment vehicles, from European local authorities to hedge funds. In the process, the flood of Japanese capital exports contributed to the credit explosion in Western economies.

Wounded Tiger: Thailand and the crisis of 1997–98

In July 1997, Thailand devalued its currency, the baht. The devaluation initiated the most disruptive economic shock to hit South-East Asia since the Second World War. Country after country followed the Thai example, allowing their currencies to float, free from the fixed pegs to the US dollar. In the circumstances, 'float' was an entirely inappropriate term: all of the currencies sank. Before the Thai devaluation, foreign investment flows had poured into the region, seeking higher interest rates and investment opportunities. The flows were encouraged by the currency stability brought about by the pegs to the dollar. Devaluations caused Western investor confidence in the region to evaporate; and as they left, so did liquidity; money disappeared just as it was to do in 2007–08. Thailand, one of the leading Asian Tiger economies, fell into a sudden and devastating depression.

Thailand had pegged its currency to the US dollar partly because its imports and exports were denominated in dollars but also because the link to the dollar encouraged foreign investors. It was also keen to develop Bangkok as a regional financial centre. Reforms in the late 1980s loosened capital restrictions to encourage these aims.

Attracting foreign capital and increasing the importance of Bangkok as a financial centre became an aim of policy. In 1993, the Thai government approved the Bangkok International Banking Facility (BIBF) to act as a 'gateway' for capital to enter and exit the country and, from the start, particularly encouraged short-term overseas borrowing by Thais. The gateway soon opened wider, with other restrictions lifted.

Allowing foreign capital unrestricted access to an emerging economy has always been a controversial policy. Emerging countries are keen to encourage growth from the capital that arrives, but critics point to the need for adjustment. There is always concern that flows devoted to investment in local securities could reverse abruptly.

Thai authorities recognised that demand for the baht might force its exchange rate higher. To accommodate this, they planned for the fixed exchange rate regime to become more flexible over time. This seemed a reasonable assumption. Thailand had shown steady progress and won plaudits from international agencies for its far-sighted policy. The World Bank said in 1994: 'Thailand provides an excellent example of the dividends to be obtained through outward orientation, receptivity to foreign investment, and a market-friendly philosophy...' The comments echo the same encouragement of financial liquidity given by central banks in America and Japan. Transactions were the measure of success.

Similar policies were introduced across the region. Indonesia removed restrictions on short-term trade finance and also on private sector project finance and capital raisings. Korea had already relaxed restrictions on short-term finance for banks, while keeping capital controls for corporations.[1]

Easing of controls demonstrated the dictum that liquidity generates liquidity. And as the liquidity rose, so the money supply expanded to meet the extra liabilities created. Foreign lending in particular surged after the introduction of the BIBF, rising to 12 per cent of GDP in 1995. Foreign bank loans through the BIBF rose from $8 billion in 1993 to $50 billion in 1996. Whereas funds had been dedicated to long-term investments, after 1993 investment was dominated by investment in bonds and shares – the riskiest sort of investment for both the investor and the country receiving the investment. In 1920s America, lending in securities also grew strongly – though then it was concentrated in equity markets rather than bonds. Similar changes occurred in other liberalising Asian countries. In Thailand, private sector debt to GDP also rose, from 64 per cent in 1987 to 142 per cent in 1996. Property investment increased dramatically.

investment in golf courses represents an epitome of conspicuous misallocation

1 Commentary on the Financial Stability Forum's Report of the Working Group on Capital Flows, Andrew Cornford, December 2000, UNTAD.

Investment in golf developments was particularly popular. If investment in residential property represents a diversion of resources from future productive capital, then investment in golf courses represents an epitome of conspicuous misallocation. Based solely on status for value, golf developments represent a 'Veblen good' of property – they signal the proximity of cash by displaying its waste, as we saw in Chapter 1. Not surprisingly, golf developments figured largely in the later property booms of Florida, California, Spain, Ireland and Portugal. Perhaps the most convincing signal of an unsustainable boom in 2008 was the news that US property tycoon Donald Trump wished to open a lavish golf resort in Scotland, the country that invented the game and probably has more golf courses per square mile than any other.

Competition within banking grew too, often an encouragement to risky lending. The BIBF offered foreign banks the opportunity to open offices in Thailand and many did. The same foreign banks used their greater access to international capital to take over high profile local companies, improve the services provided by these companies and win over local customers. Thai banks were reduced to competing for less-creditworthy customers.

As foreign lending grew, the country's current account deficit expanded. In 1993, Australian economist John Pitchford said a private sector current account deficit – such as Thailand's – was largely an agreement between 'consenting adults' and showed the preference of investors for higher returns. It should not therefore be a threat.[2] That's all very well unless the consenting adults fail to agree on repayments. Thailand's net borrowings from foreigners grew to 8 per cent of GDP in 1996. To put this into context, anything over 4 per cent is considered dangerous because it exposes domestic borrowers to the vagaries of foreign lenders. Thailand was borrowing from foreigners at about two times the rate that was considered prudent. There was little concern by investors, because almost all debt was held by the private sector, which in theory meant lenders were simply funding business. It was almost all denominated in dollars, and it was almost all short-

2 'Current account deficits: the Autralian debate', Rochelle Belkar, Lynne Cockerell, Christopher Kent, RBA Discussion paper, February 2007.

term. Similar large foreign flows entered Indonesia, Korea, Malaysia and the Philippines. More lending went to property. In the Philippines and Thailand 15–20 per cent of banks' total assets were devoted to real estate or related businesses. In Malaysia and Indonesia, the figure was closer to 20–25 per cent.[3] There were echoes here of the same scale of foreign lending to the US between 2003 and 2007 – just one of the links that led from the Asian crisis to the current global crisis. Similar foreign flows, devoted to real estate – perhaps the least productive long-term investment for a country, were a feature also of Spain, Romania, Bulgaria, Hungary, Latvia, Estonia and Lithuania – all countries that suffered badly from the 2007–08 financial crisis.

The lesson seems clear: don't borrow from foreigners. However, the lesson is mistaken. For the creation of debt is merely an expansion of a balance sheet with both sides. If the lenders insist on lending, there is little the country can do to stop it. Second-tier German banks forced lending on to (willing) Spanish property developers because they themselves could not compete in their home market. Thai property developers received loans from Japanese banks because the banks' home market was imploding.

There is a limit to the amount of money that can be jammed into a narrow investment space, as even America discovered ten years later. On 18 February 1997 the *Wall Street Journal* wrote: 'Investors in Thailand, fasten your seat belts. An increasing amount of speculative money is trying to dislodge the baht's loose peg to the US dollar, many regional financial executives say. Analysts believe Thailand's central bank will put up a strong fight against the speculators, and many say they are betting the central bank will win – but at a heavy cost.'[4] By the end of June it was evident that the domestic financial system was collapsing – money was disappearing, just as it did from the financial system of Europe and America in August 2007.

3 'Asia-Europe relations in the light of the Southeast Asian financial crisis', Walden Bello, seminar to TNI ASEM, Amsterdam, 31 October 1997.
4 'Financiers fear attack on baht; forex battle may hurt economy', Paul Sherer, *Wall Street Journal*, 10 February 1997.

On June 29, the Bank of Thailand announced the suspension of sixteen financial companies and issued a guarantee of depositors and creditors funds in the rest of the financial system.[5] It did not stem the crisis. On 30 June, prime minister Chavalit Yongchaiyudh assured Thais there would be no devaluation. Three days later, on July 2, the baht freed itself from the dollar peg and floated, downwards and fast.

Before the float, one dollar was worth 26 baht. The following day one dollar was worth 29 baht. By the end of January 1998, one dollar was worth 55 baht, more or less a halving of the Thai currency's value in six months.

Following the Thai devaluation, pressure appeared on the Indonesian rupiah, the Philippine peso and the Malaysian ringgit. On 11 July, both the Indonesian and the Philippine authorities were forced to introduce 'flexibility' to their currency – effectively a float. The central bank of Malaysia, Bank Negara, attempted to stem the outflow with intervention but on 14 July, the Malaysian authorities allowed the currency to float. On 24 July, a 'currency meltdown' occurred with speculative attacks on the ringgit, peso and rupiah. By mid-August, Indonesia had abandoned its attempts to defend the rupiah; the currency plunged, by about 20 per cent against the dollar.

In the third quarter of 1997, the outflow was 222 billion baht, in the fourth quarter it was 102 billion baht. The first quarter of 1998 saw an outflow of 200 billion baht, the second quarter an outflow of 87 billion baht, the third quarter an outflow of 128 billion baht and the fourth quarter of 1998 an outflow of 236 billion baht. In all, this was one baht for every five in the Thai economy. The banking sector experienced the greatest outflows, prompted by concerns about its exposure to risky loans, which, of course, became increasingly risky because of the financial crisis.

capital flight on this scale drains all liquidity from a domestic banking system

5 'Financial sector crisis and restructuring lessons from Asia', IMF occasional paper 188, January 2000.

Capital flight on this scale drains all liquidity from a domestic banking system. Yet this money did not leave in the form of baht, it left in the form of dollars. The baht measure overstates the value of the disappearing currency – in international terms – because the value of the baht was falling. In fact, money was simply disappearing from the financial system in the same way it disappears in any financial crisis. The paper assets denoting debts that had circulated as a form of 'extended currency' became unacceptable. In 2007, the rejection of the extended money was substituted by demand for 'central bank' money – cash and central bank reserves. In Thailand, and other Asian currencies caught up in the devaluations, there was no domestic currency benchmark acceptable. Pegged to the dollar, the dollar itself became their 'central bank' money, the only acceptable medium of exchange. Whenever there is a crisis, the same run to familiar and guaranteed liquidity emerges.

Hedge funds strike it rich

The devaluations, and the economic damage they caused, soon prompted Asian countries to look for someone to blame. A familiar list of international (especially US and/or Jewish) financiers and funds were criticised. At a meeting of the ASEAN regional forum in Kuala Lumpur on 25 July 1997, foreign ministers issued a communiqué criticising the 'well co-ordinated' efforts to destabilise currencies for 'self-serving purposes...' Malaysian prime minister Mahathir saw the handiwork of hedge funds, and specifically singled out George Soros as responsible for attacks on the ringgit. He believed Soros was behind the attack on the ringgit as punishment for the Malaysian government support for the military junta in Myanmar, which had been accepted into ASEAN in late July. Dr Mahathir also suggested that Jewish financiers gave the Jews a bad name: 'The impression created is of course that being Jewish they have lots of money. They know how to manipulate money...'

The comments about Jews were poisonous nonsense. The accusation that hedge funds had made large amounts of money from the crisis was, on the other hand, correct. Hedge funds did very well out of the episode – unlike the mauling they received ten years later during the US financial crisis, when they also got the blame. In the year that followed the Thai devaluation, the Credit Suisse/Tremont Hedge Fund Index showed returns of 23.62 per cent; we can assume most of the profit came from Asia. 'Global macro' type hedge funds, which were most involved in speculative selling of Asian currencies, returned 40.53 per cent. Tellingly, returns from macro funds had been lacklustre until July 1997, followed by a boost just at the time of the devaluations. An investor letter from Julian Robertson's Jaguar fund reported monthly net returns of 11.7 per cent in July 1997, compared with cumulative returns of only 0.7 per cent for the first six months of the year. George Soros's Quantum fund saw returns rise from 14 per cent in June to 27 per cent at the end of July and his Quota fund specialising in equity and macro-economic strategies gained 20 per cent in July alone.

The funds, of course, were merely capitalising on what they assessed as an unsustainable situation; they acted as messengers of is demise. The real trigger for the crisis was the unsustainably high borrowing from foreigners and a bursting property bubble – the same trigger for the current financial crisis a decade later. It was the realisation that the billions of dollars of investment would not be repaid that caused the money based on an imagined future to disappear.

Some hedge funds – a minority – did well in 2007–08 on the fall in mortgage bond prices. They too found their success confused with being the cause. The most successful had to appear before a US Congress committee to explain why they had the bad taste to be right in their investments.

It was not just hedge funds that were withdrawing their capital. In 1997, the region saw an outflow by foreign banks of $11.4 billion, a swing of 11 per cent of GDP for the combined five countries affected. Those that remained cut their lending and refused to roll over loans. In fact, the flows were not all one-way. While banks were leaving, Western investors were buying up the cheapened assets in Thailand and the rest. Western investors thus appeared to gain twice; by gains made through selling the currency (hedge funds and some banks) and again by direct investment in the countries after the devaluations.[6] Foreigners – mostly Western, mostly US foreigners – first pumping money into the region, then abruptly withdrawing it made a strong impression on the victims.

In fact, the reality was more complex. Among the most aggressive withdrawers were Japanese banks, which had domestic problems of their own. They had been heavy lenders to South-East Asia because Japanese manufacturers (especially electronics and textiles) had shifted many of their plants to the 'Tiger economies'. Japanese banks had made loans not only to the local branches of familiar Japanese companies but also made consumer loans, and loans on real estate – the lesson of the Japanese bubble economy apparently had not been learnt.

Although the trade flows between Asian countries and Japan were an important component of the toxic mix in the Thai economy, local attention focused on hedge funds and free-wheeling US capitalism. The stigma of predatory hedge funds and the disruption they seemed to have caused remained.

A profound effect on Chinese policy

damage from too much foreign capital affected Chinese policy profoundly

Damage from too much foreign capital affected Chinese policy profoundly. China became convinced that it needed, first, an immensely strong foreign currency reserve fund to defend itself against any conceivable attack from foreign hedge funds, and second, to control strictly how foreign money entered and left the country. To pursue this policy required the pegging of the currency against the dollar, which in turn required reserves. Thus began the accumulation of dollars which, through its narrow investment focus, was a large contributor to the disaster in Western economies a decade later.

---

6 Medhi Krongkaew, Capital flows and economic crisis in Thailand, *The Developing Economies* XXXVII–4, December 1999.

Later, the Asian crisis was summed up by academic Padma Desai: 'Financial globalisation is a complex process in which the animal spirits of risk-prone, return savvy investors from the developed market economies with global, electronic reach collide with the weak financial institutions, traditional corporate practices, and vulnerable political arrangements of emerging market economies with disastrous consequences for the latter.'[7] If 'risk-prone, return savvy investors from developed market economies' is changed to 'risk-averse, naïve reserve managers from developing economies', this description of Thai vulnerability could read as an uncanny prediction of the problems that emerged in the US.

Aftermath in property: ruin, folly and delusion

Even with interest rates high in the Far East, borrowing for investment in real estate had become a mania. Apartments, shopping centres, houses, office blocks sprang up in expanding suburbs around Bangkok. 'It would not be an exaggeration to say that half of Bangkok's landed families became real estate developers and the other half became real estate investors and speculators. During weekends, developers would set up stalls in supermarkets and department stores to market their wares and real estate associations organised roving fairs with houses for sale. Small flats became a convenient unit of investment for middle and high-income families and this drove up demand.'[8] If this sounds familiar to Western readers now, it was thought alien to the West in the mid-1990s, even though stock markets boomed.

Not surprisingly, real estate suffered badly from withdrawal of foreign lending after the devaluation. Bangkok Land Public Company, one of Thailand's largest developers at the time, was half-way through the construction of a $1 billion scheme called Muang Thong Thani (MTT), a mixture of residential and commercial property that was promoted as the largest of its kind in the world.

7 Padma Desai, *Financial Crisis, Contagion, and Containment*, Princeton University Press, 2003.
8 Yap Kioe Sheng, Sakchai Kirinpanu, Bangkok's Housing Boom and the Financial Crisis in Thailand: Only the sky was the limit, June 1999.

The third phase of the project was begun but the devaluation of the baht killed any attempt to finish the project. It quickly became clear that many of the properties had been bought by speculators on a small deposit. They were now unable to pay for the balance owed.

Over ten years later the project remains almost as it was on the day the baht began its descent. Time has rendered the development much less appealing; in some places it resembles an urban wasteland of raw concrete pillars rising 250 feet into the air, uninhabited and desolate.

MTT also came to represent an unwillingness to take defeat, and take the loss. The project continues to wait for the return of investors or buyers. It was behaviour reflected in the maxim 'Don't pay, don't close, don't run.' Many similar projects can still be seen around Bangkok and across Thailand, although few offer such an impressive vision of failure as MTT.

Examples of similar extravagant, and thwarted, ambition can be seen in Malaysia, Indonesia and the Philippines; unfinished buildings, and with internal structures unprotected from the tropical climate. There are claims that these ghost structures will not last another ten years before they fall down: the recent construction collapse in Madrid and Dublin may invite aesthetic disfigurement of these cities that may last a generation.

Lessons for China

The Chinese political elite were horrified by the disruption visited on Thailand, Indonesia and the other South Asian victims of the crisis. On no account should China allow policy flexibility that could be abused by foreign speculators. In response, Beijing tightened its grip on capital controls. Only total control over trade policy by the regime was permitted. With the control over capital, the Chinese government also acquired control of the yuan/dollar exchange rate. The counterpart to Chinese currency policy was to determine the value of its own currency in terms of the dollar. As exports continued to grow in the following years, the dollars generated had to be recycled to avoid inflation in China.

Investment in American assets was the obvious, and apparently the safest, destination for the extra dollars. The US was the global hegemon, its economy was by far the largest in the world and its bond markets the most liquid and open; surely there could be no problems from this policy? Unfortunately, there were to be serious long-term problems.

So serious, in fact, that a conspiracist might conclude that the damage this policy eventually inflicted on the American economy was part of a long-term plan by the Chinese to undermine US dominance. If so, it was spectacularly successful. On the one hand, Chinese exports undermined America's own manufacturing. The recycling of reserves would add to the undermining of US political pre-eminence in the world by almost destroying its financial system.

A conspiracy seems implausible, especially for anyone with experience of Chinese investment policy. The 'crowding out' effects that the Chinese reserves strategy created in American markets were due to the crudeness of this policy, not subtlety. There was nothing conspiratorial about the placing of so many recycled dollars into the Treasury and government agency markets. It was simply parking cash, as uncomplicated as making a bank deposit, and as unthinking.

> it was simply parking cash, as uncomplicated as making a bank deposit, and as unthinking

The lesson Chinese authorities drew from the Asian crisis was to remain deeply wary of international bodies, including the International Monetary Fund (IMF).[9] In June 2007, the People's Bank of China, the central bank, said the IMF 'should carry out its duties based on mutual understanding and respect', especially for the views of developing countries. It was a statement that managed to sound both defiant and worried simultaneously.

Lessons were drawn elsewhere in the region too. Most credit busts are followed by the now familiar witch-hunt to find who had

9 'China warns IMF over renminbi rate', *Financial Times*, 21 June 2007.

caused it. The Asian countries blamed the West, particularly the US, the IMF and hedge funds.

To ensure there never could again be speculative attacks against their currencies, countries in the region, except Thailand, began to accumulate enormous dollar reserves. By early 1999, the Philippines had rebuilt its reserves above the level that they were at before the devaluation of the Thai baht. Malaysian reserves exceeded pre-crisis levels by early 1999, and continued to grow. Indonesian reserves were more depleted than other countries and took longer to rebuild, reaching pre-crisis levels only in 2000. Korea had rebuilt its reserves to pre-crisis levels by the end of the first quarter of 1998 and reserves continued to grow at a very fast pace in the years that followed; from $30 billion in mid-1998, to $90 billion by mid-2000. The greatest reserve accumulator of all was China.

The International Monetary Fund responds

The International Monetary Fund had been intimately involved in advising Asia's economies on economic policy throughout the 1980s and 1990s. It grew concerned about the imbalances in the current accounts but its assessment was that adjustments could be gradual. On the other hand, the fund was a strong supporter of liberalising measures taken by various countries. The IMF believed that the more open the economies, the more likely they were to modernise, to the benefit of their populations. It was a variant on the doctrine followed by Alan Greenspan, US Federal Reserve chairman, in his support for financial innovation.

An IMF annual report, released on 30 April 1997, just two months before the devastating devaluation, and with money already leaving the country, 'strongly praised Thailand's remarkable economic performance and the authorities' consistent record of sound macroeconomic policies'. Indonesia and Malaysia received similar plaudits.

In retrospect, it was clear that the public pronouncements of both the IMF and local authorities did not reflect the whole picture. In June 1997, the IMF had attempted to present a report critical of

Thai economic policies. The Thai government refused to allow the report to be released. Relations between the IMF and the Asian countries were tense before the devaluation. They would get a lot worse after the devaluations.

Initial response: support at a price

As usual in a crisis, the IMF was forced into an ad hoc policy. It provided funds to the affected countries directly and also organised funding from other donors, such as public and private Japanese organisations and bodies such as the World Bank and the Asian Development Bank.

The fund itself admitted the reforms that accompanied assistance would feature 'structural reforms that had few precedents in depth and breadth'. The broad outline was to clear out the 'bad banks' and the 'bad loans', whilst tightening fiscal and monetary policies of the affected countries – exactly the opposite policies were followed in the West later.

The tight monetary conditions demanded by the IMF drove local businesses into bankruptcy. Good local companies as well as bad were simply unable to pay the cost of servicing their loans.

Fiscal policy was also toughened. The devaluations were thought to be partly due to unsustainable current account deficits and the IMF decided the governments should take a lead in savings – through controlling their spending, even though their economies were entering recession. It was akin to a surgeon insisting that the patient have no anesthetic. It was a policy unlikely to be inflicted on a developed country in difficulty. The measure of how much opinions have changed about the 'right way' to handle a crisis is to compare the IMF prescriptions with the huge fiscal stimulus unleashed by the US government in 2008.

The programmes came with another sting. The IMF readily acknowledged that 'one of the more controversial structural policies' in the support programmes was capital account liberalisation – effectively allowing foreign ownership of assets. This was particularly problematic in Korea. Now, foreigners were being given an opportunity to buy Korean assets cheaply as part of the deal with the IMF, after causing the fall in the first place. National pride, already hurt by devaluation, felt this was particularly unjust.

> financial cleansing is often accompanied by
> political cleansing

Financial cleansing is often accompanied by political cleansing. Indonesian politics was ruptured partly as a result of the IMF aid package. One component of the loan conditions was that the Suharto government was forced to eliminate subsidies on basic goods. As a result, on 5 May 1998, the price of kerosene, electricity and gasoline rose by up to 70 per cent, prompting riots. Fifteen days after the removal of the subsidies, Suharto himself was removed after leading his country for 32 years.

The headquarters of the IMF is located just off Pennsylvania Avenue in Washington, approximately four minutes' walk from the White House. Because of the IMF's response to the Asian crisis, Asia assumed the fund acted as an agent of the US government, to cheapen assets, and to hobble local governments, wringing binding commitments from the aided governments on American access to their markets, and their companies.

The Americans certainly pressed the IMF to act fast to halt contagion. The big fear was a Chinese devaluation. Chinese trade with America was much more important than Thailand, Indonesia and Malaysia. If China devalued, its cheaper goods could decimate American manufacturing.

Sell high, buy other countries low

American influence extended much further than simply protecting its own industry from cheaper competition. Its companies, along with other Westerners, having led the exodus, now returned to buy cheap – and desperate – Asian companies, much as locals had feared. In November 1997, Citibank signed a memorandum of understanding with First Bangkok City bank to take a stake of at least 50.1 per cent. In the following weeks there were other statements of interest in Thai banking groups from American International, Development Bank of Singapore, Credit Suisse First Boston, and Westdeutsche Landesbank. Bangkok Investment Company was acquired by American International Group (AIG).

Korea offered prime pickings; its economy was much larger and better developed than others in the region. The IMF stipulated Korea should allow Japanese companies greater access to the Korean market, despite a large trade surplus between the two countries that favoured Japan. As part of the IMF conditions, Korea agreed to allow foreign investors to acquire majority stakes in listed companies, with the aim of allowing full takeovers by the end of 1998. According to the *Financial Times*:[10] 'The full opening of the capital markets will pave the way for foreign takeovers of Korean companies and increase foreign competition in the financial sector...'

The aftermath, and what we should have learned

When Western commentators talk about the current financial crisis, they usually limit their focus to events that occurred after August 2007 or even after Lehman's bankruptcy in September 2008. The effect of the Asian crisis led a decade later to a credit crunch in America, and through America to Europe. There was, therefore, a line of almost constant financial crisis from 1990 through to 2008. It originated in Japan, spread to South Asia, and progressed to the dot-com boom before its final flourish in Western housing and financial markets.

The rolling crisis would moderate for a time, but it never went away. From 1990 onwards at least one banking system was in crisis, and one property market collapsing, during any year. The West largely ignored the crises; the victims were emerging economies, or Germany adapting to reunification, or Japan recovering from the 'bubble'. The apparent special cases invoked to explain each crisis mask the linkages between them.

10 'Reform schedule is price of Korean Christmas rescue', *Financial Times*, 27 December 1998.

Globalisation brought many benefits, and these will, I hope, survive the recent retreat to national protection. Yet, globalisation was also accompanied by an almost permanent dislocation in one or more financial systems. The information and financial freedom that accompanied globalisation and brought benefits to vast numbers of previously poverty-stricken people in emerging economies certainly came with a dark companion.

Over the ten years that followed the Asian crisis, the symptoms of Thai problems (overheated economy, real-estate bubble, lending mania, foreign borrowing, and current account deficit) grew ever more obvious in the US and several European economies. No-one believed that the devastation that had been visited on small, emerging economies could appear in the largest and most developed economies of the world.

America benefits, but does it learn?

The Americans welcomed the Asian devaluations. The Clinton administration strongly believed the benefits of cheaper products from devalued Asian currencies would count more than the damage done to US manufacturers by a stronger dollar. Cheaper Asian currencies did cause Republicans to worry about the effects on manufacturing, which might not be able to compete. Senator Jim Leach (Republican) said: 'The concern about lost jobs more than offsets the benefits of cheaper goods.' The administration won, together with consumers. US consumers continued their dominant influence over economic policy for the next decade; a role that was to encourage the expansion of mortgage lending after the dot-com crash.

The Clinton administration supported a 'strong dollar' (cheap goods) policy and gave it frequent backing from the Treasury secretary, Robert Rubin. With a background in Wall Street – including foreign exchange trading – Rubin offered wholehearted support to the benefits of increased trade in the aftermath of the Cold War. He was also a believer in the inherent strength of the American economy. Rubin's internationalism – with the leading role for the US – appeared in a speech he gave in June 1997 celebrating the fiftieth anniversary of the Marshall Plan – the plan that rescued the European economies after the Second World War.

It was an important speech because it laid out the ethical assumptions that had underpinned US trade policy since 1945, and which seemed even more relevant after the end of the Cold War.[11]

> 'The imperative for US leadership and engagement in the global economy have not changed since the Marshall Plan – though the circumstances obviously have. In fact, in some respects that imperative has increased, just as the centrality of economics to foreign policy, which was great then, has also in some respects increased. In 1947, 12 per cent of our economy relied on trade. Today, that figure has more than doubled. In 1947, the vast preponderance of leading US corporations viewed themselves as American companies with offices abroad. Today, they see themselves as global corporations based in the United States. In 1947, capital markets were national, with very little flow across country borders. Today, there is an enormous integrated global capital market, with vast cross-border investment and financing flows every day. Technology, political change and market openings have sped our economies towards integration and created new opportunities for growth, but also new risks. It is no exaggeration when we say that our economic well-being is enormously and irreversibly linked to the rest of the world.'

Rubin laid out in evangelistic terms the future shape of the global economy

Rubin's speech was made the same month as the Thai devaluation. The next decade would underline the links between America and the rest of the world. Rubin laid out in evangelistic terms the future shape of the global economy; including Washington's responsibility to take the lead with companies that could no longer be considered national assets, but global enterprises, flow of capital to maintain growth, and, of course, increasing US influence. Rubin believed the global economy was a moral

11 Remarks by Treasury secretary Robert E. Rubin on the 50th anniversary of Marshall Plan, George Washington University, 2 June 1997.

construct to be used to improve the lives of workers and consumers in both developing countries and America. It was a policy that dove-tailed with the leadership doctrine of the Fed's Alan Greenspan and the profit motive of US bankers.

While Rubin's stance was moral, it contained a triumphalism reflected by others in the administration. One week after Rubin gave his speech celebrating the Marshall Plan, deputy Treasury secretary Larry Summers spoke to the World Trade Conference in Denver and gave the self-interested counterpoint to Rubin's moral doctrine:[12]

> 'It is increasingly clear that we are also the world's only economic superpower. In an era of globalisation, we are the world's most flexible and dynamic economy. And we are uniquely positioned to interact with the emerging world due to our global reach, the diversity of our people and the flexibility of our institutions. We dominate or lead in virtually every post-industrial industry.... The strong position we are in benefits the American people. But it also gives us a new authority on the world stage and an opportunity to shape a world of our making. In an era of globalisation where national borders no longer define the boundaries of economies, we can use our position to encourage the free flow of goods, capital, technology and ultimately wealth across the globe. That will improve standards of living and create new markets for our goods.'

Summers' words are a celebration of America the inventor of the internet, evangelist of new technologies, defender of global finance and global integration. Despite their different statements, Rubin's and Summers' belief in the redeeming power of economic flexibility echoed the views of former British prime minister Margaret Thatcher. Thatcher's belief in market economics in her political thought was closely allied to a conviction that the Cold War could be won partly by empowering consumers. The doctrine stuck. Summers again: 'for the first time in a half century we have no obvious enemy... With the end of the Cold War and

12 'American global leadership: the Denver summit and beyond', Lawrence Summers, World Trade Conference, Denver, 10 June 1997.

globalisation of the world economy, we have a historic opportunity to further strengthen the global system.' A stronger global system meant consolidation of American ascendancy, particularly the US consumer. It was an attitude that permeated the Congress with support for housing. The primacy of the consumer, backed by finance, also became the cornerstone of Greenspan's philosophy at the Fed.

At the time, Washington seemed to have everything to win from the Asian crisis. A boost for the benefits of the strong dollar came with a nearly 30 per cent fall in crude oil prices as a result of the crisis – and the economic slowdown in the region. The fall in price caused John Lichtblau of the Petroleum Industry Research Foundation to announce: 'This is a bonanza for consumers.' He meant, of course, US consumers, not consumers anywhere else.

The 'knowledge economy', software and financial services: all of these aspects of business were dominated by American companies. In his Denver address, Summers summed up a new world full of promise: 'We dominate or lead in virtually every post-industrial industry. Think of Microsoft in software, Federal Express in shipping or NASDAQ in financial services.'[13] The new world of 'logistics and statistics' invented by America was destined to be its route to further greatness.

many of the markers of failure in Asia suddenly appeared in the home of capitalism itself

America had won the Cold War, benefited from the Asian mess and opened the world to trade. It enjoyed a sustained economic expansion with a strong dollar while other countries seemed to suffer disastrous economic contractions through devaluations. The world wanted its currency and its assets. In return, all it needed to do was to keep buying the imports from its trade partners, through its consumers. From this base of almost unbounded optimism, the lineaments of future disaster took shape. Within a decade, many of the markers of failure in Asia suddenly appeared in the home of

13 'American global leadership: the Denver summit and beyond', Lawrence Summers, World Trade Conference, Denver, 10 June 1997.

capitalism itself, exposing the same unsustainable optimism and leading to the same evaporation or flight of capital. Even the asset class most affected was the same; apartments, golf resorts, new shopping centres, together with the same sort of businesses; property developers, mortgage lenders, foreign and domestic banks. At the time, the Asian crisis seemed an almost earth-shattering event; yet within a decade its lessons had been unlearned almost completely. Partly, this was due to the overwhelming faith in US command of global capitalism, partly it was just a remarkably short memory.

Loving the dollar: lessons from a great flood of capital

I believe that all times are complex and uncertain.

Robert Rubin, 12 April 2002

The popular view is that the recent financial crisis emerged from reckless investment. In reality, the crisis was created, to a large degree, by the most risk-averse investors; those charged with protecting the foreign exchange reserves. How can the most conservative investors in the world contribute to a financial crisis? As every good school child knows, you can do anything if you try really hard; and reserve managers tried really hard.

After the Asian crisis of 1997 the world sought dollars, motivated solely by the reserve status of the currency. Despite the grand plans of Robert Rubin and Larry Summers at the US Treasury, foreigners placed little value on the economic prowess of American business. Nor did they place much value on the returns earned on their dollar investments. They just sought safety and liquidity.

As we saw in the last chapter, the Asian crisis demonstrated the damage that could occur without enough dollars to defend a currency peg. The accumulation of dollar reserves was driven by a desire to avoid future speculative attack. But the incentive to accumulate dollars was also driven by the liquidity of the investments the currency offered. Reserve managers rarely invest in anything except high-quality debt and an attraction of the dollar was the amount of debt available. Their investment, of course, created more American debt.

Saving is simply deferred consumption; so the countries investing in such debt deferred their own consumption so that Americans could borrow – and consume – immediately. This made sense in light of the trade flows that had emerged through the 1990s. Asian countries had oriented their entire export effort to satisfying US consumers and needed to ensure their products continued to find a buyer. By maintaining cheap currencies against the dollar, exports were kept at an attractive price, and dollar earnings were collected, to be recycled in reserve investments. Over time, the recycled dollars reduced the investment returns of other investors in US markets. Eventually, the low returns forced other investors, and banks, into alternative investments, some of which included mortgage bonds, collateralised debt obligations (CDOs). Thus reserve managers, and Asian countries in particular, played an important role in creating the conditions for the financial crisis.

> reserve managers … played an important role in creating the conditions for the financial crisis

The irony is that the crisis was evidence of too much capital; or too much capital in the wrong place. This was the opposite of the dearth of capital expected in the early 1990s. After the fall of the Berlin Wall, there was a profound fear that the world simply did not have enough capital to fix the dilapidated infrastructure of the newly liberated countries and invest in new business. In 1995, international equity portfolios held about $1.5 trillion. The anticipated cost of new infrastructure in the next decade was at least $1 trillion, leaving little for business investment.

In fact, the pool of capital seemed to be shrinking, not growing. The second-largest economy in the world, Japan, was nursing wounds from its 'bubble economy'. Japan was a major trading partner for East Asian countries and had previously provided large amounts of capital into the region. Japan remained the largest single lender, but by 1993 it had reduced its role as Asian financier.

Eastern European countries, newly liberated from the communist bloc, were also demanding a slice of the capital pie. Infrastructure in the region was often beyond repair. Factories contained machinery that had operated since the 1950s. Some factories even used machinery liberated by the Red Army at the end of the Second World War. New roads were needed, airports required upgrades and social infrastructure was way behind the West. Some funds could be provided by agencies such as the European Bank of Reconstruction and Development and some came from joint-ventures with Western companies. More capital came from asset sales to Western companies. But there seemed never to be enough. Three years after the fall of the Berlin Wall, some East Berliners still opened their front rooms as makeshift bars for passers-by to attract a little extra income. It was symptomatic of a region desperate for foreign money.

The shock appearance of money

So, how did the capital drought turn into a flood? Where did the money come from? Like money everywhere and at all times, it was created, by banks themselves or their agents or by the rising number of transactions and by increased trust in debtors. With rising international trade, the debt eventually reappeared in recycled foreign reserves; that is, from generally poorer, emerging-market countries that decided that instead of investment in their own infrastructure it was better to lend to the richest countries of the world, to whom they exported their goods. Eventually, the reserves of developing countries provided the largest source of funding for Americans yet seen. It was a policy of mutual convenience, but it certainly did not follow a logic of development, which suggests America should lend to aid Chinese development, rather than the other way round.

At the end of 1996, Western countries were winding down reserves. They were a waste of money in a world that seemed increasingly secure. The global holdings of foreign exchange reserves totalled $1,518 billion, and were still dominated by developed countries – Western economies and Japan – which collectively owned $707 billion. 'Newly industrialised' Asian countries held the next largest portion, of $262 billion. Of these reserves, 68 per cent was held in dollars.[1]

1 BIS 67th Annual Report, exchange rate section, 1997.

Following the Asian crisis, a trend for accumulating reserves emerged, led by Asia. At the end of 1998, total foreign exchange reserve holdings stood at $1,636 billion,[2] of which 70 per cent was in dollars. Asian countries now held almost as much foreign exchange reserves ($563 billion) as industrialised countries ($690 billion).

The following year the total holdings of foreign exchange reserves again had increased (by $110 billion) and dollars now accounted for 79 per cent of all holdings. Asian foreign exchange reserves (excluding Japan) were once again leaders in accumulation of dollars, with holdings rising 14 per cent in the year to the end of 1999, double the overall growth rate of their total reserves.

A switch to dollars was also taking place elsewhere in 1999. The launch of the euro single currency in 1999 meant that Deutschmarks and French Francs previously held by member countries were no longer required in reserves. The old reserves did not disappear, but were simply switched into dollars. After 1999, the dollar was the only real reserve currency in the world – the yen had lost favour because of the shrinking international influence of the country and low interest rates and it would take several years for reserve managers to gain confidence in the euro.

For the ten years that followed, Asian foreign exchange reserve accumulation outpaced all other regions, concentrating on dollars. By the end of 2001, Asian countries (excluding Japan) held almost the same quantity of dollar foreign exchange reserves as all the dollar reserves of industrialised countries put together. Other countries, notably Latin America and oil producers, including Russia, also decided to accumulate dollar reserves. Japan, too, had switched to steadily buying dollars to maintain a competitive exchange rate. Japan increased its foreign exchange reserves by an average of $50 billion every year from 1999 to 2002, and at an increasing pace. The Chinese led every other reserve manager; in 2002, China increased dollar reserves by $74 billion, an increase of 39 per cent in a single year.

2 BIS 69th Annual Report, exchange rate section, 1999.

A trillion-dollar proof against the capitalists

The Chinese motivation for accumulating reserves also changed; from defence against speculative attack to defence against appreciation. The Bank for International Settlements (BIS) wrote 'the sizeable accumulation of official reserves in China and India appeared consistent with a policy preference to resist large appreciations'. The BIS also suggested the Chinese policy might damage other countries. The annual report tactfully suggested that China (and Japan) should allow an appreciation of their currency against the dollar to avoid a rise in 'global imbalances'.

The appeal fell on deaf ears. In 2003, Japan added another $201 billion to its reserves and China added $117 billion. Dollar reserves at the end of 2003 totalled $2 trillion dollars, a 17 per cent increase on the previous year. The Japanese were now regularly intervening to stop the yen appreciating against the dollar, which left them with dollars to invest.

By 2002, in a complete turnaround of outlook compared with 1997, speculators began to bet that both the Chinese peg and the Japanese yen would be forced into a large appreciation (not depreciation). Persistent trade surpluses with the US in both Japan and China created the expectation that both currencies needed to rise against the dollar. Chinese fears of devaluation in 1998 needed to be adapted, in just four years, into a determined policy to stop a rise in their currency against the dollar.

Oil producers were keen buyers of dollars. From early 2004 till mid-2006 the price of oil rose from $30 a barrel to nearly $80 and the US current account deficit rose as a result. Dollars spent on oil were returned to the US as yet more reserves, or through growing sovereign wealth funds. In 2003, the US current account deficit was, for the first time, entirely funded by reserve accumulation by foreign states, both goods producers, such as China, and oil producers.

It was around 2003 too that markets began to show serious deviation from traditional patterns: long-end yields failed to respond to central bank policy; corporate spreads continued to contract despite higher official interest rates; and financial insurance costs fell. Housing refinance also began its second boost as available dollar investments by reserve managers pushed other investors away from the Treasury and agency markets into non-agency mortgage bonds. Collateralised debt obligations on mortgages began to appear.

Foreign civil servants oust private investment

Private foreign investment was replaced by foreign reserve investors in America between 2002 and 2004. Private sector investors found higher returns elsewhere. Instead, the major part of foreign investment was dominated by civil servant investors in the form of reserve managers.

Those private sector investors that remained discovered the higher returns available in US (and later Spanish and British) mortgage bonds. Mortgage financing continued strongly through the recession, providing better returns. New products such as mortgage CDOs were offering even better returns, along with high credit ratings, which attracted even conservative investors. Some mortgage bonds (those packaged into agency bonds) were also being bought for the first time by reserve managers, who favoured their higher returns, their liquidity and their implicit guarantee by the US government. Thus the investment landscape was increasingly colonised by supposed ultra-conservative investors, whose weight of funds forced them, and others, into increasingly risky areas.

> one in every twenty dollars spent by Americans was provided by foreign bond holders

In 2003, foreign exchange reserve managers purchased bonds worth nearly 5 per cent of US gross domestic product. One in every twenty dollars spent by Americans was provided by foreign bond holders. Asia held $3 trillion, the lion's share with China. Chinese reserve accumulation increased by record amounts each year in 2004 ($207 billion), 2005 ($209 billion) and 2006 ($247 billion).

The Chinese would, presumably, have bought more had they not changed their foreign exchange policy in 2005 to allow appreciation of the yuan against the dollar. Nevertheless, imbalances of this size do not continue indefinitely, and the longer they continue, the more likely the adjustment, when it comes, will be as devastating as it was in Thailand.

America and its foreign suppliers of consumer goods and oil had discovered a mutual interest. The Chinese and Japanese economies needed exports and US consumers wanted their exports. On the other side of the ledger, the American economy required foreign capital to sustain its consumers' borrowing and, increasingly, the housing market that was the main object of that borrowing.

Unlike Bill Clinton's administration, from 2000 the George W. Bush administration showed little interest in international financial flows. As long as the money continued to come in, and consumers were happy, the Bush administration was happy to leave discussion to the central bank. In April 2005, the future chairman of the Federal Reserve,[3] Ben Bernanke, suggested a 'combination of diverse forces has created a significant increase in the global supply of saving – a global saving glut – which helps to explain both the increase in the US current account deficit and the relatively low level of long-term real interest rates in the world today'. Not many people worried about the savings glut, especially as it seemed to provide almost limitless lending to Americans, who, of course, could be trusted to pay it back.

The poor lend money to the wealthiest

Why was it necessary for non-American savers to invest in US assets rather than in their own countries? After all, these countries needed investment, sometimes desperately. Americans fooled themselves that foreigners were choosing America for its booming economy. Bernanke said 'the technology boom of the 1990s and the depth and sophistication of the country's financial markets

3 Ben Bernanke,'The global savings glut and the U.S. current account defict', Sandridge Lecture, Virginia Association of Economic, Richmond, Virginia, 14 April 2005.

(which among other things have allowed households easy access to housing wealth) have certainly been important'. Actually, it was a more prosaic reason, also mentioned by Bernanke in the same speech: 'Another factor is the special international status of the US dollar.'

America had to accept a current account deficit, if so much money was intent on coming into the country. It offered its bond markets to the world and the world bought them because they were American. The quantities involved dictated this would create a current account deficit. Bernanke's boss, Alan Greenspan, considered the possibility of a future shift of reserve assets out of the dollar.[4]

> 'What could be the potential consequences should the dollar's status as the world's reserve currency significantly diminish, especially if foreign investors reduce their rate of accumulation of claims on US residents?' Most analysts would contend that US interest rates were lowered by the world's accumulation of dollars. Accordingly, in the event of a significant diminishing of the dollar's reserve currency status, U.S. interest rates would presumably rise... Any diminution of the reserve status of the dollar, should it occur, is likely to be readily absorbed by a far more flexible US economy than existed in Britain immediately following World War II. This, of course, presupposes that we in the United States in the years ahead maintain and, I trust, enhance our economy's degree of flexibility and our involvement in the highly successful globalisation of recent decades.'

Bernanke and Greenspan suggested there was no means to stop Americans borrowing from foreigners.

Reserve managers are conservative investors; they usually concentrate on low-risk investments such as government bonds. Increasingly, the mortgage bond market offered alternatives. Chinese reserve managers began to buy bonds issued by mortgage agencies Freddie Mac and Fannie Mae in large quantities from 2004 onwards, aiding the expansion of the mortgage market. Those who charge American borrowers and lenders with dangerously

4 Alan Greenspan, 'Stability and economic growth: the role of the central bank', 14 November 2005.

irresponsible behaviour should question the competence and motives of these so-called conservative investors.

Larry Summers, reviewing global capital flows years after the Asian crisis prophetically said:[5]

> 'it is impossible to predict economic and other developments, and that countries should be careful what they wish for. In the wake of the East Asian financial crisis, many analysts – including me – recommended that emerging market economies build up reserves to reduce the risks of future crises. I still think that was good advice. But in today's international financial system the largest net flow comes from the world's richest, most powerful country borrowing on a massive scale from countries containing a significant portion of the world's poorest people. ... Having such a huge flow of borrowing from the world's richest country... raises questions about how well the international financial system is working.'

Yet, the international financial system seemed to prosper so well without addressing international capital flows that many simply ignored the imbalances; imbalances that would eventually create perhaps the greatest financial crisis in history.

The unbalanced globe

Foreign capital flows were not limited to reserve managers, nor were they limited to China, Japan and the US. The relationship between the Asian capital exporters and America was mirrored in lesser amounts around the developed world in a pattern repeated worldwide. Countries with trade surpluses – such as Japan, China, Switzerland and Germany – lent to those requiring borrowing such as Spain, the UK, Ireland, Australia and most importantly, the US.

Within the European single currency an added incentive for cross-border lending was the absence of currency risk. Opportunities for

---

5 Larry Summers, 'Development lessons of the 1990s,' in *Development Challenges in the 1990s: Leading policymakers speak from experience*, ed. Timothy Besley, World Bank Publications, 2005.

higher returns in countries such as Spain were offered to banks elsewhere in the region. German banks were especially keen to invest.

By September 2007, lending to Spain by German banks stood at $250 billion, by far the largest foreign lender to the Spanish. German banks lent to Spain for the same reason that the Japanese sought overseas investments; for higher returns. These were not reserve managers seeking safety. But there was a crucial difference to the Japanese. Since the introduction of the single currency, there was no longer any currency risk between Germany and Spain. Unlike Japanese lending overseas, which risked losses if the yen appreciated, German lenders did not face this risk, and so thought their investments were more secure. A similar argument had fooled investors in Thailand, before the devaluation.

Much of the German lending took the form of bonds, backed by Spanish mortgages. As long as the bonds did not default, German investors gained better returns than they could find in their own country. The Spanish mortgage bond market grew rapidly as a result, just as there was growing demand for US mortgage bonds. The UK was also a popular issuer of mortgage-backed bonds, which were also bought largely by European investors – mostly German. Total German bank claims on the UK amounted to $600 billion in 2007, with an increasing amount in the form of mortgage bonds from issuers such as Northern Rock and Bradford & Bingley: lenders who relied on the bond buyers to maintain their business model.

In the aftermath of the stock crash in October 2008, caused by the year-long credit crunch, the German ambassador was interviewed on the BBC. He expressed annoyance that German banks seemed to be having problems when, as far as he was concerned, the credit problems were caused by profligate mortgage borrowers. Germany had never had a housing boom; its house price index had remained unchanged for ten years while most other European countries followed America in a housing boom.

The ambassador failed to realise that while he was blaming Anglo-Saxons for lax lending standards, his country had acted as banker for the entire European continent, with similarly lax lending standards. When house prices turned down, more-or-less simultaneously, across America and Europe, all lenders were hit by rising delinquent loans, defaults, and declining value of collateral. Europeans protested that they had no subprime problem, yet there were numerous examples of lax lending that amounted to subprime lending. Loans were given for more than the value of the house being bought; valuations of houses were stated above the purchase price specifically to obtain larger mortgages; mortgages were offered for higher multiples of earnings. Some companies – such as Bradford & Bingley – built businesses on providing loans to high-risk borrowers such as 'self-certified' earnings, and 'buy-to-let'. Semantically, there was no subprime in Europe, but only because it was an American term; Europeans simply do not categorise so readily. Yet, the problem was the same.

Crowding out the usual crowd

In the US, the Federal Reserve Bank of New York has confirmed[6] that foreign reserve managers became the most important buyers of Treasury bonds. Treasuries are sold by regular auction. Since 2003 reserve managers' share of the total bids often exceeded 30 per cent. Dealers would bet how large the 'indirect' bidders were, which signalled the reserve manager purchases, because they bought indirectly, using accounts held at the Federal Reserve.

> dealers also wondered what would happen to Treasury prices if reserve managers failed to bid

Dealers also wondered what would happen to Treasury prices if reserve managers failed to bid at the auctions. In November 2004, the week of the US Thanksgiving holiday, *China Business News* reported that the Chinese central bank had begun to cut its holdings of Treasuries, to limit the losses from a falling dollar. Chinese officials at the central bank denied there was any truth to

---

6 Michael J. Fleming, 'Who buys Treasury securities at auction?', *Current Issues in Economics and Finance*, vol. 13, no. 1, January 2007, Federal Reserve Bank of New York.

the story, but as the *Financial Times* wrote at the time, 'a seed of doubt had been planted'. The suggestion that Chinese buyers might be losing interest caused a sharp fall in Treasury prices. The *FT* quoted a bond expert on the subject: 'A cynic would suspect the timing of the allegedly erroneous report was not a coincidence. It came at the quietest time of the year. This has been a reminder to the Americans of the influence that China wields over the Treasuries market.'

Certainly the reserve managers – mostly Chinese – had become the most important investor group in Treasury securities, the most liquid market in the world. Their effect was pervasive and long-lasting. Their concerted buying caused 10-year maturity Treasury yields to fall between 0.4 per cent[7] and 0.9 per cent[8] lower than they otherwise would have been at the end of 2004. This kind of fall in the bond yield produces a huge boost to economic growth; perhaps as much of a boost as a central bank can create through cutting interest rates five or six times, perhaps more.

Even this almost certainly understates the extent of the stimulus created. The buying flattened the yield curve and, as we saw in the first chapter, a flatter yield curve is a sign of rising risk appetite, because it shows long-dated bonds are approaching the value of cash, and that private money is likely to pervade the system (buyers switch to buying other forms of debt to gain higher returns). Sure enough, investor confidence increased and they moved into riskier assets – such as lower-rated mortgage bonds, CDOs as well as longer-term securities. A paper from the European Central Bank (ECB) suggested 'an increase in purchases of treasuries may, in theory, divert investment from other markets'.[9] The concentration of such large buying by reserve managers on the US capital markets, the largest in the world, would reveal that even these markets, big as they were, simply were insufficient to

---

7 'The accumulation of foreign reserves', International Relations Committee Task Force, European Central Bank occasional paper 43, February 2003.

8 Francis Warnock and Veronica Warnock, 'International capital flows and US interest rates', NBER working paper 12560, October 2006.

9 Teresa Balcao Reis, Emiliano Gonzalez Mota with input from Lucia Cuadro-Saez and Sergio Gavila, The Impact of Asian Reserve Accumulation on Asset Prices, subsection of ECB Occasional Paper No. 43, quoted above.

accommodate the amount of dollars. The overwhelming investment had to go somewhere, and the easiest destination was 'private label' mortgage bonds (bonds issued by non-agencies).

The reserve managers, particularly from China, increasingly bought mortgage-related bonds in the form of agency bonds of Freddie Mac and Fannie Mae. Thus foreign buyers directly supported the US mortgage market. Their investment had similar effects on their yields to what had happened in the Treasury market. The mortgage agencies estimated that without Asian purchases of reserve assets mortgage rates would show 'perhaps a 40 to 50 basis point increase'. They also noted that 'such an increase in mortgage rates would have quite a chilling effect on US housing and mortgage markets'.[10] If, for any reason, the buyers stopped buying, the housing market would be in trouble. Long-term corporate rates fell by over 1 per cent.[11] Low rates meant less need for corporate bonds and loans, so there was more demand for mortgages and credit card bonds as replacement investments. Lower interest rates also led to more cash at companies to invest in bank deposits – which allowed more lending. There was also incentive for banks to concentrate on home loans as new mortgage bonds produced higher fees than corporate bonds. Bank profits rose, boosting bank capital, which was largely held in bonds, which meant there was less need to issue shares.

The effect of lower borrowing costs on the government alone was considerable. New Treasury bonds at lower rates produced cumulative savings between 2003 and 2006 of well over $40 billion,[12] enough to run the justice department for a year ($35 billion in 2004) or the homeland security department ($45 billion in 2004).[13] Taking account of the savings throughout the economy, the effects of lower rates were colossal.

---

10 'The Impact of Global Capital Flows and Foreign Financing of U.S. Mortgage and Treasury Interest Rates', Ashok Bardham and Dwight Jaffee, Research Institute for American Housing, June 2007.

11 'Corporates are driving the global savings glut', Jan Loeys, David Mackie, Paul Meggyesi, Nikolaos Panigirtzoglou, 24 June 2005, JP Morgan.

12 A crude calculation, I admit: $7.4 trillion, 4/5ths rolled with a saving of 65bp (0.65 per cent) = $38.5 billion.

13 US government financial statements for year ended 30 September 2004.

Alan Greenspan was, as usual, acute in his observation. He noted the flattening of the yield curve and the fall in risk premiums and linked the effects to the 'break-up of the Soviet Union and the integration of China and India into the global trading market' and identified the 'greater integration of financial markets'. He also noted the generally benign economic conditions that pertained – low inflation, high growth, which supported higher mortgage borrowing, and higher investor confidence.

The slow flow from Japan

To be fair, it was not just reserve managers who flooded the West with cash. The outflow of money from Japanese banks between 2002 and 2007, mostly to Western investments, was larger than the growth in the entire Japanese economy over the same time. The Japanese economy grew by $744 billion in the five years from 2002. During the same period, Japanese banks increased their foreign claims by $770 billion.[14] Japanese banks collectively had decided there were better opportunities outside their own country than within it. Even after the events of the past two years it is clear they have not yet changed their minds; export of capital from Japan's private sector remains a dominant theme today.

The most popular destinations for Japanese money from 2001 till 2007 were countries that experienced the highest degree of financial innovation; the US, Europe, the UK, Australia and Caribbean offshore banking centres – a synonym for offshore hedge funds.

Hedge funds in particular benefited through funding themselves in low-cost Japanese yen to invest in higher-yielding products. Foreign banks too found the funding levels attractive. Some, such as Swiss banks, could access cheap funds in their own currency; they too provided cheap funding for foreign investors. The most popular source of funding was the yen. The 'carry trade' pervaded the financial system from the peak of the dot-com recession till 2007. It continues to this day.

---

14 BIS banking statistics at www.bis.org.

Not just racy hedge funds and foreign banks turned to cheap funds from Japan. European local authorities, municipalities and companies were also keen borrowers of the yen via the carry trade. A local authority could issue a note in yen with a low coupon and assume the currency risk for the term of the note, often five years. The enthusiasm of local authorities for 'structured finance' products occasionally worried French officials. If the yen strengthened during those five years the cost would be borne by local taxpayers, not the official who initiated the trade.

'Housewives of Tokyo' disrupt international finance

While Japanese banks concentrated on servicing hedge funds and foreign banks, Japanese households looked elsewhere for returns. With low interest rates offered in Japan for so long and savings growing continuously among households, savers were enticed into foreign currency bonds that offered higher yields. A special class of bonds, known as *uridashi* bonds, sold directly to households, was approved by Tokyo in 1994. The money of Japanese households has been leaving the country every since, and continues to do so.

With the yen stable after 2000, the bonds became much more popular, as a period of zero interest rate policy (ZIRP) in Japan reduced income on domestic bonds and savings accounts to nothing.

The Japanese were convinced the yen would not strengthen against a foreign currency. The finance ministry had 'stabilised' the yen against the dollar by the end of the 1990s. With 'credible', long-term currency stability, private investors began to buy *uridashi* again in large amounts. Good initial returns created repeat business, and drew in more investors.

The range of currencies offered by the *uridashi* bonds was initially limited to G7 countries, although other currencies were soon offered. The choice of currencies depended on its interest rate; so when US interest rates fell from 2001, the focus switched to Australian dollars. By 2003, very low interest rates in the US ensured Australian dollar issuance accounted for the majority of *uridashi* that year. New Zealand received an overwhelming amount of *uridashi* issuance from 2004 onwards. In both August and October 2005, the New Zealand dollar was the most popular currency in which to issue *uridashi* bonds and by the end of 2005, total outstanding issuance in NZD amounted to 16 per cent of New Zealand GDP, and was equivalent to over 70 per cent of outstanding New Zealand government bonds. This kind of dominance had profound effects on interest rates, reducing them and forcing central banks to attempt to compensate – and occasionally complain.

Uridashi averaged US$24 billion a year from 2004 till the beginning of 2008. More exotic products emerged to cater to the desire for investing in foreign currencies. The most notorious product was the power-reverse dual currency bond, which offered long investment horizons (up to 36 years) and many options. The basic aim remained the same; to gain higher interest from a foreign currency than was available in Japan. In 2000, just less than Y1 trillion of power-reverse dual currency bonds were issued. The subsequent three years saw well in excess of that figure issued each year. Each year took capital from Japan and placed it into the banking systems of other countries.

The New Zealand Reserve Bank reported that *uridashi* tended to depress swap rates in the 2–3 year part of the NZD yield curve, an area typically linked to mortgages. The Reserve Bank commented that 'this has reduced the effectiveness of, and increased the lags involved in, the transmission of increases in the Official Cash Rate'. The high quantity of *uridashi* bonds issued in New Zealand was interrupting the usual mechanisms of the country's monetary policy.

The Japanese household investor attracted international attention in other areas too. In a speech made in early July 2007, Bank of Japan board member Kiyohiko Nishimura said: 'The arrival of Japanese households as major investors seems to have affected foreign-exchange markets. The gnomes of Zurich were accused in their day of destabilising markets. The housewives of Tokyo are apparently acting to stabilise them.'

The 'search for yield' drives Japanese banks abroad

Japanese banks were even keener to export capital than households

Japanese banks were even keener to export capital than households. The Bank for International Settlements reported Japanese bank overseas assets grew strongly after 2000. In December 1999, Japanese banks held $744 billion in loans to overseas borrowers. By September 2007, total outstanding loans from Japanese banks to overseas borrowers stood at $1.6 trillion. The increase is about the same as the entire annual production of a medium-sized developed economy such as the Netherlands.

Japanese bank lending increased particularly strongly to countries most closely associated with securitisation and hedge fund activity, especially after 2004. These included securitisation centres such as US and UK and a collection of countries collectively known as 'other offshore banking centres'. These 'offshore centres' were countries in which large numbers of hedge funds registered their businesses to benefit from a low tax regime.

Where did the money go? Some went into home loans, or to finance shopping centres, equity markets, and cars. As the Western world's manufacturer, some of the money was recycled into China. But before it reached the consumer the money went to expanding credit in Western economies, both on-balance sheet, if it could be accomplished within regulations, and off-balance sheet – into structured investment vehicles, conduits and securitisations.

Hedge funds took a large amount of this exported capital. Japanese banks lent particularly heavily to Caribbean offshore banking centres. The Cayman Islands were the favourite. The outstanding lending to these Caribbean countries at the end of the third quarter of 2007 was $300 billion, compared with Japanese lending to the UK of $200 billion, and to Germany of $123 billion, and to the US of $727 billion. Japanese banks were lending roughly half as much to hedge funds as to the US, the largest economy in the world, and the biggest borrower.

Hedge-fund borrowing on this scale marked a turning point for the industry. Hedge funds responded to the new set of investors with explosive growth: between 2001 and 2007 the amount of money managed by hedge funds rose from $400 billion to $2 trillion.

It was not just Japanese bank lending, for sure. Swiss banks too were very active, due to the low interest rates offered by that country. Between them, Japan and Switzerland dominated the funding of the hedge fund industry, helping to raise the power of the industry, and indirectly aiding the expansion of securitisation and leveraged investment. Using a conservative average leverage of two times, the financial muscle that hedge funds could wield would be $4 trillion – roughly equivalent to the GDP of the UK and Canada. It is almost certain this estimate vastly understates the extent of the financial power wielded by hedge funds. Many of their investments were designed to reduce the reported leverage used. Products such as CDOs contained inbuilt gearing, yet could be reported as though there was none.

An early global tremor

In early 2006, the Japanese economy was robust enough for the Bank of Japan to begin to consider tightening monetary policy. The first step was to reduce the amounts of money available to Japanese banks through their current accounts held at the Bank of Japan. From a peak of Y32 trillion the central bank reduced the current account balance to Y16 billion in just a month after May 2006.

As international borrowers realised the money available was finally shrinking, they cut back on their investments and bought the yen. The rise in the yen caused the 'carry trade' to register the first losses since 2001.

The effects of Japanese monetary tightening rippled through the financial world. Credit spreads widened, equity prices fell, the cost of financial insurance rose, the Australian and New Zealand dollars fell sharply, indicators of financial stress rose. The first indications of fragility in credit markets appeared, to emerge much more strongly one year later in the full-blown credit crunch.

Japan's capital exports: still more to come

In October 2008, *The Economist* estimated Japanese corporations were sitting on Y60 trillion ($600 billion). Corporate Japan found itself thwarted in its own country – the economy was sluggish, takeovers were hard to accomplish, the population was declining – so it had to turn abroad. The deals have tended to be strategic: Takeda Pharmaceuticals took over Millennium Pharmaceuticals in the US; TDK took over the electronics division of Epcos in Germany; Tokio Marine bought an American insurer, Philadelphia Consolidated. The stream of money from Japan has not been plugged by the bursting of the subprime bubble and the 2008 banking crisis.

It is also clear that Japanese households have not given up on their overseas adventure. There is no real sign that households are tempted to repatriate their investments and *uridashi* issuance continues. After a rush for Japanese yen assets in September and October 2008, which seemed largely driven by unwinding of hedge fund positions, the flow has slowed sharply. If the yen settles into a range against the dollar again, and it seems likely, then outflows may rise again. They will face a hurdle in locating any economy with interest rates high enough to interest them – at least for the next two years. For corporate investors, a time horizon of two years is not a big problem – it is just enough time to settle into ownership in time for the wider economy to recover. For households, two years is probably too long to wait. It is more likely that current household overseas savings remain in offshore bonds.

Echoes of Japan in the West

The experience of Japan after the bursting of its bubble has now been visited on Western countries. All have now experienced a calamitous decline in their economies, driven by investors' refusal to buy the bonds that had previously financed economic expansion. For a time, the banking system stopped lending. All these things happened in Japan. There are other parallels too. While the Japanese had 'zombie' loans with corporate customers, most Western banks now have 'zombie' mortgage clients. As governments pump more money into the banks, there will inevitably be political pressure to avoid 'foreclosures'. Already this has happened in the US, Germany and the UK. Residential real estate markets are deeply political. The Japanese showed how intractable an asset bust can be. The paradox of the Japanese banking crisis is that its alleviation appears, indirectly, to have helped create a similar bust in Western countries a decade later.

The euro: an exercise in imbalance

The third stage of European monetary union introduced the euro in 1999. The bloc using the new currency consisted of eleven original members, joined later by a further four countries.[15] The single currency was a financial innovation in its own right. Mature economies such as France, Germany, Italy, the Netherlands and Belgium joined with a number of 'converging economies' such as Spain, Portugal and Greece. With currency risk eliminated between the member nations, the project was promoted as an opportunity for cross-border investment. Intra-zone investment offered higher returns for investors from France and Germany through 'convergence' – the process by which economic performance equalised across the region, together with bond prices. Spreads between government bonds began to tighten before the project began and did not stop tightening till the beginning of 2007.

This process of 'convergence' was exactly the process that Long Term Capital Management had tried to exploit until 1998. They were right about the long term, but disastrously wrong about the possibility of short-term setbacks.

---

15 France, Germany, the Netherlands, Belgium, Luxembourg, Finland, Ireland, Austria, Italy, Spain and Portugal joined the eurozone in 1999. Greece joined in 2001. Slovenia joined in 2007. Malta and Cyprus joined in 2008.

Convergence creates its own challenges

The same monetary policy operated across the zone, controlled by the European Central bank based on aggregate economic performance. As Germany and France made up the major part of the eurozone, the economic conditions of these two countries dictated monetary policy for the entire area. Appropriate monetary policy for Germany and France was too loose for Spain, Ireland, Greece and Portugal. High growth and consumption among these 'converging economies' was the result, along with house price rises. Fed up with low growth and low returns, Germany banks saw the higher returns from Spain and others as a huge opportunity, particularly from mortgage bonds. Cross-border lending within the euro area became one of its most distinctive features, with Germany providing the lion's share of the funding. Just as in Japan, the rate of lending to foreigners consistently exceeded the rate of growth of Germany itself. Spain was the largest beneficiary of German investment, mostly in the form of mortgage bonds. During the most expansionary 'mania phase' of lending between 2005 and 2007 nearly half of the growth of the Spanish economy can be explained by an increase in German bank lending alone.[16]

> the rate of lending to foreigners consistently exceeded the rate of growth of Germany itself

The lending was not confined within the euro area; the money was often recycled into third countries. Germany lent to Spain, which in turn lent to the UK, which in turn lent to the US. A flow of funds passed through various countries, sometimes financing growth locally, but with excess lending always moving further up the current account chain, destined for the largest borrower in the world, America.

Austrian banks became the largest lenders to Romania and Hungary in what appeared to be an attempt to resuscitate a financial equivalent of the Austro-Hungarian Empire.

---

16 According to BIS statistics, between 2005 and 2007 the Spanish economy expanded by $205 billion (constant dollars at 2005 rate). Over the same period, net lending to Spain from Germany amounted to $93 billion, roughly 45 per cent of the total growth of Spain within that period.

The eurozone was merely a microcosm of wider cross-border investment opportunities opening up around the world through 'globalisation'. And running through all the financial innovations over the decade from 1997 is the idea of 'convergence'. Robert Merton, the Harvard academic, described the 'convergence' of investment techniques offered through derivatives; Long Term Capital sought to exploit convergence across the globe to create the biggest hedge fund yet seen; the euro area explicitly sought to 'converge' economies. For a few years the visions of Robert Merton, the Harvard academic, LTCM and Eurocrats met, and were realised.

The large euro area economy created conditions that were particularly suited to financial innovation. The ECB in October 2002 released a paper[17] that argued the establishment of the euro area caused companies and banks to increase in size, and for market-based lending (rather than relationship-based) to dominate. The single currency created an environment ready for CDOs and securitisation as well as cross-border lending.

The introduction of the single currency also led directly to the development of a single interest swap curve. The Euribor swap market became the most liquid in the world, with turnover exceeding that of the dollar swap curve and extending to maturities of fifty years, well beyond the thirty-year maximum maturity of the US swap curve. Euribor's success was partly due to the lack of a single bond curve that could be applied across the economy – the German curve was the most important, and provided the futures contracts, but failed to provide a convincing benchmark curve for all issuers. The rise of asset swappers was a direct result of the tying of different bond markets into the swap curve; creating floating rate instruments and financing them at bank rates. Asset swappers represented pan-European financial innovation, directly caused by the single currency. There were few questions asked about the limits of innovation.

---

17 Banks and Markets: the changing character of European Finance; Raghuram G.Rajan and Luigi Zingales, NBER working paper 9595, 2003.

Opportunity for second-rate banks

Germany has had a problem in its banking sector for many years. The federal state allowed regional banks owned by Länder (the states) to become important providers of credit to the economy, yet they are perennial underperformers. When the European Union forbade the one competitive advantage these banks enjoyed (state guarantees) in 2001, the Landesbanks sought opportunities in other countries. They became among the largest providers of credit to Spain, Ireland and to the Eastern European countries.

The Landesbanks were following the lead of other German banks into the financing of peripheral countries. Since the beginning of the single currency, banks such as Depfa, previously a specialist mortgage provider for the public sector, had realised there was a great deal of money to be made by applying its securitisation expertise to European government bonds. Between 2001 and 2004 Depfa became perhaps the largest buyer of long-dated Italian government bonds. It also bought regional Italian bonds, and the bonds of Greece and other lesser credits. While the funding costs of Depfa remained low, its profits were good. Potential profits were enhanced by the company's change of domicile (and relocation) to low tax Ireland.

Lending to emerging European economies is the equivalent of the move banks made into riskier assets in the US and the products used were the same – securitised mortgage bonds, collateralised debt obligations. While Wall Street was moving west and south in America, German, French, Belgian, Swedish and Austrian banks were moving south and east. Whereas New York acted as the hub for financial products in America, in Europe it was London that assumed a similar role.

'Convergence' was assumed to be a permanent process. Bond spreads between European sovereign issuers converged to a few hundredths of one per cent by 2005. Candidates for admission to the EU saw their costs of borrowing – and the cost of borrowing for their citizens – fall to record lows.

Spain, in particular, found its bond market consistently

outperforming all others in the single currency, as its ratings improved and foreigners were willing to lend to the strongest major economy in Europe. Convergence among sovereign bonds within the single currency spread after 2004 to convergence of aspiring joiners of the single currency such as Hungary, Slovakia, and the Czech Republic. New joiners to the EU such as Romania and Bulgaria also found they were popular with foreign investors, usually from within the single currency, and often investing in euros, not local currency. This left these countries vulnerable to shocks, with their debts denominated in foreign currency – just like Thailand had been.

Investment combined with financial innovation in the case of Spain and securitised bonds issued in support of mortgages grew strongly. What had begun as convergence of sovereign bonds had spread to lending to the entire economy.

The imbalances that emerged look, in retrospect, very similar to those that emerged in South-East Asia before that crisis. A dominant investor, keen to take advantage of higher returns, and able to invest in its own currency, was tempted into countries that would turn out to be unprepared for the withdrawal of foreign credit. The difference is that the situation in Eastern Europe makes the Asian crisis look a minor problem. The imbalances in Romania, Bulgaria and others dwarf those of Thailand in 1997. However, they have the advantage of geography and lenders will probably not desert as they did in the Asian crisis. Nevertheless, most of the former Eastern bloc countries face a difficult decade.

The global meaning of money

Banking – and therefore all lending, including that from reserve managers – is a matter of looking after a balance sheet. The notion of bank profit used to be secondary to ensuring that the borrower repaid and that investment was matched by an ability to find funding. Successful investment, in other words, is a form of money exchange; a matching of assets and liabilities.

Neither reserve managers nor cross-border lenders were concerned with matching their assets and liabilities. For the German banks who invested in Spain, or Eastern Europe, the aim was to maximise their returns, without any consideration of funding ever being a problem. For reserve managers, the aim was simply to park money in an asset. The bonds bought were viewed as a large money-box, holding wealth for some future need. It does not seem to have occurred to the foreign buyers of Treasury bonds and mortgage bonds that their asset was someone else's liability, and that there was a limit to the amount that could be absorbed even by the American financial market. In both Europe and the US there was a familiar disconnection between money as debt and money as a medium of exchange.

Was this uncritical investment driven by greed? Reserve managers openly accepted lower returns from their investments than they could gain from investing in their own countries, so greed was no motivation. Cross-border lending in Europe was more openly driven by returns, but more as a matter of survival. The returns were good, for a few years, but the initial motivation of Landesbank investors was simply to continue to exist. That the result may hasten their demise says something about the flaws in the ECB project to integrate the single currency without concern for the risks along the way. An example of this is the way the ECB encouraged the spread of cross-border 'synthetic credit derivatives' and securitisation in the euro area. In early 2007, the central bank wrote:[18]

> 'In contrast to cash instruments, synthetic CDOs generate exposure to underlying assets not by buying bonds or loans outright, but by referencing names or assets through credit derivatives. This technique is particularly attractive in Europe because there continue to be some restrictions in the underlying cash market (e.g. national regulatory barriers, legal difficulties in transferring loans, limited issuance of corporate bonds, a less developed market infrastructure) that limit the capacity to diversify credit risk portfolios across countries.'

Here, the ECB actively encouraged the use of what turned out to be the most dangerous tool in the financial box, the synthetic collateralised debt obligation (CDO).

18 Financial Integration in Europe, April 2007, March/ECB report.

the ECB actively encouraged the use of what turned out to be the most dangerous tool in the financial box

The ECB was also a supporter of integrating and standardising mortgage lending across the region. Some European securitised mortgages were almost as toxic as US subprime. Again from the ECB:[19]

> 'The Eurosystem strongly supports further integration in mortgage markets. More integration would lead to a Euro area wide availability of a broad range of mortgage products, which would affect the transmission of monetary policy impulses and contribute to a more stable financial system as a result of improved risk diversification.'

Financial integration is a noble long-term project within Europe. Hasty implementation produced contradiction. The president of the ECB, Jean-Claude Trichet, warned of 'under-priced risk' in financial markets several times, without, apparently, realising that the second mandate pursued by his own bank was dedicated to supporting the instruments that were later blamed for causing the damage. Explaining the origins of the crisis later, Trichet said:

> 'The under-pricing of the unit of risk related mainly to inadequate assumptions made about the distribution of returns to highly complex, new financial securities. Let me mention a few examples. First, take the fact that, in calculating the probability of default of mortgages in a large economy, the possibility of a drop in real estate prices or the ongoing deterioration in lending standards, were not properly factored in, or even totally disregarded.'

This is so easy to say after the event. The fact is the ECB was, and remains, a keen long-term promoter of any available mechanism to integrate European financial markets. If securitised mortgages or synthetic CDOs proved useful, then they were to be included in the grand plan.

---

19 Financial Integration in Europe, April 2008, ECB report.

The imbalances in the euro area mirrored the imbalances in the wider world. In addition, European banks also took part in the great American expansion of credit. There still remains a question over how much damage the European banking system sustained by the combined effects of the US financial crisis and the home-grown crisis that quickly followed. The IMF estimates the eventual cost will fall more heavily on European banking than on US banks. This is a shocking conclusion for a central bank (the ECB) that prides itself on conservative actions based on calm deliberation.

this is a shocking conclusion for a central bank (the ECB)

For reserve managers, their objectives were varied, but rarely strayed into the realm of either making a profit or considering the balance sheet effect they were creating. They were much more concerned about the transactional convenience of their investments, and the requirements of trade policy. For every dollar that entered the US economy from China, or Japan, or Saudi Arabia, America added a dollar to the bill it owed to the world. After the Asian crisis, a large, and growing, part of the world learned that acquiring dollars was an integral part of globalisation. The myth of unbounded America is something from Western movies, and a belief in unlimited investment opportunities had been propagated by that country's elite such as Treasury secretary Robert Rubin and his successors. It was a belief that proved as much of a myth as the Wild West.

When reserve managers invested in American bonds, they thought they were simply parking money, not creating a debt. What could possibly go wrong? What could go wrong was the overwhelming of the heart of financial capitalism. Myopic, trade-oriented investment strategies, intent only on liquid investment, were the single most important cause of the financial crisis. The deluge was aided by willing borrowers in America, and by the blithe acceptance of the flood of foreign money from America's central bank, political elite and its banking system. The enthusiastic borrowing turned the great cycle of financial crisis that had been wheeling round the world since 1990 back onto America itself, the sponsor of globalisation. The financial history of the past twenty years is always intimately connected with global capital flows. None was larger, or ultimately more damaging, than the flood of money that sought dollars. The greenback may yet be permanently tainted by the unbalanced capital flow unleashed by globalisation. The dollar may yet find that it has been loved to death.

How central banks lost their grip

These wise men that give fools money get
themselves a good report – after fourteen
years' purchase
Twelfth Night, William Shakespeare

C entral banks should be the first line of defence against
crisis. They are probably the most important institution
within an economy; their existence is based on protection
of the value of a currency. Central banks are charged with a role of
caution. As the saying goes: 'Take away the punchbowl just as the
party gets going.' These institutions are the guardians against
financial excess. Yet all the major central banks contributed to the
build-up of excesses that led to the recent crisis.

After Paul Volker's chairing of the Federal Reserve ended in 1987,
central banks abdicated responsibility for financial stability,
concentrating solely on growth and inflation. Their policies
focused on control of short-term interest rates to contain consumer
prices, or to stimulate growth. It was as if the police had decided
to enforce traffic restrictions, and ignore all other illegal behaviour.
Little effort was devoted to understanding the growth in liquidity,
or the behaviour of money other than its empirical effects on
inflation. As the role of central banks increasingly marginalised
their previous role in financial stability, they became effective
advocates of transactional finance. It did not matter whether the
central bank was European, British or American; their sole
purpose became promotion of growth (increasingly through
financial transactions) and containment of inflation.

From 1999, the emergence of the European single currency introduced, for the first time, a major competitor to the Fed, and challenged the status of the dollar as reserve currency among EU nations. This led to a certain amount of competition between central banks. After 1999, the US central bank's prestige was measured not only by its guidance of domestic activity, but also by how much better its economy was doing compared with Europe. There was an international imperative to enhance the attractions of the dollar, and financial support by the central bank was an important part of the attraction. The single currency also introduced 'financial integration' to the euro area, a policy that encouraged enormous cross-border lending and imbalances. It was a policy encouraged by the ECB.

> 'financial integration' … encouraged enormous cross-border lending and imbalances

The Bank of Japan (BoJ) has found policy dominated by its own, seemingly permanent banking crisis, lasting almost two decades. The BoJ's quest to rescue the domestic Japanese economy also had important international effects. Its policies unleashed a flood of capital that spilled into the wider world, fuelling growth in countries such as Australia and New Zealand.

Japan's lost decade: prelude to international disorder

Financial crises are cultural and historic events. A crisis changes the way a nation thinks about itself, and how others see it. Japan has been in more-or-less permanent financial crisis of one sort or another since 1990 and looks set to continue to suffer for several more years. As a consequence, an advanced economy – in the early 1990s perhaps, the most advanced economy – and a highly ordered society has been forced to accept lower expectations, lower living standards, social upheaval and a fall in international influence. The adjustment has so far taken almost two decades. Japan now has a shrunken aspect, with an ageing population edging to decrepitude.

This image of Japan is, of course, a false one, but it is potent. Similar self-examination and adjustment is likely in those countries and regions badly affected by today's crisis – the US, Britain, Ireland, Spain and Eastern Europe. Japan, despite or because of its travails, seems resigned to difficulty, accepting of the limitation on its ambitions. There were no riots, no meaningful right-wing – or left-wing – clamour, few scapegoats, no loss of dignity. The social mix in Britain and the US is, perhaps, more combustible than Japan; it is not safe to assume that Japanese stoicism will be a model for the disappointments of younger and more diverse societies in the West in the aftermath of crisis.

Alone among the major central banks, the BoJ was forced, through the 1990s, to concern itself with the problem of money as a practical, rather than a theoretical issue. The problems of its banking system and the response of the BoJ were the first time a major developed economy had to face such issues in the modern world. The subsequent dislocation of the monetary system of most of the developed world almost certainly means the problems and confusions of money will dominate policy making across the globe for the foreseeable future. Money everywhere faces a crisis of meaning.

On 25 December 1989, concerned that the economy was overheating, the BoJ under new governor Yasushi Mieno raised interest rates by 50 basis points to 4.25 per cent. It was a decision that marked the beginning of at least nineteen years of economic pain and social uncertainty in Japan.

Finance minister Ryutaro Hashimoto said the rate rise 'should help to maintain price stability by controlling inflationary pressures and to sustain economic growth led by domestic demand'. The Japanese economy had grown strongly since the early 1980s, and prices in share and property markets were rising. The Nikkei share price index initially shrugged off the rate rise and achieved a record level of 38,915 on 29 December 1989, just a few days after the rate rise. But by August 1992, the index had fallen 63 per cent to 14,194. So began the 'lost decade' of Japan, characterised by growing banking strains, rising unemployment, huge increases in government spending and almost no growth.

We've seen that the Japanese recession that followed the bursting of the 'bubble economy' spread through Thailand and other emerging economies and was to have an indirect bearing on the current global crisis. Policy reaction from the BoJ in particular drove domestic investment abroad, and encouraged international borrowers to look to Japan as their provider of funds. With almost no attractive lending opportunities in Japan, banks and households looked for higher returns elsewhere. Japanese policy appears to have exported the 'bubble' to America and Europe. The queue of ineffectual measures attempted to remedy the situation, and the frustration both of the Japanese themselves and their trading partners may also signal some of the problems to come in dealing with financial adjustment today.

The origins of the Japanese banking crisis

The Japanese financial crisis, like many crises, was preceded by bank deregulation which introduced new financial products to companies. From the 1980s, Japanese corporations turned to bonds to finance themselves, and away from bank loans, which had been the main source of funding. By 1991, 24.5 per cent of corporate funding came from bond issuance, a huge increase on the 3.6 per cent of funding backed by bonds in 1984. Unfortunately, the counterpart to the rise in bond issuance was that Japanese banks lost the stable revenue generated from making loans. For a while, rising property and stock prices provided substitute business through lending for investments and construction.

Influence of 'globalisation' on Japan's economy

The link between globalisation and financial crises is a theme running through this book and the emergence of an offshore manufacturing industry in Asian countries such as Malaysia and Thailand played a part in undermining economic relationships in Japan, which contributed to later Japanese financial problems.

Japanese companies were often arranged in *keiretsu*, interlinked webs of suppliers with a dominant producer at the centre, usually with a bank attached. As international trade grew in the 1980s, suppliers in the *keiretsu* found it increasingly difficult to compete against manufacturers in South-East Asia. The Japanese electronics industry experienced sustained 'hollowing out' of smaller suppliers in the *keiretsu* in the early 1990s because of foreign competition. Exports of Japanese electronic goods fell progressively. By 1990, imports of electronic goods were 20 per cent higher than exports, a reverse of the situation in the mid-1980s. By 2000, imports were worth half as much again as exports. Japanese suppliers were undermined and with the economic downturn after the 'bubble' economy in 1989, *keiretsu* suppliers began to fail. Yet banks' long-standing relationships encouraged them to continue to lend to these companies despite their precarious financial condition; many of them were, in effect, insolvent.

Japan's banks initially shrugged off a deflating stock market and problems in the *keiretsu* as property prices continued to rise. Anxious to prevent a bubble moving from one asset class to another, the government stamped on lending against real estate. From 1990 onwards both real estate and equity prices fell catastrophically. Real estate values halved between 1991 and 1998.

the collapse eventually took valuations below the historic values banks had on their balance sheets

The collapse eventually took valuations below the historic values banks had on their balance sheets. In response, many banks tried to raise capital to offset their losses. Amazingly, the Japanese bank regulator discouraged capital raising because of the depressing effect it had on already low share prices.

Starved of capital, banks extended the term of loans, increased the use of overdrafts, gave flexible repayment terms and relaxed their lending standards. Two weaker institutions (Anzen Credit Cooperative and Tokyo Kyowa Credit Cooperative) nearly doubled their lending and deposit taking between 1992 and 1994 in an effort to generate profits. In a similar 'resurrection gamble', in the last months of 2006 subprime originators ramped up mortgage lending simply to generate fees to cover rising costs. Both strategies ended in failure.

In 1995, the Japanese finance ministry moved to liquidate seven *jusen*, housing loan corporations hit by non-performing loans – supposedly the beginning of dealing with the crisis. Even by Japanese standards the clean-up was slow. It took two years just to establish the vehicle handling liquidations – the Housing Loan Administration Corporation.

Deep problems in its many more banks eventually caused Japan to enter a prolonged recession in 1997 that rolled on for a decade. Japan lost 15–17 per cent of expected GDP in 10 years. If anyone is in doubt about the seriousness of banking crises in developed economies they should consider the experience of Japan.

The Asian crisis, bail-out and a regional disaster

The Asian crisis of 1997–78 introduced another set of problems that spread into far-flung reaches of the Japanese economy. Japanese politicians, alarmed at the prospect of a regional recession on top of their own, proposed a $100 billion Asian Monetary Fund to aid stricken Asian Tiger economies. US Treasury secretary Robert Rubin thought the fund would undermine Washington's influence in the region and vetoed the idea. Japan played out its painful adjustment, now encumbered by losses in South-East Asia. In November 1997, as an indirect result of the Asian currency crisis, Sanyo Securities defaulted on borrowing and filed for protection from creditors.

The knock-on effect of the Asian crisis spread through Japanese money markets, where much of the Sanyo borrowing had been sourced. Lending between banks declined sharply, liquidity in the Japanese banking system collapsed. Japanese officials were finally galvanised into taking action. The finance ministry ordered Hokkaido Takushoku Bank and Yamaichi Securities to suspend operations in September 1997.

Hokkaido Takushoku's failure, the first commercial banking casualty in Japan, had a big effect on the island of Hokkaido where the bank lent to 60 per cent of local businesses. Hokkaido is the northernmost of Japan's four largest islands. Its distance from Tokyo, dominance of agriculture and severe winter weather mean it has always depended on government assistance and infrastructure projects. The Japanese recession actually encouraged more building in Hokkaido as an antidote to the island's problems, and increased the property crash when it came. When Hokkaido Takushoku collapsed, a rash of bankruptcies followed, a third of them among construction companies.

Belated regulation: worse than nothing

Japanese regulators bolted the stable door long after the horse had gone. Laws were introduced in 1997 to 'ensure the soundness of financial institutions'. Had the rules been in place before the bank crisis began, they might have prompted a swift writedown of bad loans. Instead, the late introduction of the rules made matters much worse. There is, of course, now a danger of new rules hampering recovery in the West.

The Japanese rules caused problems immediately. There were early signs of a run on weaker banks and the finance ministry was forced to guarantee all deposits in local and foreign currency in trust bank accounts. By this time, government aid for the entire sector was becoming inevitable. The same kind of escalation tipped US, British and European governments into more and more action in the autumn of 2008.

Washington's pressure on Tokyo to fix its banks escalated after Russia defaulted on its government debt on 17 August 1998. A Japanese government package for the banks was supposedly agreed in time for a meeting between prime minister Keizo Obuchi and US president Bill Clinton. Two days before the meeting, on 20 September 1990, the hedge fund Long Term Capital was rescued by a combination of investment banks and the New York Federal Reserve. The added market turmoil was too much. Within a month, a Japanese bail-out of $510 billion had been agreed; recapitalisation, deposit protection and acquisition and finance of bad loans led the Diet to allocate funds equal to 12 per cent of Japanese GDP. The delay in dealing with the banks undoubtedly cost the Japanese more than it would otherwise. Dealing with the banks had been a history of denial, prevarication, more denial, hope and finally fear. One of the more hopeful aspects of the 2007–08 crisis was the speed with which the Western governments reacted in recognising and addressing the problem. It does not mean the consequences will be less severe than Japan, but it is a good start.

Quantitative easing, its wider impact and the flow of money

Far from an end to the problems, the end of the 1990s signalled that things were about to get a lot worse, and to encompass the financial globe. The collapse of the dot-com bubble in 2001 threatened Japan's economy with recession once again. The economy was at risk of self-reinforcing deflation. Prices had already been falling, as had retail sales. It was important to stop the rot, and encourage households to spend again.

> consumers assumed troubled retailers would
> sell for less in future, and held off from buying

First, the BoJ again emphasised its commitment to ultra-low interest rates. From a peak of 8.3 per cent in 1991, official interest rates fell to virtually zero by 1998. Interest rates were to stay close to zero for at least the next ten years. Yet, instead of encouraging Japanese spending, consumers assumed troubled retailers would sell for less in future, and held off from buying. Retail prices fell, more or less continually from the mid-1990s until 2003. The BoJ could not lower official interest rates below zero, so instead, it began a policy of 'quantitative easing' in which it hugely increased the money held by banks' own accounts at the central bank in the hope this money would increase risk appetite, and create an expectation of future price rises.

The policy began in March 2001 when the BoJ switched from focusing on the interest rate level – already at zero – to targeting the quantity of money in the Japanese economy. The central bank flooded the financial system with liquidity and committed to continue with 'quantitative easing' until 'the consumer price index (excluding perishables, on nationwide statistics) registers stably zero per cent or an increase year on year'.

Current account holdings held by commercial banks at the central bank rose from Y4 trillion (about $40 billion) to Y33 trillion, about $330 billion. The BoJ injected the equivalent of 5 per cent of GDP into the banking system in the hope the banks would eventually pass it on to customers. Over time, the policy caused Japanese money supply to expand by Y60 trillion. A similar solution was deemed necessary in 2009 in the Western economies. First the Bank of England, then the Federal Reserve and the Swiss National Bank followed the trail blazed in 2001 by Japan. They followed it much earlier in the economic cycle than the BoJ had done, conscious that the downturn this time was not just in one country, but the entire globe. The BoJ and the other central banks all found they needed to replace vanished money after the bursting of a credit bubble.

The BoJ's 'quantitative easing' policy continued until March 2006. During those five years, Japan's deflation gradually eased. But it led to changes as profound outside Japan as inside the country.

The quantitative easing created a historic migration of capital from Japan to the rest of the world. Data from the Bank for International Settlements show that following quantitative easing, the overseas holdings of Japanese banks increased by $900 billion in the six years to September 2007 – more even than the total amount of money created by quantitative easing. The increase in foreign lending grew particularly strongly from 2004, as the credit boom in the US picked up. And of the $900 billion lent abroad, perhaps $174 billion appears to have gone to hedge funds.

How could this have happened? How could the BoJ allow the money that was supposed to help its own economy be diverted into foreign funds? In fact, it shows the recurrent pattern of unintended consequences of a global, open trading system. If there are no investment opportunities in a country, then capital export to gain higher returns is a sensible strategy. Money is not bound to wishful thinking. Why lend to Japanese who have demonstrated economic ineptitude, when foreign banks and funds will pay higher rates?

The Japanese flow of money into other countries was often so large it distorted policy in smaller countries and the previous chapter showed us that the central banks of Australia and New Zealand frequently complained about the flood of Japanese *uridashi* bonds, which depressed interest rates in those economies and cheapened mortgages. Both countries have experienced a housing boom partly on the back of cheap borrowing costs.

The flow of Japanese money eventually distorted investments in America and directly contributed to the subprime catastrophe through flattened yield curves, compressed credit spreads and increased risk appetite among US investors for all manner of higher yielding products; especially mortgage bonds and structured credit products. In this way, it acted in much the same way as reserve management capital.

There was a quiet desperation in Japan's belief that foreigners could behave more sensibly than they themselves. As it happened, the flood of money from Japan ensured the foreigners would have ample opportunity to demonstrate their own incompetence.

The size of Japan made it special. The catastrophic collapse of the Japanese financial system encouraged its savers – and lenders – to focus on foreigners. Japanese capital increased the liquidity available in dollars whilst simultaneously denying the recovery of their own financial system.

The Fed and the bail-out of Long Term Capital Management

Two episodes during the ten years after the Japanese bubble burst demonstrated the US Federal Reserve was also a promoter of economic growth rather than a protector of its currency. These were the collapse of the hedge fund Long Term Capital Management (LTCM) in 1997 and the implosion three years later of the dot-com bubble. At the time seen as isolated incidents, we can now look back and see that both marked patterns of behaviour that grew more pronounced from 1990 onwards, and directly contributed to today's crisis.

LTCM: birth and growth

John Meriwether, founder and senior partner of LTCM, previous leader of the arbitrage group at Salomon Brothers investment bank, recruited Robert C. Merton and Myron Scholes to join him setting up a hedge fund in 1994. Merton was Harvard's foremost finance scholar – and a persuasive advocate for derivatives. He had played a key role, with Scholes, in devising the Black–Scholes option pricing formula that has been at the heart of much financial innovation since the 1980s. Scholes and Merton were to become co-laureates of the 1997 Nobel Prize for Economics, just as the Asian financial crisis was exploding. Merton's contribution to the development of derivatives had been theoretical; here was a chance to be practical.

> ## the $1 billion was just a fraction of the investments actually employed by LTCM

The reputation of its principals allowed LTCM to open its doors in 1994 with $1 billion of investors' money. Through leverage, the $1 billion was just a fraction of the investments actually employed by LTCM in strategies known as 'relative value arbitrage'. Scholes once described the technique of the fund as 'earning a tiny spread on each of thousands of trades, as if it were vacuuming up nickels others couldn't see.' As the Scholes analogy suggests, the fund needed to invest huge amounts, a strategy that demanded large borrowing.

The investment strategies employed with the borrowed money were, in fact, just sophisticated versions of the 'convergence trades' that attempted to profit from a seemingly inevitable convergence of global markets, representing a victory of transactional finance ideas. Far from striking out on an untrodden path, the fund was, from the start, part of a wider progress of international expansion, emulated in different ways in emerging market funds and international bank lending.

In the first year of LTCM operations in 1995, the fund delivered a huge return of 43 per cent after fees. Investors clamoured to join. The equity capital grew from $1 billion to $3.6 billion. The increase in investors required even more gearing to achieve similar returns and by the end of that year the fund controlled assets of $102 billion by borrowing $28 for every $1 invested. The pattern continued the following year. By the end of 1996, LTCM had equity of about $4.5 billion and controlled assets of $140 billion – borrowing $30 for each $1 invested. Returns that year were 41 per cent after fees. The borrowing was colossal, and risks were high, but no-one questions risk when returns are seemingly stable and high.

'Convergence': politics and profit

It was a costly omission. Globalisation encouraged funds of all types effectively to bet on the same 'convergence' strategy as LTCM. German banks followed one local version by investing in Russia; Templeton Funds, specialists in emerging markets, followed another in Asia. The success of the fund also attracted outright emulators, whose competition reduced potential returns. In addition, LTCM replicated, unwittingly, the same trade across different investments and different economies.

The partners' bet on 'convergence' appeared in almost every investment they made. There were some good reasons for their commitment. The approach of monetary union in Europe had given a strong political incentive for bond prices in the continent to come together, to converge. Investors had been backing this trade since 1994 as it became increasingly clear the single currency would go ahead on schedule and had made millions of dollars in profit. Some have suggested the political aspects of 'convergence' dove-tailed with the theoretical precepts of the fund. In particular, the Italian government had much to gain from promoting convergence ahead of monetary union, and the fund was undoubtedly heavily invested in Italian government assets. Alberto Giovannini was, from 1992 to 1994, co-chairman of the council of experts at the Treasury in Rome where he ran Italy's international debt programme. The fund employed Giovannini as senior strategist.

Convergence is a topic close to Giovannini's heart and his influence on European monetary union continues to this day with the reports of the Giovannini Group, a group of experts that advised on the removing of financial barriers within the single currency. The single currency has always been committed to convergence. A coincidence of potential profit and the political and economic aspirations of Italy aligned in the trades of LTCM.

In November 2007, Giovannini was able to put his first-hand experience of calamity to use when he wrote about the disturbance caused by subprime mortgages:[1]

> 'When ... as a result of a shock, all agents, simultaneously but independently, seek liquidity, the intermediaries' balance sheets go under stress, there is no demand for less liquid assets and disruptive liquidations may threaten financial stability...'

This seems a reasonably accurate description of what he must have observed at LTCM in 1998.

Beginning of the end

From July 1997 onwards, the devaluation of the Thai baht and the propagation of risk throughout emerging economies threatened the all-star LTCM fund. The effects, though, took time to be realised. The US stock market reached a high by June 1998 and the disturbance of the Asian crisis had encouraged funds like LTCM to add positions in expectation that 'convergence' would quickly resume. Yet far from heralding a new era of profits, 1998 would see the end of the fund.

On 17 August 1998, pressured by events in Asia and a broken tax system, the Russian government and central bank jointly issued a moratorium on foreign exchange transactions and unilaterally converted debt securities into longer maturities with new coupons. The Kremlin insisted the arrangements were not a default, but investors interpreted the news as a default.

losses were highest among those holding the 'convergence' strategy

1 Alberto Giovannini and Luigi Spaventa, Filling the Information Gap, 5 November 2007,

Illiquidity spread throughout the international financial system, and immediately alarmed central banks in the US and Germany. Three-month deposit spreads over government bond yields rose acutely in the US and Canada, followed by the UK and France. Emerging bond spreads rose sharply. Losses were highest among those holding the 'convergence' strategy. LTCM had been losing money since May, and after Russia's move things got a lot worse. On 21 August alone, the fund lost $553 million, 15 per cent of its equity.

LTCM now suffered from being unable to unwind its positions; partly because it was so big, partly because the positions themselves were complex. In a financially integrated world, illiquidity in a fund is similar to a financial crisis in a small country. Thailand in 1997 suffered from a withdrawal of financial support from its foreign bankers. Similarly, LTCM suffered a withdrawal of liquidity from banks located half an hour down the road in Manhattan. Both LTCM and Thailand were dollar-denominated baskets of assets funded by outsiders who suddenly lost confidence in the ability of the borrower to repay them. While Thailand had a population of 64 million and was the second-largest economy in South-East Asia, its entire economy was worth a similar amount to the assets controlled by LTCM.

Just as in the Asian crisis, liquidity had been assumed by LTCM and now money evaporated fast. Sensing problems, the fund's counterparties demanded higher prices to unwind positions, which compounded the losses in the fund. On 2 September, Meriwether wrote a letter to investors telling them the fund had lost $2.5 billion that year, 52 per cent of its equity. Yet it still controlled a large portfolio. If it was forced to sell the remaining $120 billion of assets, it would bankrupt the fund and propagate problems throughout the financial system.

On 23 September 1998, fourteen brokers and banks from Europe and the US met in the New York Federal Reserve Bank with the principals of LTCM and arranged a recapitalisation of $3.6 billion. Six days later, the Fed cut federal funds rates by 25bp. Other central banks followed the Fed with rate cuts of their own – the Bank of England and some European central banks included.

The combined actions failed to stop the panic. Investors who had borrowed in yen were forced to close their positions, which caused a rise in the Japanese currency, causing more losses, which forced other investors to reduce their investments. Credit conditions continued to deteriorate. Instead of rising, the price of government bond markets now began to fall as cash was demanded elsewhere. Other hedge funds began to fail. Ellington Capital Management in the US was forced to auction $1.5 billion of mortgage securities on 11 October to keep itself in business. Traders and investors began to say that conditions threatened to get a lot worse unless something drastic was done.

The Fed saves the world

The rising problems led the Fed, on 15 October 1998, to announce, unexpectedly, a rate cut of 25bp. Several members of the Federal Open Market Committee objected but it was 'generally concluded that the risk of adverse market reactions was worth taking and that the easing actions under consideration were more likely to settle volatile financial markets...'[2] It was a decision that was to mark Fed policy for well over a decade.

Financial markets reacted immediately. The S&P 500 equity index rose from around the time of the rate cut to the end of the year, reaching record highs. Spreads between different grades of bonds fell and so did the cost of stock options. The fear had not only subsided, but turned straight back to greed. It seemed the Fed had saved the world. And through its actions, the Fed learned that future instability, seemingly, could always be addressed through rate cuts.

For all the relief, the behaviour of the Fed was questionable. It was not obvious that financial panic had any effect on the wider world. Why deliver a rate cut when the US high street had not noticed a problem? Official reports into LTCM did nothing to calm the disquiet. The US president's Working Group on Financial

2 Minutes to the Federal Open Market Committee Conference Call, 15 October 1998.

Markets[3] (otherwise known as the 'Plunge Protection Team') reported first. The group included Robert Rubin, secretary of the Treasury; Arthur Levitt, chairman of the Securities and Exchange Commission, the body charged with supervising US financial markets; and Alan Greenspan, chairman of the Federal Reserve. In other words, the report was written by the same people who had authorised – or sanctioned – the Fed's rate cut. No wonder it failed to elicit confidence as an independent assessment.

The Greenspan put

The report on LTCM suggested that 'market-based constraints can break down in good times as creditors and investors become less concerned about risk'. The fund, controlled by fifteen or so partners, owned a portfolio the size of the annual output of Thailand; it was probably obvious that constraints had broken down. Yet the report failed to address this risk concentration and did not look at the risks of similar positions at banks, many mutual funds and other hedge funds. LTCM was, above all, an example of the instability of financial globalisation and the tendency for investment positions to be replicated many times over; it was far from unique. Why did the Plunge Protection Team not consider the wider ramifications?

In light of the recovery of the stock market after the Fed's rate cut in October 1998, there was doubt about the need to cut rates at all. A group of economists introduced a lasting image of a central bank that 'cut first, asked questions later'. They suggested investors would be persuaded that the Fed 'would take decisive action to prevent the market falling but not to stop it rising... So the Fed is apparently insuring them. The effect is like a put...'[4] So was born the 'Greenspan put', which described a supposed asymmetry of Fed policy; encouraging risk, while bailing out disaster through rate cuts.

3 'Hedge Funds, Leverage, and the Lessons of Long-Term Capital Management', Report by the Presidents Working Group on Financial Markets, April 1999.
4 Marcus H. Miller, Paul A. Weller and Lei Zhang, Moral Hazard and the US Stock Market: Analysing the 'Greenspan Put', *Economic Journal*, Vol. 112, pp. C171–C186, 2002.

Greenspan ... believed that central banks could not prevent asset bubbles

Surprisingly, Greenspan himself agreed. He believed that central banks could not prevent asset bubbles. Instead, central banks must be prepared to avoid widespread economic damage after the bursting of a bubble – something he felt the Bank of Japan had never done. So Fed policy became defined by avoidance of Japan's malaise at any cost. By following a policy determined to avoid the fate of Japan, the Fed actually ensured it was much more likely to suffer the same consequences.

Some believed the Fed's actions encouraged risky investment behaviour similar to that of LTCM. A later BIS report suggested that the Fed's arrangements to unwind LTCM had benefited banks 'holding proprietary trading positions similar to those of the hedge fund'. As the majority of the loss-making trades held by LTCM rose in value massively after the Fed-sponsored bail-out and rate cuts, the institutions involved in the bail-out actually made large profits. Those that took part in the fund rescue were rewarded particularly. 'It is an unhappy set of circumstances,' one bank executive involved in the rescue told the *New York Times*,[5] but, he added: 'We hope there is a reasonable chance of turning it around, and even making a profit.' Another executive in the same article seemed to relish the opportunity to take over the positions: 'Our people are going to try to capture the value in that portfolio.' As the LTCM portfolios were unwound over the next eighteen months, the return for the sixteen banks involved was indeed positive. For the five investment banks in the supervisory team, the returns were particularly good.

A disastrous lesson of overreach had turned into another opportunity to replicate the same positions, with the same world view. Bank interest in the LTCM portfolio was testament to the prevailing view that global 'convergence' was a certainty, led by America. Furthermore, it was a destiny underwritten by the Fed.

---

5 Joseph Kahn and Peter Truell, 'Investors Fear Trouble at Another Hedge fund', 29 September 1998, *New York Times*.

Much later, Fed president William McDonough said: 'I believe we did the right thing, but I certainly understand why others could say we went a little too close to the edge or we went over the edge.'

In some respects, the rate cut of 15 October 1998 conclusively confirmed the global reach of the Fed and America in the post-Cold War world. The rate cut endorsed the Fed's ability to calm all markets during a crisis. The collapse of LTCM, ironically, also highlighted the central role of US financial markets for all investors, a role that had increased over the previous decade after the fall of the Berlin Wall and was to continue and grow in importance for another decade.

Greenspan and dot-com

LTCM was an episode that challenged, briefly, the aura of growing US confidence. It was also an episode that should have raised a wider awareness that the novel features of the post-Cold War environment were not all benign. The link between unbalanced globalisation and financial disruption was perceived only dimly by authorities. For bankers, LTCM was mostly seen as an example of isolated hubris, rather than an example of what would happen to most of their own companies within a decade. The second episode that demonstrated the move away from traditional central bank concerns grew out of the steady increase in share prices through the 1990s, and it is to that I want to turn now.

The growing conviction of Greenspan that American economic ascendancy depended on his assistance became, later, an important element in creating the conditions of the credit bubble. This had been seen with LTCM, but it was also obvious in the Fed chairman's approach to the dot-com boom – and bust. The US stock market reflected, from the early 1990s, the peace dividend that accompanied the fall of the Berlin Wall and the new investment opportunities. The dollar's influence grew in countries that had previously remained outside the web of global trade; China, Eastern Europe, Russia and India. The ascendancy of the dollar was due largely to the perceived inadequacy of local currencies – an inadequacy dramatically reinforced after the Asian crisis. Nevertheless, it gave Washington enormous leverage, and it allowed Americans to sell their debt to foreigners at lower rates than would otherwise be possible. Above all, the American ascendancy reached new heights with the commercial exploitation of the internet from about 1993 onwards.

American business methods dominated finance. International investors added to the portfolio of shares and debt on Wall Street. Dollars were in demand not just to avert the risk in emerging markets but because the American future really did seem the most assured available. In the circumstances, it was rational for US stock prices to rise.

Greenspan confuses progress with irrationality

Initially, Greenspan seemed to disagree. In October 1996 he said the stock market might be suffering from 'irrational exuberance'. It became the chairman's single most famous comment and seemed to suggest his disquiet at rising share prices. Yet it was also a view he was to change in the following years, even though share prices continued to rise, to the detriment of the stock market and the US economy.

In fact, Greenspan's concerns coincided with a fundamental change in his thinking. From the October speech onwards, Greenspan convinced himself that the changes in the economy were historic; that the country could look forward to an age of expansion and prosperity. His growing conviction of this rosy future also extended to the advances made in finance, which he saw as part of the wider US dominance of information technology. Share price rises were far from irrational.

In any case, the stock market, backed by technological, political and military ascendancy, was always unlikely to be derailed by Greenspan's comments. There was a 'crowding in' of investment into stock markets round the world as the implications of mass communication via the internet sank in. The American economy was further boosted by an improving government budget.

A milestone in low inflation was passed in 1998; personal consumption expenditure prices rose just 0.8 per cent in the year as a whole. The stock market, even in the face of problems from the Asian crisis, rose strongly. By the end of the year, the NASDAQ stock index was up 39.6 per cent, adding to two years of strong gains. The Dow Jones Industrial Average too rose by a (then) record 380 points in a day on 9 September 1998.

> an expanding world, focused on liquid
> American markets, would not be distracted

The gains of the first three quarters of the year were tested in the final three months with the collapse of LTCM. Yet little long-term damage seemed to have been done by the dislocations. The S&P 500 index gained nearly 29 per cent in the year to the end of 1998. An expanding world, focused on liquid American markets, would not be distracted by problems in apparently far away countries. So the equity rally continued.

A law for financial expansion

In 1999, an important piece of legislation made its way through the US Congress, and gained approval of the Treasury and the Federal Reserve, which was to have consequences later. The Financial Services Modernization Act (otherwise known as the Gramm–Leach–Bliley Act) replaced the Glass–Steagall Act of the 1930s. The earlier act prohibited the overlap of business by banks, insurance companies, brokers and fund managers and was designed to stop the banking system using its regulatory and financial power from distorting securities issuance business. For years, foreign banks, particularly Japanese banks, had been able to offer services to their American clients that local banks could not. Globalisation had placed US banks at a disadvantage and Gramm–Leach–Bliley aimed at freeing them.

The new act was designed to encourage competitiveness within the financial system, a system that was already becoming relatively crowded. Added competition, in finance, almost always raises problems of lending standards. The Gramm–Leach–Bliley Act was one of a series of precursors to crisis.

Greenspan jumps on the Exuberance Express

Meanwhile, Greenspan's comments on exuberance appear to mark his conversion to the very exuberance he had appeared to criticise. Greenspan later said: 'My idea was that as the world absorbed information technology and learned to put it to work, we had entered what would prove to be a protracted period of lower inflation, lower interest rates, increased productivity and full employment...' The chairman went on: 'The depth and persistence of such technological changes, I noted, appear only once every fifty or one hundred years.'[6] He was, as usual, right in detail, if underestimating the broader difficulties that would be associated with technological change.

Greenspan increasingly focused on gains in productivity, which he saw boosted by technology. In 1999, he said:[7]

'When we look back at the 1990s, from the perspective of say 2010, the nature of the forces currently in train will have presumably become clearer. We may conceivably conclude from that vantage point that, at the turn of the millennium, the American economy was experiencing a once-in-a-century acceleration of innovation, which propelled forward productivity, output, corporate profits, and stock prices at a pace not seen in generations, if ever.'

Greenspan may be good enough to tell us what he thinks of the productivity miracle now that we are approaching 2010. America will surely need a large amount of productivity to regain the wealth lost as a result of the financial crisis.

Y2K: the crash of optimism version 1.0

In hindsight, the technology boom of the late 1990s always had an inbuilt cut-off date in New Year's Day 2000. The 2000 date changeover, it was feared, would cause old computer programs to crash if they were unable to process the date correctly. The Fed

6 Alan Greenspan, *The Age of Turbulence*, Penguin/Allen Lane, 2007, p. 167.
7 Alan Greenspan, 'Technology and the economy', speech to the Economic Club of New York, 13 January, 2000.

had been among the most insistent advocates of spending to fix the problem.

Again, it faced the problem with the assistance of lower rates. Before New Year, the Fed injected $100 billion in repurchase agreements[8] – an unusually high amount. It was a policy resurrected after the September 2001 terror attacks, and in 2007 when the credit crunch began. In the days before the millennium, the Fed had also placed vaults of cash around the US in case the banking system could not access the national payments systems.

In the event, the millennium celebrations went off with only minor hitches: Telecom Italia sent out bills for the first two months of 2000 with the wrong date and an Australian bus ticket system failed. Not much else happened. There was no real problem even among systems that had performed no remedial work – such as US school computer system.

the deadline and the official encouragement definitely pushed up the cost of programmers

The total cost of fixing the problem was put at between $300 billion and $600 billion; much of it spent in 1999, just as the technology boom was peaking. Did the amount of money spent on the millennium bug add to the last 'manic' phase of the dot-com bubble? It seems probable. The deadline and the official encouragement definitely pushed up the cost of programmers and with them, the cost of information technology in general. The last price rise in dot-com stocks coincided with the push to fix the bug. It seems highly likely that such costs exacerbated the overvaluation of stock markets as a consequence.

The fix had other effects too. With a lack of programmers, US companies began to place tasks offshore, particularly in India, Israel and Ireland. Demand for IT drove a rise in international outsourcing. The millennium deadline gave an unquantifiable

8 Larry Meyer, 'Executing monetary policy without treasuries', 12 October 2001, 52nd International Atlantic Economic Conference, Philadelphia, Pennsylvania.

boost to the global services industry; another example of the link between market liquidity and globalisation.

Then, from 1 January 2000 no further spending was needed. As a sector, information technology had feasted. As New Year 2000 chimed, the sector needed to adjust, fast, to tighter constraints.

Downturn in the new century

Bad news did not take long to arrive. In January 2000, Amazon.com laid off staff as costs grew while revenues stagnated. In March 2000, *Barron's* magazine published a list of 51 internet companies it expected to fail due to 'cash burnout' where the companies had simply run out of money. The party was well and truly over.

Stock market sentiment began to turn too. April was a particularly volatile month. The government declared Microsoft to be a 'monopolist'. Microsoft's shares fell abruptly and the NASDAQ index suffered its worst day, falling 10 per cent. It was the start of a slide for all stocks, particularly technology stocks. By the end of the month the NASDAQ had fallen by a third. It was not just dot-com companies that suffered; the information sector as a whole contracted, partly as a reaction to lower IT investment after the millennium. After such a rise, the spectre of Japan's decline and prolonged recession was never far from sight.

ILoveYou: a new disease

Something new appeared in May 2000, too. From the Philippines, the ILoveYou virus spread around the world in just twenty-four hours. Along the way it crashed the UK's Houses of Parliament computer system and was rumoured to have caused the CIA to shut down its email systems. Technology had become a matter of national security. It is estimated the virus caused $5.5 billion of damage.

Greenspan had focused narrowly on one benefit of technological change. Failing dot-coms, expensive Y2K preparations and the

ILoveYou virus reflected an unacknowledged dark side of technology. From 2000 onwards it was clear that worldwide connectivity brought waste, time-consuming repair work, unreliable information, and inefficiency along with wealth. Colossal waste of investment was revealed as stocks crashed and much of the new fibre-optic infrastructure lay 'dark' from lack of traffic.

The focus switches

Greenspan continued to praise the productivity gains of technology throughout 2000. However, a full year of market decline undermined the Fed chairman's support. In his public speeches, Greenspan mentioned productivity 145 times in 2000, but only 24 times in 2001.

Rather than the unbounded optimism that Greenspan had expressed one year earlier of a 'once-in-a-century acceleration of innovation... productivity, output, corporate profits, and stock prices...' the economy now faced recession. To save his vision of an unbounded future, the chairman needed a saviour for the consumer and he was to find it in mortgage borrowers, who responded to his reduction in interest rates.

The Fed began 2001 with an unscheduled rate cut in the first week of the New Year, the first unscheduled cut between meetings since the LTCM collapse. The rate cut came just as employment began to rise sharply across the economy. Over the next two years unemployment rose from below 4 per cent in December 2000 to 6.3 per cent in mid-2002.

The Fed continued to cut rates in early 2001. The central bank based its decisions both on the rise in the number of jobless and the poor performance of the stock market. A fall in market liquidity was met with rise in central bank liquidity.

September 2001

Then on 11 September 2001, economic problems were overshadowed, and seemingly compounded, by the terrorist attacks on the World Trade Center and the Pentagon. The Federal Reserve reacted to the terrorist attacks by running the emergency procedures it had planned for the millennium.

In the event, the four-day break in stock trading was considered a triumph and would have been much worse without the millennium training. The Fed cut rates by 50 basis points immediately after the attacks and used repurchase agreements to inject huge amounts of liquidity.

Over the course of the next six months the Fed cut rates five times. By mid-2002 the Fed funds interest rate was at 1.25 per cent. Inflation was relegated to a second order issue. What was paramount was to provide support for the economy – and its financial markets – in the face of attack.

> there was actually less evidence of economic collapse than might be expected

Yet, there was actually less evidence of economic collapse than might be expected. The economy grew in 2001 and again in 2002. In both years, it was noted that the national trend of house price rises that had begun six years earlier had continued. International trade had been declining in 2000 but picked up after mid-2001. By 2002, international trade had exceeded the previous peak of 2000. House price rises added to consumer confidence and encouraged people to borrow against their houses. The mortgage 'refinance wave' created by lower Fed interest rates had ridden to the aid of the economy by converting price rises into cash in consumers' pockets.

Japan's dark presence

In spite of continued growth and house price gains, official US inflation had been declining since the millennium, partly as a result of the lower cost of imports through a strong dollar, and partly because of the decline in economic activity.

In November 2002, Ben Bernanke, then a Fed governor, made a speech entitled 'Deflation: making sure "it" doesn't happen here.'

Bernanke believed the overwhelming probability was that the US would avoid deflation because of the resilience of its economy and its entrepreneurial culture. Nevertheless, the spectre of deflation was so terrifying that he announced it was the duty of the Fed to 'take whatever means necessary to prevent significant deflation in the United States...' It was essential that the Fed would never find itself in the same position as the Bank of Japan. It must deal with the problem pre-emptively.

Bernanke's speech suggested his favoured method for tackling deflation was to ensure that long-term rates were forced lower. In one suggestion, Bernanke advocated setting upper limits on Treasury bond yields, to be defended by the Fed. Not surprisingly, long bond yields fell after the speech, flattening the yield curve.

The liquidity generator unleashed

As we saw in Chapter 1, a flatter yield curve without higher interest rates expands financial market liquidity. From November 2002, markets began to react to the promise of additional liquidity in the Bernanke speech. A floor in equity markets was found, mortgage borrowing began to increase, retail sales picked up. This is when a central bank would normally expect to raise interest rates as the country recovered from a recession. Instead, the Fed was considering reducing rates again. These last rate cuts by the Fed now look a foolish incentive to the lending boom that followed.

There is no doubt that Japanese deflation was a concern for international policy makers in 2002. In March 2003, the BIS held a conference attended by central bankers from all of the developed countries.[9] The conference outlined contemporary thinking about the threat to the global economy from Japanese deflation. The paper from the Japanese delegation[10] listed the woes of the Japanese economy and suggested the government should begin to

[9] 'Monetary stability, financial stability and the business cycle', 22–29 March 2003, Bank for International Settlements, Basel.
[10] Mitsuhiro Fukao, 'Financial strains and the zero lower bound: the Japanese experience', March 2003, Keio University.

purchase mutual funds and real estate and also announce an explicit inflation target to persuade the Japanese public to spend.

The threat of US deflation seemed overstated. The economy continued to grow in 2003 at a quickening pace and falling interest rates prompted increased mortgage lending. Average house prices increased 7.5 per cent each year from 2001 to 2003. Some cities such as New York experienced double-digit house price inflation. While the official measures of inflation were causing Bernanke to consider 'whatever means necessary', parts of the economy were expanding dramatically.

There was plenty of evidence that interest rates should already have been higher, not lower. Tax cuts by Washington beginning in 2001 had boosted growth by 1.5–2.0 per cent of GDP in 2002. By 2003, private consumption was rising along with the house prices. The stock market had also stopped falling. None of this stopped the Fed from cutting rates to 1 per cent in June 2003. It kept rates at this historic low level for a full year, stimulating the housing boom and adding to the strong recovery that had begun in stock prices.

The speech by Bernanke in November 2002 was to mark a milestone in the history of the Fed and the economic history of the US for it signalled the beginning of the great credit boom.

Even as the Fed cut rates to 1 per cent in June 2003, the committee acknowledged growing market confidence. 'The gains in equity prices and a narrowing of risk spreads also appeared to reflect more upbeat assessments of underlying business conditions and, partly in concert with reduced geopolitical risks since the end of major military activity in Iraq, growing convictions that the downside vulnerability of the domestic economy had diminished.'[11]

The assessment failed to mention any analysis based on an expanded stock of money. One simple reason for the combination of a rise in equity prices and narrowing of spreads was the increased availability of dollars; either from the added liquidity

11 Minutes of the Federal Open Market Committee, 24–25 June 2003.

from reserve managers recycling their wealth, or from the creation of credit through use of collateral and highly liquid market conditions.

From the second quarter of 1998 until the third quarter of 2006, the US house price index[12] never fell below a growth rate of 5 per cent a year, even through recession. After the final rate cut in 2003, both the number of transactions and price growth accelerated. House price growth rose to an annual rate of 9.7 per cent by the second quarter of 2005 and remained at similar levels for the following year. Heightened liquidity had expanded from pure financial assets into the wider economy.

> heightened liquidity had expanded from pure financial assets into the wider economy

Far from trying to moderate such price rises, Greenspan welcomed the housing boom. The strength in prices was regarded as a sign of US ascendancy, perhaps replacing pure technology. Greenspan said in 2002:

> 'Since early 2000, this market [for secondary mortgages] has facilitated the large debt-financed extraction of home equity that, in turn, has been so critical in supporting consumer outlays in the United States throughout the recent period of stress.'

The housing boom had helped the country to avoid a much deeper recession in 2001. The housing mortgage agency Freddie Mac wrote: 'During 2002 and 2003 families converted more than $200 billion of home equity into cash at the time of their conventional mortgage refinance, which they ploughed back into the economy.[13] Greenspan estimated that every realised dollar of house price led to 10–15 cents of consumption.

The range of mortgage products expanded to allow a wider use for borrowed money: refinancing an existing mortgage at a better rate; paying off existing debts; as a line of credit to buy a car or pay for a holiday. Based on the historic safety of mortgage finance and the

---

12 House price index, Office of Federal Housing Enterprise Oversight (OFHEO).
13 Frank E. Nothaft and Yan Chang, 'Refinance and accumulation of home equity wealth', Freddie Mac working paper No 4–2, February 2004.

confidence of financial innovation, there was little excluded from the list. So the seeds for destruction of a two-decade boom were sown.

Long-term faith in an American future

Greenspan always retained a faith in America's ability to innovate to a brave new future:[14]

> 'Technology continues to bring rapid change and, hence, considerable uncertainty, to the global marketplace. Monetary policy, supervision and regulation activities, and payments system operation will need to be calibrated to respond to the influences of that technological change.'

He remained acutely aware of the risks too. At the height of the housing boom in August 2005, Greenspan explained how slower house prices were likely to moderate the current account deficit:

> 'The surprisingly high correlation between increases in home equity extraction and the current account deficit suggests that an end to the housing boom could induce a significant rise in the personal saving rate, a decline in imports, and a corresponding improvement in the current account deficit. Whether those adjustments are wrenching will depend, as I suggested yesterday, on the degree of economic flexibility that we and our trading partners maintain, and I hope enhance, in the years ahead.'

Yet despite acknowledging the possibility of 'wrenching adjustments', he was unable to see his policies had contributed to them. His mistake was to remain a celebrant of US primacy long after 'global imbalances' had tipped towards disaster. The Fed repeatedly cut interest rates and/or injected liquidity whenever there was a problem – in response to the LTCM collapse, ahead of the millennium, in response to the dot-com bust, as an answer to the terrorist attacks. Some of the cuts were undoubtedly justified. The pattern also encouraged investors, borrowers and banks to accept greater risk, because they became increasingly convinced that any difficulty would lead to lower borrowing costs.

---

14 Closing remarks at a symposium sponsored by the Federal Reserve Bank of Kansas City, Jackson Hole, Wyoming, 27 August 2005.

In Europe: equal rates for unequal countries

Unlike the Federal Reserve, the European Central Bank maintained
a very close watch on developments in the money supply of the
single currency. Yet while the ECB publicly espoused a hard
monetary outlook, it was also driven by an unspoken mandate to
promote the financial integration of the single currency as much as
inflation. A coincidence of objectives between the hedge fund
LTCM and the Italian government has already been noted, and the
mutual convenience for investors and European authorities of
'convergence' extended into central bank policy. The ECB was
driven by a contradictory policy; on the one hand it sought to
contain inflation, yet it also saw its role as promoting growth and
spreading liquid markets across the area. In the end, even its
interest rate policy tended to follow that of the Fed, while its aim
to integrate the financial markets of its new currency allowed and
even encouraged huge imbalances to emerge that would later
cause almost as much disruption as those of US subprime.

Follow the Fed

The same month that the Fed reduced rates to 1 per cent, June
2003, the ECB cut its main interest rate by 50 basis points to 2.0
per cent, a relatively large reduction and the lowest ever level of
rates in the area. The central banks of both America and Europe,
despite denials, were contesting for the role of global leadership.
And as is often the case in competition, while their constitutions
and outlook differed widely, the policies that emerged were forced
to follow a similar path; both concentrated on growth and inflation
at the expense of developments in credit. Whether they liked it or
not, international markets yoked the two central banks together in
a policy embrace.

The ECB did point to some uncomfortable problems
unacknowledged by the Fed. It noted that 'the euro area economy
has continued to accumulate liquidity significantly above the
amount needed to sustain non-inflationary growth'. Later, it would
become clear that this strong growth in liquidity was due to the
growth in the 'shadow banking system' of conduits, special

investment vehicles (SIVs) and hedge funds that expanded with the easy money.

Local imbalances

The ECB also had to consider its effect on what remained an economy of unequals. Unlike America, the single currency was a combination of highly developed and increasingly competitive economies such as Germany and 'convergence' economies – the others, such as Spain, attempting to catch up.

> cross-border lending represented by far the most obvious innovation of the single currency

Economists worried about the size of borrowing in America from the rest of the world – reaching nearly 6.5 per cent of GDP by mid-2004. In Europe, a microcosm of similar imbalances was also developing. Countries such as Spain and Greece financed spending by borrowing. And banks within the eurozone, particularly second-tier banks from Germany, were happy to oblige. Cross-border lending represented by far the most obvious innovation of the single currency in its first decade.

The arrangement suited all parties. The Spanish continued their long 'convergence' to the leading countries, France and Germany. In 2004, Spain acquired an AAA credit rating. Its property developers were intent on creating the California of Europe, and in many ways they succeeded, building miles of unsold homes, just like the Golden State of California.

And just like California, Spain became the destination of investment from banks who found competition too fierce on their home turf. German Landesbanks saw securitised issues from Spain as a way to compete. At one time they were buying as much in Spanish asset-backed securities as it took to fund the entire foreign borrowing needs of Spain. Meanwhile, other eurozone members were expanding eastward, lending foreign currency to ex-communist states, both in and outside the EU. Just as the dollar had encouraged global liquidity, so the euro had a similar regional effect.

Integration persisted as a dominant, though rarely stated, policy for the ECB even after the financial crisis. In a report published in April 2009, the ECB conceded[15] that 'early indications suggest signs of retrenchment within national borders. Going forward, heightened vigilance and monitoring of the functioning of the single European financial market will be necessary.'

Collusion in liquidity

From 2003 on both sides of the Atlantic, interest rate policy was low, encouraging financial activity. The BoJ was pumping money into Japan, and onward into the globe. Rather than slowing or reversing risk-taking, the policies of the three biggest central banks, the Fed, the BoJ and the ECB, were adding to investor 'exuberance'.

The world's biggest central banks had, in their different ways, shown they were less interested in financial stability than the success of financial market liquidity. The Fed was the most overt in its encouragement of market solutions, through liquidity. The ECB and the Bank of Japan too promoted market liquidity as a matter of policy with similarly unbalanced results. Central banks are supposed to be guardians of the value of the currency; in the past twenty years all have clearly lost their grip on this central function.

15 Financial Integration in Europe, European Central Bank, April 2009.

Going fishing: lessons of financial innovation

6

> Only a crazy person would have a mathematical model just running – (and) you go off fishing.
>
> Robert C. Merton

The eruption of the financial crisis has been accompanied by a chorus of criticism aimed at the financial products deemed to have created the problems. Criticism has been levelled even at financial innovation itself. Disputes about the benefits of innovation in finance are not new. The new is always suspect, and easy to blame.

To say anything meaningful about financial innovation, it is at least necessary to start with an idea of what financial services provide to an economy. Robert Merton, one of the most important financial innovators of the past generation, identified six main functions of finance:[1]

- to move funds between borrower and lender across time and space;
- to pool funds together to engage in projects in an efficient way from a collection of smaller contributions;
- to manage financial risk;
- to extract information to help in making decisions;
- to make information more widely available to society as a whole;

---

1 Robert C. Merton, 'Financial Innovation and Economic Performance', *Journal of Applied Corporate Finance*, Winter 1992.

▌ to help in the sale and purchase of goods or services through a payment system.

Of all these functions, only the last function, payments, is really familiar to most people, yet almost everyone uses finance for the other functions too, usually without knowing. To be worthwhile, financial innovation must improve one or more of these six functions of finance. Because our borrowing and lending habits need to match a more sophisticated environment, they need to adapt to change; that is the purpose of innovation. But innovation at an individual level is quite different from innovation at a wholesale level. The changes to wholesale financial markets have been radical, and disruptive.

> ▌ changes to wholesale financial markets have
> ▌ been radical, and disruptive

Finance, for Merton, is certainly not just about transactions and payments. Merton believed advances made by option theory in particular would lead banks and investors to perform roles that would become almost indistinguishable. We would all become bankers. The theme of conflict between debt and transactional finance that runs through this book therefore ensures Merton is among the most important thinkers on modern finance. His work on option pricing, which is at the heart of recent financial innovation, led, in 1997 (the same year as the Thai devaluation), to the Royal Swedish Academy of Sciences awarding Merton and Myron Scholes the Nobel Prize for Economics.

Why innovation is needed

There is often an inherent bias against financial innovation, often from those who should know better. The American economist J. K. Galbraith[2] said: 'The rule is that financial operations do not lend themselves to innovation. What is recurrently so described and celebrated is, without exception, a small variation on an established design... All financial innovation involves, in one

---

2 John Kenneth Galbraith, *A Short History of Financial Euphoria*, 1990, Penguin.

form or another, the creation of debt secured in greater or lesser adequacy by real assets.'

Galbraith was wrong to dismiss financial innovation so glibly. Contrary to his assertions, financial operations need constant adjustment, and thus innovation. Galbraith's idea that all finance is just secured debt is tantamount to complaining that drama is just acting, or bridges are just a route over an obstacle. It is an accurate description, but contains no consideration of efficiency, robustness, or elegance. Financial innovation, despite its recent critics, offers all of these.

New financial products are needed in the same way new road surfaces are needed; as an update to worn-out structures. It is sensible to seek further innovation, not retreat from the innovation we already have. Some of the structures have been shown to be less robust than we need. That does not mean we go back to a dirt track, it means we repair and relay. The world of global competition will not stop, so neither should finance. Innovation is valued in all other industries. Finance should not abdicate behaviour that is accepted, and encouraged, in the wider world.

Technology is frequently the cause of financial innovation. Since the financial crisis began, investors in the US and the UK have increased their interest in exchange traded funds as a result of the changed market conditions. The popularity of such funds depends on the sophistication of the technology on which they depend. Options and many other markets simply would not exist without modern technology. If we cannot make technology stand still, we cannot make finance stand still; innovation is baked into our culture, including our financial culture.

Regulation itself is perhaps the most potent force behind financial innovation. Lack of co-ordination and lack of consistency across financial products are a constant and fruitful source of innovation. Some see the growth of financial derivatives almost entirely as a response to inhibiting regulation.

Regulation, technology and the changing economic environment together explain not only the reason why financial innovation is required, but also the details of the products that emerge. In the

1970s, high inflation and volatile interest rates and bond markets created a demand for instruments to hedge that volatility, and so led to the emergence of financial futures. In the past ten years, financial innovations were aimed at extracting higher yields and increasing liquidity – in many cases at great cost. The same desire to circumvent obstacles or make the market operate more efficiently has always driven financial innovation, and will continue to do so.

It is one of the great benefits of crises that an opening is provided to challenge entrenched interests, and introduce more appropriate responses. Demand for products that had not previously existed will emerge, or demand for existing products changes. This always happens.

The Eurodollar market that emerged in London in the 1970s grew as a response to the restrictions of the US banking system, a demand that rose with the price of oil during the oil price shock. One could say, therefore, that the beginning of modern financial innovation began as a reaction to a financial crisis of sorts (the 'oil shock') and an avoidance of regulation. The innovation – Eurodollar bond issues – was subsequently welcomed by the US authorities whose regulations were circumvented because it was recognised as providing access to more capital. Eurodollar bonds were also one of the innovations that allowed London to re-emerge as a major financial centre from the 1970s onwards. Avoidance of someone's regulations is an incentive for other countries to take advantage of; we will see more of this in the aftermath of our crisis.

The dangers of uncritical acceptance of orthodoxy

Many of the problems since mid-2007 were caused not by too much financial innovation, but by reliance on a financial establishment view of how the world operates. The dominant financial theory, the Efficient Market Hypothesis, assumes decisions are based on independent 'agents' who always act in their own best interests to maximise their own benefit, and who are aware of all the known facts. The theory is flawed. At any time it is often not clear what best interests are. It is impossible to know whether all the facts are known. And investors do not act independently, but tribally, just like everyone else. What can appear 'best interests' in one environment can turn out to be anything but once the environment changes. Some circumstances suit high borrowing, some suit low borrowing; confusing the two can be disastrous in either case. What now looks foolish behaviour may previously have been required for survival.

> what now looks foolish behaviour may previously have been required for survival

Many of the innovations of the past twenty years aimed to increase the number of transactions and the speed at which they could be processed, rather than improving creditworthiness. These were inherently unstable, because liquidity can disappear, as we saw earlier. But the most dangerous innovations were those that attempted to increase the number of transactions through using quantitative techniques to refine the definition of creditworthy borrowers.

The scandal of financial innovation in the past decade was the lack of challenge to underlying assumptions. Rather than too much innovation, there was probably too little, or too little of a radical nature.

The risk revolution: innovation for all

Financial innovation that grew from the late 1970s was dependent on the same changes that accompanied globalisation. Technology allowed processing of information and formulae on a massive scale and linked creators, buyers, sellers and intermediaries as never before. The same technology underpinned the organisation of global trade routes. Information technology also distributed financial power away from banks into hedge funds, companies, sovereign wealth funds, individuals and households. Computers and the internet have been the greatest source of financial competition and innovation. Competition came from within the industry, between the financial industry and its customers and from the entry of newcomers. The innovation that originated in Western banks was not only based on new technology, it was driven forward as a response to the levelling effect such technology had on finance.

As a result of technology, finance has changed forever, even without the banking crisis. Can you imagine banking without the web now? Or investment accounts without online trading? The cumulative long-term effect of these forces has been a permanent revolution in finance that is probably far from over. As new instruments and methods of business are introduced, their usefulness and expertise almost never remain limited to their inventors. There is no patent system for financial designs. The current crisis may demonstrate an underlying fragility of a banking system that competes too hard, but it is no more likely that competition goes away than that the internet goes away. Yet, in another way, technology, together with the expanded user base of financial services, simply introduced another environment to which innovation sought to respond; so technology is both the solution and the obstacle. Compared with even a decade ago, we are all bankers now.

Efficiency or avoidance?

Economically, financial innovations can be divided into two categories. The first I will call 'innovations of efficiency' and is concerned with the distribution of financial risk, liquidity or transparency of prices and reduction in the cost of financing. The second I call 'innovations of avoidance'. These innovations seek to reduce tax or circumvent regulations. The first category simply tries to help finance run as fast as possible while the second attempts to avoid the institutional hurdles that may be placed (sometimes arbitrarily) on the race track.

Both innovations of efficiency and innovations of avoidance require the processing of large amounts of information. Communication with large numbers of people, often simultaneously and often over large distances, is also necessary.

Banks used to be world leaders in these functions. Since the advent of the personal computer, and especially the web, there are more people with the technological capacity to challenge, and directly compete with, banks than ever before. Most of the time, both competition and innovation were encouraged by regulators and governments as a way to provide ever more financial resources to the public, and as a result, higher economic growth. As with most developments, the benefits are emphasised but the risks are often not considered.

Why derivatives are so important

A financial derivative is simply an instrument that 'derives' its value from the price of another security, or commodity, or even a set of circumstances. There is often, therefore, no requirement for a principal investment; yet while derivatives can be made to emulate any sort of financial transaction they do so at a fraction of the outlay. This enhances innovation through efficiency. In addition, derivatives are often, as we shall see, used as an innovation of avoidance.

The method designed by Fischer Black, Merton and Scholes was what mathematicians call a closed form – in other words it was self-contained within its own notation. This ensured that once described it was programmable and so applicable to a wide range of circumstances. In essence, the formula offered a means to price protection against any future event, as long as a number of parameters were known (or assumed). The subsequent success of the Black–Scholes formula shows that, in broad terms, it replicated the behaviour of the real world. Although there will be some carping about that claim, theory and practice do offer protection against unforeseen losses on investments. Protection on this scale had never been offered so widely before the advent of 'scientific finance' that this formula represented.

The appearance of Black and Scholes' paper was well timed. The year of publication, 1973, was the year the Chicago Board Options Exchange opened. Before the opening of this exchange, each option traded was tailor-made, a much more laborious procedure than exchange-trading. The opening of the options exchange was an 'innovation of efficiency'. Together with the Black–Scholes formula, the exchange initiated a new world of financial products.

Merton's views dominated banking from the 1970s onwards. He envisaged a financial system made up almost entirely of derivatives managed by experts, who were able to distribute their value across the entire financial system. It was a vision that has largely been fulfilled, to the benefit of companies and individuals across the developed and emerging worlds. I have no doubt that the financial world will continue to be dominated by derivatives. The backlash against leverage will be moderated by concern about losing the benefits these instruments offer. Already, governments in Europe, the US and the UK recognise the damage done to their economies by the abrupt halt in securitisation, one of the key innovations of the last half century. The world needs these cogs of finance, or the machine will stop altogether.

the backlash against leverage will be moderated by concern about losing the benefits

Certainly there were mistakes. An important member of the European Central Bank, Francesco Papadia, has summed up his interpretation of this:[3]

> There was a hope that credit risk transfer helped banks distribute risk. We found out that there was a transfer of risk, from the US to Europe, but not outside of the banking system... The brilliant idea of securitisation has been nearly destroyed by very poor implementation.'

So another apparently appealing facet of innovation might include the ability to correct past mistakes, including mistakes in previous innovations. Yet, had Merton's prescriptions for risk distribution been followed, the damage to the banking system might have been lessened.

3 The director general of open market operations at the ECB was speaking at the IMN ABS conference on 2 June 2009.

There is no escaping the downside of innovation either. In the past decade too much money chasing too few investment opportunities encouraged bankers to find new ways to invest more in similar products. Innovation provided the mechanism by which the uncritical investment was channelled into the economy. As the American investment environment – and smaller local markets such as the UK, Ireland and Spain – became super-saturated, innovation provided a (temporary) fix – and a source of revenue too.

Merton and 'convergence'

Merton was evangelistic about derivatives. He believed they would lead to global 'convergence' of economic performance, living standards, healthcare, and social equality. Derivatives would allow connections to emerge between systems. The 'diverse financial systems of individual nation states would lead one to question how effective integration across geopolitical borders could have taken place since those systems are rarely compatible in institutional forms, regulations, laws, tax structures and business practices. Still, significant integration did take place.'[4] This was made possible in large part by derivative securities functioning as 'adaptors', which could transform investment in one area into something acceptable to another area, or jurisdiction. This 'convergent' behaviour across countries, which derivatives were expected to encourage, was a theme taken up by hedge fund Long Term Capital Management, for whom Merton was a partner as we've seen in Chapter 5. Convergence was also an important factor behind the European single currency. The worlds of the financial academic, the hedge fund and the political aspirations of Europe collided regularly, and with different actors, throughout the 1990s as the area readied itself for monetary union, The use of derivatives, especially such products as 'total return swaps', will continue to break down barriers for investors, whatever rules are likely to be put in place.

4 Robert C. Merton, Finance and the role of financial engineering in the 21st century, 12–13 December 2001, paper delivered at Kyoto University, Japan.

Yet, words often betray faulty assumptions, and in the case of 'convergence', the word contains the assumption that there is a single, predetermined destination to which behaviour should 'converge'. There is plenty of evidence that some permanent convergence does occur in a globalised world. Cars tend to adopt similar features, similar TV formats seem to be successful, and similar products (MP3 players) seem to have universal appeal. These products differ from finance in that they perform a simple function, or elicit simple, and universal, emotions. Convergence of product design is also often driven not by the buyer, but by standardisation of the seller; something that may not be possible in the provision of credit. While both seller and buyer may be pleased with the result for a music player, or a game show, the area of finance depends on much more subtle interaction of social and economic assumptions, some of which are difficult to change.

Critics argue the Black–Scholes formula is flawed because the single parameter needed to determine the price of an option, the level of uncertainty, is itself subject to a very wide variety of interpretations.[5] It is impossible to standardise. Supporters reply that the criticism is misdirected. You could argue that building a house does not match the ideal imagined by the architect. Variations in earth, the level of the water table, and local bye-laws are important. The question is whether there is enough tolerance in the plans to accommodate local, non-ideal factors. Mostly, the answer is 'yes'. Black–Scholes, as a closed formula, was by definition idealised. It is not, and never has claimed to be, a theory that could be applied in all circumstance without local adaptation. There is a great deal of interpretive work to decide when and to what degree the idealised formula needs to be adapted.

Merton said:

> 'Like other scientists, we had no practical objective. We simply found the options-pricing problem interesting. It was an engaging puzzle, a difficult challenge. And we know that just as the model helped shape the markets, the markets in turn helped shape the evolving model.'

5 Espen Gaarder Haug and Nassim Nicholas Taleb, 'Why we have never used the Black–Scholes–Merton option pricing formula', January 2008.

Swapping efficiency

Almost all derivatives require an application of the Black–Scholes formula in some form, and it has been applied to many contracts that do not appear to be derivatives. Insurance is one common contract that is, in effect, simply a payment contingent on a certain event, and therefore an option. Shares too are an option on the terminal value of a company. Eastern European bonds behave as if they contain an option on entering the European single currency, as did Italian bonds a decade ago.

One of the most common, and basic, forms of derivative is an interest rate swap; an agreement in which two counterparties swap fixed cash flows for floating. It is worth looking a little closer at swaps because they are so common, and also because they represent a very good example of innovation of both efficiency and avoidance.

As most swap agreements by design begin with matching cash flows, though with different types of cashflow, they are normally valued at zero – both sides of the swap balance each other. This means a swap is also an instrument without capital investment, yet it offers a return that is linked to the two reference cashflows. If one cashflow is a fixed rate of ten years and the other is a floating rate, the effect is very similar to owning a bond funded by a short-term deposit, without the capital outlay on either side. As yields (or rates) move up, the receiver of cashflows based on the long maturity will lose money, while the payer of those cashflows will gain. If rates move down, the reverse occurs.

An interest-rate swap is a 'bank-in-a-box'. Just as a bank typically borrows short-term deposits and lends long-term loans, so a receiver of a long-term fixed rate swap will perform the same operation by paying short-term rates (equivalent to a bank deposit) and receiving a long-term fixed interest rate. The interest rate swap is certainly an 'innovation of efficiency'; it offers the ability for companies, and even banks, quickly to switch their funding requirements to suit their circumstances. For banks, this has become essential, and explains why the number of outstanding swap agreements – bilateral contracts between two parties – far exceeds the total productive capacity of the globe, and with maturities that extend far into the future – as far as fifty years.

An interest rate swap is also an example of an innovation of avoidance. A swap contains two cashflows that are functionally equivalent to the income from a short-term deposit and a bond contains the cashflow components of both an asset and a liability, yet it has capital of neither, because it is simply an agreement to exchange two cashflows. There is no way to include this type of instrument on a balance sheet.

> the move off-balance sheet ... is the key to
> 'innovations of avoidance'

The move off-balance sheet has been an important feature of financial innovation and is the key to 'innovations of avoidance'. The capital requirements of banks are costly, and based on the recognised assets held on the balance sheet. The more that can be shifted away from the balance sheet, the better. Swaps are associated with a further advantage (or problem, depending on your point of view); they deliver exposure to large amounts of risk without any initial cost, no capital cost at all, and they are inherently leveraged. All these features ensure interest rate swaps account for the vast majority of outstanding custom-made derivatives. Swaps have revolutionised fixed income investment since they were first traded in 1982, through their flexibility, liquidity and the cost advantages. They also revolutionised banking through their ability to carry considerable risk off the balance sheet. These are all features in the growth in liquidity, and transactional finance.

Bringing liquidity to the illiquid

Another great financial innovation, which predated swaps by approximately ten years, was financial futures. Futures contracts have existed for hundreds of years in commodity markets; standardised contracts promising future delivery and payment of goods. Financial futures began only in the 1970s. Their success was to bring cash-like properties to markets that would otherwise demand much greater outlay of capital. The emergence of financial futures coincided with the publication of the Black–Scholes option pricing model. While futures are much simpler products than options, as are most swaps, the products share many features. In fact, options can be thought of as futures with embedded insurance protection.

Originally introduced to hedge against volatile bond prices during the high inflation of the 1970s, futures have proved even more useful by adding liquidity to underlying bond markets. They do this by demanding only a small portion of the full price of the instrument they hedge (similar to the inherent leverage of a swap), and therefore freeing the rest of the price to be invested in cash, or anywhere else, including in more futures. The liquid cash surplus of the futures investor is high, while the liquid cash surplus of the bond investor is low.

The most common futures contracts are for government bonds, though these are not the only important market. There also exist futures markets for short-term interest rates and central bank rates. Futures also transfer liquidity to the underlying bond. This is clear because the bonds on which the futures are based trade at a premium to other bonds. Higher turnover in the futures contract leads to greater liquidity of the underlying bond, and to a higher relative price. A higher price must mean a lower return, but it also means greater investor certainty, which is usually treated as a valid trade-off. Just as cash is highly liquid and sought after, but offers a low return. The extra liquidity offered by the financial future, the exchange-traded derivative, therefore provides the bond with more characteristics of cash. If this behaviour becomes prevalent, and it often does, the underlying bond can be almost equivalent to a cash addition to the economy.

What can go wrong?

There is a dark side. The liquidity provided to investors by futures – or any other derivative using margin adjustments – can reverse abruptly. An investor committed to the cash bond investment knows he has no cash surplus. Unfortunately, for the futures investor the high cash surplus is unstable. A price fall will cause a payment of margins, reducing the surplus. If this cash had been allocated to other investment projects, they would need to be liquidated to pay the margin.

There is always another holder on the other side of the transaction. This holder would then be 'short' the future and making money as our first investor was losing, exactly offsetting the original futures position. As the price of the futures market is linked directly to the bond market, the transfer of the liquid cash surplus between the two parties can be thought of also as a transfer of liquidity to the underlying instrument – i.e. to the bond. Margined or collateralised derivatives of all types perform a similar function. The advantage of futures over other instruments is the use of the exchange as the counterparty in each transaction, which when combined with an appropriate initial margin has meant these markets distribute risk with a low possibility of default. Even when users have gone bankrupt the exchange has absorbed the shock.

the convenience of futures contracts caused an explosion of listed derivative trading

The convenience of futures contracts caused an explosion of listed derivative trading. Outstanding financial futures contracts rose from 26 million with a face value of $10 trillion in 2001 to 155 million contracts outstanding with a face value of $28 trillion in 2007. Turnover rose even more dramatically, directly reflecting the rise in liquidity. In 2001, futures transacted 345 million contracts with a face value of $109 trillion. In 2007, there were 1.5 billion futures transactions with a face value of $457 trillion, nearly ten times the estimated annual GDP of the globe – $53 trillion.[6]

While futures are an important addition to financial products, many innovations have concentrated on 'over-the-counter' (OTC) solutions, which tailor solutions to specific requirements but depend on the creditworthiness of each side of the transaction. Interest rate swaps are the most successful example of OTC

6 Futures and options figures from Bank for International Settlements, www.bis.org.

instruments, but there are many more. A boom in OTC credit default swaps, and the potential disruption this might cause during the financial crisis, have led to them being moved (by regulators) to a clearing house, so reducing the exposure of counterparties.

The credit default swap acts as an insurance policy against a company default; the seller of the swap promises to pay the face value of a bond if the issuer experiences a 'credit event' – most likely a default. In return, the buyer promises to pay a stream of payments every quarter to the seller. In effect, the buyer is buying a put option on the debt of the underlying company.

A combination of interest rate swaps and credit default swaps can create an investment position similar to owning corporate bonds, but without the necessity to pay out much capital. By mid-2007, the BIS estimated there was $45.2 trillion of notional protection of credit default swaps outstanding[7] – close to total global GDP.

Credit default swaps transfer cash surplus into illiquid markets in a similar way to futures markets. An investor can keep most of his money in the bank and still remain exposed to potential gains in corporate bonds. The additional cash available to investors is a means of liquifying the balance sheets of counterparties, so encouraging more investment.

Derivatives have increased liquidity, and both protection and exposure to financial risks, but they also concentrate risk, which can be very dangerous. They also standardise the characteristics of the instruments they are hedging, which can also bring risks if liquidity dries up. This standardisation usually includes regular dates on which they expire. These dates usually occur in the middle of the last month of the quarter. These dates are called International Money Market (IMM) dates. The concentration of payments this has caused creates stress even during normal times. During a crisis it can add to tensions to an alarming degree. The IMM dates have been associated with a series of high profile failures of the financial system.

7 'Triennial and semiannual surveys on positions in global over-the-counter (OTC) derivative markets at end-June 2007', Bank for International Settlements, November 2007.

Close to the IMM date in September 2007, the British mortgage provider Northern Rock collapsed. Just before the next IMM date, December 2007, the Federal Reserve was forced to inject huge amounts of liquidity. In the week of the March 2008 IMM date, Bear Sterns collapsed; in the period around the June 2008 IMM date, the US mortgage agencies Fannie Mae and Freddie Mac were taken into 'conservatorship'; in the week of the September 2008 IMM date, Lehman Brothers collapsed. Most of these difficulties would have occurred anyway, but the trigger was the stress of concentrated payments around the IMM dates. In a crisis, this encourages banks to become even more wary of counterparties, and might have triggered the collapse of the weaker companies. With regulators suggesting more instruments should go on to exchange as a solution to the crisis, this problem may get worse in future.

Lower cost, higher competition

The single most important driver for the explosion of derivatives is the ease with which an investor or a bank can access liquidity. This includes the relatively low cost. Let's return to Merton, noting that he wrote:[8]

> 'Costs of implementing financial strategies for institutions using derivatives can be a tenth or a twentieth of the cost of using underlying cash-market securities. Looking to the future with such cost savings, we are not going back. Derivatives are a permanent part of the mainstream global financial system.'

He might have added that if we did go back, the decision would be accompanied by very heavy costs for both borrowers and investors.

There is no escape from competition for banks. The low cost of derivatives is double-edged for those who invented them, for the products have increased the number of investors able and willing to use them to compete with banks. Competition came not only

8 Robert C. Merton, 'Financial Innovation and the management and regulation of financial institutions', *Journal of Banking and Finance*, 19, 1995.

from institutions with large amounts of capital but from anyone able to borrow enough to enter the market, such as hedge funds, and even individuals. The explosion in derivatives also increased what is known as 'counterparty risk', the danger that the other side of the deal might renege. Some of these contracts can last for fifty years. The potential for unexpected calls on the 'surplus cash' increased sharply, which can be disruptive for investors, and their counterparts, if the investor is unable to pay, or perceived to be at risk of not paying.

This is paradoxical, as a system of contingent claims – rather than fixed claims – is the basis of derivatives. Contingency is widely accepted to be the best means to reduce financial risk through spreading it more widely. In theory, securities that transfer payments from one period to another, or from one location to another, can be used to spread risk across time and space (as we've seen, this is one of Merton's functions of finance). This should reduce volatility and risk for all involved.

> the problem is that transfer of financial risk can take place in two directions

The problem is that transfer of financial risk can take place in two directions. The lower costs of transaction and accounting, plus the highly efficient off-balance sheet exposure, encourage concentrated use of derivatives. The transfer of risk still takes place, but instead it can take the form of borrowing risk from other places and future periods, rather than transferring it. This is what happened to many banks, including USB, my previous employer, during the credit bubble. Far from transferring risk to others, banks assumed more.

The star innovation of avoidance was securitisation

Traditional securitisation brings together pools of loans within a special purpose vehicle and issues fixed-income securities to investors, which derive their principal and cashflows from the pool of underlying assets. Even when there are no capital constraints on banks, securitisation can reduce the cost of credit by, in effect, expanding the balance sheets of the banking sector beyond banks. Buyers of securitised assets, such as insurance companies or pension funds, become providers of credit. This is the basis of what became known as the 'originate and distribute' model; the arrangement whereby banks made loans and distributed the resulting securitised assets to investors.

The process is of great benefit for all of society in the way it spreads credit risk around many parties. Yet, since its first introduction in the 1970s, it has always been used to move risk off the balance sheet of banks. This is dangerous if the off-balance-sheet vehicle requires support from the sponsor bank, as many of them did in 2007.

If financial innovations are disturbing to traditional measures of investment, they are also disruptive to the regulatory assessments, as the process of securitisation shows. Merton gives an example of how regulations may cease to have much meaning in a world of derivatives.[9]

> 'Regulations say banks have to allocate more capital against mortgages than against lower risk Treasury bonds. This is obviously costly. Derivatives offer a way round this problem. If instead, it [the bank] were to continue to operate in the mortgage market in terms of origination and servicing, but sells the mortgages and uses the proceeds to buy US government bonds, then under the BIS rules, the government bonds produce no capital requirement and the bank would thus have no capital maintenance.
>
> The bank could receive the economic equivalent of holding mortgages by entering into an amortising swap in which the bank receives the total return on mortgages… and pays the returns on US Treasury bonds to the swap counterparty. The net of that series of transactions is that the bank receives the returns on the mortgages as if it has invested in them directly. The BIS capital calculation, instead of being 4 per cent, appears to produce a capital requirement using the swap route of about 0.5 per cent…

9 'Triennial and semiannual surveys on positions in global over-the-counter (OTC) derivative markets at end-June 2007', Bank for International Settlements, November 2007.

These remarks are not intended to be critical of those who set up the regulations. It is instead an attempt to underscore that, fundamentally, many of those institutional categories will have to be redefined to be operationally effective in setting regulations. This is both frightening and exciting.'

Anyone who thinks this process, or securitisation, is somehow against the rules or that the moving of lending off the balance sheets of banks was frowned upon is mistaken. Securitisation was encouraged by the US government precisely for the reason that it freed banks to generate more loans for their capital. A similar encouragement came from central banks and regulators in Europe. Securitisation was successful because demand for housing finance exceeded the ability of banks to provide money in the traditional way. The provision of mortgage credit since the Second World War was always limited by traditional banks and securitisation was acknowledged by the government to satisfy the demand, without changing the rules of bank capital. There was, of course, an inherent contradiction in government encouragement to banks avoiding regulation while officially adhering to capital rules. Much of this contradiction was based on the political benefits provided by financial innovation, plus the increasing international competition.

> much of this contradiction was based on the political benefits provided by financial innovation

The key element of securitisation is converting loans into securities. Loans have always been difficult to value. When loans become securities, on the other hand, they also acquire a price and therefore an observable value. The supporters of securitisation could justifiably claim that the process revealed information that had previously been hidden, an innovation in efficiency. Securitisation was, therefore, both an innovation of efficiency and an innovation of avoidance.

The downside to securitisation

Over time, securitisation introduced misaligned incentives and greater complexity. In particular, the fees attached to creating securities, the stacking of securities within other securities and the promises of high ratings have been attacked as contributors to the credit crunch. Some 'higher' forms of securitisation, such as CDOs, far from solving a problem, often (though not always) merely invented an apparent solution based on high liquidity – till circumstances revealed the unsafe premises on which they were built. The search for yield that followed the low-point in central bank interest rates in 2003 promoted more of these products as investors sought returns.

In his report into the response to the global banking crisis published in March 2009, Lord Turner said:[10]

> 'Securitised credit intermediation could reduce risks for the whole banking system, since while some of the credit risk would be held by the originating bank and some by other banks acting as investors, much would be passed through to end non-bank investors. Credit losses would therefore be less likely to produce banking system failure. But that is not what happened. Because when the music stopped... the majority of the holdings of the securitised credit, and the vast majority of the losses which arose, did not lie in the books of end investors intending to hold the assets to maturity, but on the books of highly leveraged banks and bank-like institutions. The new model left most of the risk still somewhere on the balance sheets of banks and bank-like institutions but in a more complex and less transparent fashion.'

New mortgage securitisations in the US rose from $684 billion in 2000 to peak at $3 trillion in 2003, declining slightly thereafter, but still running at $2 trillion in 2007.[11] If mistakes made were on such a colossal scale of lending there was a risk that failure in one product would propagate throughout the rest of the system.

---

10 'The Turner Review: a regulatory response to the global banking crisis', Financial Services Authority, March 2009.
11 Securities Industry and Financial Markets Association, www.sifma.org.

> there was a risk that failure in one product would propagate throughout the rest of the system

There is a parallel between the rise in mortgage bonds in the past twenty years and a similar spectacular rise in the 1920s, which, of course, led to the Great Crash in 1929. In 1922, there were $682 million outstanding mortgage bonds. By 1929 this had risen to $4 billion. In this way at least, the latest boom – and bust – was almost exactly 1,000 times greater than the 1920s. The reason for such growth was the liquidity that bonds provided, compared with the illiquid mortgage loans that sat on the balance sheets of banks and 'building and loan associations'. The mortgage market in the 1920s also saw new entrants to take advantage of increased liquidity when life insurance companies increased their investment in mortgages. Increased participation always breeds competition.

Staggering growth rates

The growth rates of derivatives of all sorts were astounding. We have already seen the numbers associated with futures. Exchange-traded equity option turnover rose from 334 million to 985 million contracts between 2001 and 2007, a growth rate of 25 per cent a year. As contingent claims, options can enhance confidence, and therefore liquidity. Unlike many other financial products, options have continued to rise in turnover since the beginning of the financial crisis. As a form of insurance they look likely to retain their recent rate of growth.

Credit derivatives grew enormously in turnover too. Default swaps (CDS) – a form of insurance on company debt – grew at an annual rate of 210 per cent a year from 2004 onwards. In common with options, turnover of CDS continued to grow strongly after the financial crisis began, a sign of their properties of contingency and insurance. The move to exchange settlement may enhance their attractions.

Collateralised debt obligations (CDOs) were the illegitimate child of securitisation and a notorious credit derivative. A CDO slices a portfolio of bonds into different pay-off profiles; the lowest rated, or 'equity', tranche receives a coupon only if all the other tranches can be paid from the bonds that underlie the structure. Losses are apportioned up the structure so that the most senior tranche is always paid unless a catastrophic event hits the entire portfolio of bonds. CDOs, like investment trusts in the 1920s, offered access to asset classes that would not otherwise be available.

CDOs packaged illiquid bonds with lower ratings into a supposed higher-grade product. A CDO therefore attempts to improve underlying credit ratings – without much success recently. They were often treated as a means of getting higher-risk loan portfolios off bank balance sheets, supposedly maintaining only the higher-valued portions. Of all the many instruments designed to bring liquidity, the CDO did more damage to the financial system in the recent crisis than any other. It was not the first time the structure had proved controversial. CDOs created losses after the dot-com bust, although this time the underlying instruments were corporate loans, rather than mortgage bonds.

Global CDO issuance rose from $4 billion in 1995, to $25 billion in 2004, to $180 billion in the second quarter of 2007. It then collapsed to $5 billion in the fourth quarter of 2008.

Working ever faster

We can pick on particular villain securities, such as CDOs, but in reality, financial innovation simply built on previous concepts. The logic that led to CDOs was embedded in many earlier products, notably securitisation of loans. There was a difference in the capacity to process, price and market larger numbers of contracts, which encouraged these racy products to emerge. This did bother regulators at times; not because the products increased credit risk per se, but because the efficiency of trading and the speed with which trades were conducted caused bottlenecks in their settlement. In 2004, regulators in America and Europe insisted that transactions in CDOs must be assigned more quickly after trade to reduce counterparty risk. In effect, the regulators were complaining that bank back offices were not keeping pace with the rapidly increased turnover. It was a telling sign; regulators had no qualms about the products that added so much efficiency to the system, but they were worried by delays in the system. Faster production was an aim of regulators, as well as banks themselves.

The shadow banking system, distorted money and SIVs

Rules introduce distortions, which innovation seeks to exploit. Regulations that limited bank loan and mortgages led to the first securitisations. And securitisation later prompted an entire industry of avoidance. In his Nobel Prize lecture in 1997, Scholes said: 'It is nearly impossible to maintain regulations that restrict activities in one industry when new competitors not subject to costly regulations are attacking the profitable businesses of that industry.' Scholes could have been talking about the banking response to the imposition of Basel 1 rules on banks on capital adequacy. Basel rules led directly to the creation of structured investment vehicles (SIVs) and 'conduits'. These were innovations designed to avoid banking regulations.

Deregulation of the banking industry from the 1980s onwards led to more mortgage brokers, car finance companies and credit card companies. The imposition of capital adequacy rules by Basel rules was designed to ensure the banking system aligned its risks and capital appropriately to avoid risks to the system. The rules meant also that banks were at a perennial disadvantage compared with specialist lenders. It was necessary to innovate to circumvent the rules.

Structured investment vehicles allowed banks to expand their lending activities outside regulatory capital rules. In this way, SIVs were similar to securitisation. The new vehicles were always linked to securitisation because they mostly used securitised bonds as their main investments. Their creation, therefore, both expanded securitised credit and provided a captive investor for the products banks created from lending.

SIVs thus represented the 'shadow banking system', a term coined by Pimco's Paul McCulley[12] to describe a set of companies operating outside the traditional banking system whose intention was to provide credit, without the costly structures required of banks. It was a process also known as regulatory arbitrage, and was an 'innovation of avoidance' *par excellence.*

> without the growth in regulation it is doubtful whether such vehicles would have been required

Without the growth in regulation it is doubtful whether such vehicles would have been required. Nor were there any objections to the quite open operation of these vehicles by banking regulators at the time. The system had appeared to work well for an extended period. Alan Greenspan said in 1998:[13] 'Regulatory capital arbitrage, I should emphasise, is not necessarily undesirable. . . That is, arbitrage may appropriately lower the effective capital requirements against some safe activities that banks would otherwise be forced to drop by the effect of regulation.' There was widespread collusion between banks and regulators on such avoidance of regulations on both sides of the Atlantic.

An SIV is a finance company that invests in long-dated bank debt (frequently securitised products) and structured finance securities, such as asset-backed securities, and funds itself using short-dated paper and share capital. The share capital of the company may be owned by sponsoring banks that benefited from a structure outside the capital adequacy rules.

It is important that the SIV remains highly rated because that means it can fund itself at a cheap rate, usually through a commercial paper programme, while investing in assets that produce a better return, effectively mimicking the traditional behaviour of a bank. The vehicle would obtain its high rating by

---

12 Bill Gross, 'Beware our shadow banking system', 28 November 2007, *Fortune.*
13 Alan Greenspan, 'The role of capital in optimal banking supervision and regulation', *FRBNY Economic Policy Review*, October 1998.

investing only in AAA rated paper. The purpose of creating a SIV is to generate returns above Libor on the assets, while funding at below Libor rates.

The SIV can act as an investor in securities issued by its sponsoring bank, while simultaneously paying a return to the same bank that the bank itself may not be able to earn, because of the nature of its funding and the constraints imposed by regulation.

The first SIV was launched in 1988 and was named Alpha. It was created by Citibank and together with its twin, Beta, they had the SIV universe to themselves until the emergence of Gordian Knot in 1995, which launched a vehicle called Sigma. Gordian Knot was an independent company that offered its services to banks needing to shift lending off their balance sheets. In the ten years that followed the appearance of Sigma, another twenty SIVs were launched. The importance of SIVs comes not from their numbers, but from the way they reinterpreted regulatory capital rules for banks and the encouragement they gave to the securitisation market in the US, the UK and continental Europe.

SIVs bought mortgage-backed securities in the US, the UK, Spain, Ireland, France and Germany. Banks from all these countries used SIVs to hold and finance new securities while they took fees on the transactions. Detailed money aggregates are not available in the US, but their activity in Europe and the UK is clearly evident in the money supply data,[14] outside the control of the central bank or regulators. In the nineteenth century, the Bank Charter Act sought to suppress the creation of credit outside officially sanctioned money. In the past twenty years, the practice was officially encouraged, even by central bankers, as a means of providing enough credit, while at the same time seeming to adhere to the rules.

---

14 See Bank of England Other Financial Corporation component of M4 and European Central Bank Other Financial Intermediary component to M3. See Bank of England quarterly breakdown of M4 lending for 'other financial corporation' component: www.bankofengland.co.uk/statistics/fm4/2009.htm. For ECB's other financial intermediary' component of M3: www.ecb.int/pub/pdf/mobu/mb200907en.pdf.

Computers change everything

The financial innovation that swept through banking over the past decade is often an expression of a bigger innovation in information technology. The communications revolution has affected all aspects of life in the developed world, and a good part of developing world. Information technology has fractured accepted investment techniques and the provision of credit across advanced economies. Access to instantaneous news flow and transactions is now available not just to banks and funds, but to anyone on the web. Comparison and analysis techniques were just starting at the beginning of the last decade and were often limited to banks able to invest large amounts in research. Deep analysis of information and instantaneous transactions were not available outside specialist finance houses until the late 1990s.

All are now commonly available to anyone with an interest, or the tenacity, to investigate. In the past decade these techniques expanded rapidly beyond banks and can now be used by almost anyone in some form. The democratisation of Western financial transactions and analysis has profoundly reduced the ability of banks to benefit from their control of information. Corporate treasurers, hedge funds, mutual funds and others have access to information previously available only to banks.

The general public too has been able to access information that had previously been the preserve of bank trading rooms. IG Index was one of the first companies to launch an online dealing platform for financial spread betting. In 1998, the company had just over 5,000 clients using its services in financial products. By 2001, it had about 15,000 and by 2008 the number had risen to 56,000. The range of products offered by the company expanded from traded shares in the UK to interest rate futures, bonds and currencies; only a decade ago these products were available only to professionals. It is now possible for an individual to construct the same trades on IG Index as those that caused problems for the hedge fund Long Term Capital Management in 1998.

> the information challenge posed by the internet can also cause direct disruption to banking

The information challenge posed by the internet can also cause direct disruption to banking. Consider the website YouWalkAway.com. In the aftermath of the subprime mortgage boom, the site allows borrowers to 'stop your mortgage company from calling you'. The site offers advice on how long a defaulted borrower can live in a house without paying any mortgage payments. It also offers to explain what procedures are needed to ensure foreclosure does not damage a borrower's credit rating, despite default. The internet generates a scale that can undermine lenders' assumptions about how to regain some money from defaulting borrowers. In so doing, the internet undermines (if not destroys) statistical relationships previously used by banks, known as the Law of Large Numbers. In the past, bankers relied on a stickiness of information so that the average borrower could be relied on to pay. Sites like YouWalkAway undermine assumptions that the average borrower will pay. Now, the average borrower has access to information dedicated to avoiding payment.

Communications technology is so deeply embedded in the financial industry that modern banking can be seen as purely a transfer (or in some cases a retention) of information, for which a bank expects a return, or a fee. It is the role of a bank to discover who is willing to lend and who is willing to borrow. If the two parties are able to discover each other without a bank, as is now possible, they may transact together without the help of the bank. A move away from the banking model is not impossible; securitisation was already half-way there and the credibility of banks themselves is now badly damaged. 'Social network' banking may rise as a credible alternative.

What's the future of financial innovation?

Two suggestions for the future of innovation seem likely to preserve the benefits and attempt to avoid the dangers. One suggestion is to demand more capital from banks to enable them to trade these products, or force them to retain an economic interest in the products they originate. Willem Buiter, an economist who used to sit on the Bank of England's Monetary Policy Committee, explains this as a need to 'force the originator to hold on to a sizeable chunk of the first-loss or equity tranche of the securitised commodities' as this 'keeps the incentive for gathering information and monitoring the relationship intact'. This sounds sensible.

The second suggestion is to encourage products to trade on an exchange, or to clear (match buyers and sellers) though a central body, and so remove the risk of counterparties. Credit default swaps already follow this route, and other products will do so. There is a limit to exchange trading, however. The tailored nature of many products – for example swaps – does not suit exchange trading. Nevertheless, standardisation does look increasingly likely for many products. Clearing of products looks highly sensible, and likely. Paul Tucker of the Bank of England has proposed 'common margin standards, common valuations and greater transparency'.

But these suggestions shirk the difficult issues. Only the most liquid or most standardised products can benefit from clearing or exchange trading, and the decision of how much value to retain in risky positions to ensure a monitoring interest assumes the products are able to be valued, or that the values mean much. Our recent problems came from instruments that do not easily fit into neat prescriptive solutions, and those that do did not contribute to the crisis.

Innovation is always a response to an environment; the environment that created CDOs no longer exists. These innovations are likely to wither in the new environment. Regulatory prescriptions on these products are probably futile. We simply do not know enough about the new world we are entering.

As usual, Greenspan had the issue on his radar: 'With the virtually unprecedented surge in innovation that we have experienced over the most recent half decade, many of the economic relationships embodied in past models no longer project outcomes that mirror the newer realities.'[15] A restriction on innovation will make a bad situation a good deal worse.

[15] Alan Greenspan, 'Monetary policy in the face of uncertainty', *Cato Journal*, vol. 21, no. 2, Autumn 2001.

7

In God We Trust: banks and their errors

Bank failures are caused by depositors who don't deposit enough money to cover losses due to mismanagement.

Dan Quayle

In God We Trust' is the motto on US coins and notes. It first appeared on the currency at a time of national crisis, the American Civil War. The war ended, but the appeal to God and trust remained. Behind the assertion is a belief that with trust, adversity can be overcome. It is a brave phrase to place so openly on currency. I presume the motto on the dollar bill implies that a failure of a bank is a failure of trust and not a failure of God. The continued use of the motto does highlight the permanent fragility of money and through money perhaps the fragility of the society that uses it. The motto is almost a prayer, maybe uttered every time a paper note is passed between citizens. It is an admission of the limited control society has over the behaviour of money. It is an unusual admission of fallibility. Most currencies are intent on declaring their security, not their fallibility.

Both in America and in Europe it was a shock in 2007 that the collapse of one seemingly small part of the system could break so completely trust among banks themselves and between citizens and their banks. The financial crisis has exposed how much of our currency relies on trust which, once broken, is very difficult to mend. The problems were compounded by what Lord Turner, chair of the Financial Services Authority, described as 'global finance without global government' – a loss of control over finance, and money, at least at a local level.

The bill so far

The International Monetary Fund (IMF) estimates[1] the total losses to banks on loans and securities will exceed $4 trillion, of an estimated total of $54 trillion outstanding – a loss rate of 7.4 per cent. Past financial crisis have been thought to be bad when losses exceeded 5 per cent. This episode will be extremely costly for society, with by far the largest bill in the short term presented by the banks themselves, but with a much larger longer-term bill potentially presented to taxpayers. There is simply not enough private capital available at present to make good these losses; government assistance was inevitable. In spite of the large amounts of government capital committed, there may be more needed, even now.

The IMF also pointed out that although the crisis began in America, and concentrated on its assets, the effect will be felt by banks elsewhere, particularly in Europe. Losses on loans and securities among European banks – not including those from the UK – are expected by the IMF to amount to $1.1 trillion, about 10 per cent higher than the losses expected by US banks. Partly, the added losses are due to investments made by European banks into America, but they also reflect their higher exposure to emerging European economies, an exposure US banks largely avoided. UK banks alone are expected to accumulate losses of $316 billion, a third of the losses of America, for an economy that is approximately one tenth of the size.

> ᴵ the bill from the banks may continue to be
> ᵢ paid by citizens for another generation

The bill from the banks may continue to be paid by citizens for another generation. The discussions about how to reform the system to avoid a similar calamity in future are already well

1 IMF Global Financial Stability Report, April 2009.

advanced. How did banks get here? What do the losses represent in geo-political terms? These are the questions we'll look at in this chapter.

Tensions arise

American capitalism focuses on market-delivered lending and consequently emphasises a form of money based on the 'medium of exchange' as much as debt. But as we saw in Chapter 2, money grew from the transfer of debts and the settlement of these debts. The tension between the two has become unbearable. These tensions have always existed, even at a local level, but they have become much greater with the worldwide financial marketplace. The resolution of this tension, or amelioration of its worst effects, is essential if the benefits of globalisation are to continue.

It is also of more immediate concern. A failure of a banking system is a potentially a failure of an entire society. This is what almost occurred in late 2008, in the aftermath of Lehman Brothers' bankruptcy. For two weeks in late September and early October there was no banking system capable of more than the most trivial transactions, and sometimes even these transactions failed. Transfers mysteriously arrived late, or did not arrive at all. Banks refused to deal with other banks. Several European banks (Dexia, Hypo Real Estate, Fortis, Royal Bank of Scotland, Barclays and HBOS) almost followed Lehman into administration. Governments across the developed world were forced to provide aid and the European Central Bank and Bank of England provided huge loans to prevent another major lender from collapse. Lehman's collapse triggered a systemic financial crisis of unprecedented proportions. No other crisis had spread across so many countries and continents so fast before. For a few weeks it seemed better to hold gold coins than a debit card in case the system collapsed. Some people did so.

The crisis had been burning for over a year before Lehman crystallised the frightening prospect of a collapse in the payments system. The surprise, in retrospect, was not that the collapse of an American investment bank would cause such devastation. The surprise, to those who work in finance, is that those who allowed it to happen did not realise the likely consequences of insolvency, especially when there had been such ample warning of the fragility of the system. In addition, US Treasury secretary Hank Paulson, the man who made the bankruptcy inevitable, had worked at an investment bank, Goldman Sachs, for thirty years before joining the Bush administration. During that time it is surprising he did not learn how serious the implications of a bankruptcy would be, even for a relatively small bank such as Lehman. How did the Western banking system get to this state?

Originate and distribute becomes 'originate and hoard'

Banks perform three roles: they create credit through a balance sheet entry; they take savings from one set of customers and lend to another set of customers; they are commercial custodians of a system of payments based on trust. When banks create credit they expect that credit to be balanced by a lender; if not immediately, then sometime in the future. A bank's role is to move money to where it will be used; they are intermediaries for the transfer of money in the financial system. For that to continue they must ensure that their own privileges in creating money do not overshadow their accepted role in payments. The utility role of banking, the payments system, has traditionally been separated from the investment banking role, which sees payments merely as the end result of transactions. This is a good example of the clash between the role of money as debt and as medium of exchange.

In the past twenty years the role of banks in the payments system and the increase in transactions caused a tension between the two purposes of money. 'Originate and distribute' is a model of banking that shifts the creation of credit into a creation of securities sold to investors; the debt is originated and distributed to investors in packages as securities. This was an important change in the way credit had been created in the past. Freed from the necessity to find a lender to create credit, banks saw credit creation as a series of transactions, rather than as debt. It was a system that had a great deal going for it; more efficient use of capital, a way to gain market share without a large balance sheet, a way to spread risk to those best able to look after it.

Unfortunately, while most of the expectations were met, 'originate and distribute' failed to transfer risk to those best able to manage it; it seemed rather to transfer risk to those least able to understand it, or not to move it at all. Many banks faced with competition for investment returns chose to keep the securities themselves and receive a better-than-average yield. As a consequence, they were left with the problems once the assets were rejected by other investors.

Would it have made a difference if the banks had sold the securities to other investors? The damage to the payments system might have been avoided. If the securities had been passed on, as intended, the losses would probably have been treated under different accounting rules. This might have avoided the catastrophic collapse that occurred in October 2008, even if eventual losses were very large. Why did banks not pass on the securities?

competition had grown to such an extent that extra earnings from securities were needed

One reason why banks held on to securities was that they needed to have their cake and eat it to survive, or at least to be regarded as competitive by their shareholders. Competition had grown to such an extent that extra earnings from securities were needed. Banks were also persuaded of the benefits of securitisation because they were involved in constructing the vehicles. Low real rates encouraged banks to keep larger amounts of securities on their balance sheets and fund them in the wholesale market. The Federal Reserve (and other central banks) had shown they could be relied upon to deliver liquidity if there were temporary difficulties and the cost of funding was favourable compared with the higher rate of return obtained from the securities. The objective of banks turned from providing credit into managing assets backed by credit, or gathering fees from originating these assets. For a while this worked splendidly, as the annual returns and the share performance of banks from 2002 until 2007 testified.

Ways were found for banks to benefit directly from the securities they issued, rather than pass them on to investors. Structured investment vehicles – which extended the balance sheets of banks outside international banking regulations – were extended. More importantly, fund management arms of banks were extended.

The most attractive form of fund management was that practised by hedge funds. Hedge funds can make the highest returns, and generate the highest fees, using the lowest overheads of any fund management technique. Banks saw the hedge fund industry was becoming increasingly mature, and concentrated. If banks were to continue to benefit from an industry that had provided an increasing stream of income since 2001, they would have to emulate it. From 2002 onwards, hedge funds were either established by the banks themselves or bought from outside banks. JPMorgan took a majority stake in Highbridge Capital, which became the largest hedge fund in the world. My own employer, UBS, established a hedge fund of its own, Dillon Read Capital Management, to gain from the fees and high returns of the sector.

Acquisition of fund management arms was, in retrospect, a dangerous overextension within banking. But it was no more than a continuation of a cycle of competition that has always dogged banking. The most successful hedge fund managers tended to come from bank trading rooms. Banks had been losing their best brains for years before they responded by either taking stakes in the funds their traders were establishing, or establishing funds of their own to keep traders while still offering them similar incentives.

The ease with which banks sourced low cost of funding, through deposits or through wholesale markets, also supported the move to holding securities that gave a better return.

An era of free money

Much has been made of the effect of ultra-low levels of interest rates offered by the Fed between 2002 and 2005, during which rates were below 3 per cent. I have commented on this as one of the causes of the crisis elsewhere. The Fed certainly over-stimulated the US economy. The European Central Bank has received less focus but it too provided easy money. In addition, the wide variety of collateral accepted by the ECB when it lent money to banks enhanced the policy of low rates further. The acceptance of asset-backed bonds as collateral by the ECB encouraged banks to issue more of these securities and to hold them on their balance sheets for presentation to the central bank. Through accepting lower quality assets as collateral in its finance operations, the ECB widened the definition of 'central bank money' to include the types of debt that would later cause problems.

Cheap funding became the norm on both sides of the Atlantic. Some banks were able expand their cheap funding through their customers. Private banking and derivative management systems often required large amounts of low-cost cash and this was delivered to banks, either as collateral or as funds on deposit awaiting investment. Many of the structured investments created during the boom years were prompted by an aim to fund banks cheaply. Investors would receive a coupon above the market interest rate as long as a particular event occurred, perhaps a steepening of the yield curve. The yield curve exposure was hedged, leaving solely a low-cost source of funding for the bank.

Funding costs also seemed guaranteed to remain low for a long time. Inflation rates were low and central banks felt they could afford to relax their vigilance over prices. Rate increases after 2004 were slow despite a strong economic recovery in the US. They were also flagged well ahead of time, allowing banks the opportunity to plan ahead. Central banks had also demonstrated their willingness to cut rates if there was a financial problem – as in the Long Term Capital Managaement episode and after the dot-com bust. This encouraged risk-taking because any difficulty was expected to be met with a swift reduction in rates. With many funding products tied to Libor rates – the benchmark rates set in London every day that reflect the cost of bank funding – and central banks apparently intent on keeping rates predictably within a defined, and low, range, the funding of assets became much more attractive. Not surprisingly, leverage ballooned.

The growth in repurchase agreements (repos) reflects the confidence in the source of funding. A repo is the lending of an asset in return for a loan of cash – or lending secured on a bond, or share. The huge increase in repo transactions and outstanding amounts of repo from 2003 onwards shows the extent to which the banking systems of America and Europe were creating their own medium of exchange through the transference of commercial debts. In June 2001, outstanding European repo positions stood at €1.8 trillion. By June 2007, their peak, the outstanding repo positions stood at €6.8 trillion, a growth rate of 25 per cent a year, much, much faster than the rate of economic growth. A similar strong rate of growth was also recorded in the US.

Why mortgages?

But why was there such an explosion of mortgage lending? One reason is that following the dot-com bust, the finance industry had run out of investable opportunities, yet the dollars kept coming into the country in recycled deficits. The 'sunny uplands' of technology innovation never captured the financial imagination again after 2001. Ironically, the profitability of web-based companies improved and the web went on to produce the most spectacularly successful service firm in history with Google. However, banks chose not to pursue the equity route after 2001. Equities appeared inherently less stable than fixed-income products, and more difficult to price reliably.

> the finance industry had run out of investable opportunities, yet the dollars kept coming in…

Fixed-income products are usually more amenable to analysis than equities because their cashflows are more predictable. After the financial and regulatory problems of the dot-com bust, investment banks chose to turn to the more certain asset class of fixed income. Of course, what you need to price fixed income reliably is consistent funding and predictable default rates. The lack of both would prove that fixed income can be as unreliable as equities. But in the dark days of equity markets in 2002, fixed income was a ray of hope.

The dominance of real estate lending among American investment banks was not just due to financial innovation. The dot-com bust of 2001 removed equities and venture capital as a source of funds and the investment banks that did worst in 2001–2003 were those that had concentrated on equities. The banks that had a market lead in mortgages reported consistently record results. Leading the industry were Lehman Brothers and Bear Sterns, both of whom would later collapse.

Regulators also encouraged the mortgage bonds from 'private label' issues, those outside the agency model, which would later prove the most toxic. In 2003, the US regulator of the agencies (OFHEO) placed limits on the balance sheets of Freddie Mac and Fannie Mae following revelations of manipulation of their earnings over a number of years. We now believe this was a political gain for the Bush administration, and allowed banks to provide the securities that investors had previously sought from agencies alone.

Investors had been keen to buy mortgage-backed bonds throughout the 2001 recession; now they switched to non-agency bonds in increasing amounts. The agencies never recovered their dominant position until it was forced on them by the government in the aftermath of the credit crunch.

With the agencies hobbled, investment banks were keen to package and sell the bonds, acting with mortgage originators across the country. Lehman Brothers and Bear Stearns had always been dominant in the sector. After 2003, they were joined by Merrill Lynch, Goldman Sachs and Morgan Stanley. From 2003 till 2006 the fee income from mortgage issuance for these banks – and related securitisations such as CDOs – outgrew all other major streams of revenue.

Morgan Stanley's annual report of 2002, at the depths of the equity decline, was depressing:

> '2002, it was a most difficult year. We began the year with the memory of 9/11 still fresh in our minds. In the months that followed, we had to contend with the continued decline in equity markets and a highly publicised investigation of Wall Street research and investment banking practices.'

In 2003, net income declined from $3.5 billion the year before to less than $3 billion, but signs of recovery were building in the fixed income market. The company shed 14 per cent of its workforce during the year but reported 'fixed income had an excellent year'. Fixed income contributed to the improved results again in 2004. '2004 was a very good year for your firm. I am pleased by the strategic initiatives we put in place. Record revenues from our fixed-income division.'

By 2005, Morgan Stanley confidently announced:

> 'We are masters of complexity and engineers of creative solutions... We boast a superb investment banking franchise, pre-eminence in key businesses such as prime brokerage and commodities, and leading positions in high-growth emerging markets... In 2005, we achieved record fixed income sales and trading revenues, record prime brokerage revenue... We will expand our capabilities across fixed income, equities and investment banking by creating structured products and more innovative solutions for clients.'

Even in 2005, there was more than a whiff of hubris. The following year, the annual report was even more celebratory.

> 'Net revenues rose 38 per cent to $21,562 million driven by record results in fixed income and equity sales and trading and fixed income underwriting, along with strong results in advisory revenues... Fixed income sales and trading revenues were a record $9,577 million, up 41 per cent from a year ago.'

Since 2004, Morgan Stanley had been retaining securitised assets on its balance sheet, presumably in the form of highly-rated tranches that were efficient in terms of meeting the regulatory capital rules of Basel I set in 1988. The Annual Report of 2006 reported: 'increase in other revenue was attributable to an increase in the fair value of the Company's retained interests in securitised receivables.'

The bank did not take on the risks with its eyes shut. In the 'risks' section of the annual filing with the Securities and Exchange Commission, Morgan Stanley listed 'liquidity risk' as the number one risk to its business.[2] In the event, it was exactly this liquidity risk that brought down many in the credit crunch – though not Morgan Stanley.

Merrill Lynch and Goldman Sachs followed a similar business development path to Morgan Stanley. As with Morgan Stanley, they worried about 'liquidity risk'. Goldman Sachs indicated its concern as early as 2003:[3]

> 'We also perform various scenario analyses, asking "What if?" about any number of possible events. Access to liquidity remains the single most important issue for any financial services firm... We place major emphasis on assuring our access to liquidity. The cornerstone of our approach is a "cushion" we maintain in the form of cash and highly liquid securities that averaged some $38 billion in 2003.'

It was a policy that stood the company in good stead; Goldman Sachs emerged as perhaps the strongest investment bank in the world in the aftermath of the financial crisis; ready to take over the shrunken franchises of its previous competitors.

Lehman and Bear Stearns had the advantage of being 'first-movers' in fixed-income markets. The 2003 annual report of Lehman Brothers wrote: 'The firm's fixed-income business produced record revenues of $4.4 billion, an increase of 68 per cent versus the previous high achieved in 2002.' Lehman's also reported its continued push into mortgages. 'The company acquired a controlling interest in Aurora Loan Services (ALS), a residential mortgage loan originator and servicer.' The company's profit 'increase was principally driven by strong institutional customer flow activity, particularly in mortgage related products'.

by 2005, Lehman was forging ahead in fixed income, mostly related to mortgages

By 2005, Lehman was forging ahead in fixed income, mostly related to mortgages. The company's report for that year said:

---

2 Annual reports of Morgan Stanley 2003–2007.
3 Annual reports of Goldman Sachs 2003–2007.

'[In] fixed income capital markets the notable increases were in commercial mortgages and real estate, residential mortgages and interest rate products.

Revenues from our residential mortgage origination and securitisation businesses increased in 2005 from the robust levels in 2004, reflecting record volumes and the continued benefits associated with the vertical integration of our mortgage origination platforms. We originated approximately $85 billion and $65 billion of residential mortgage loans in 2005 and 2004, respectively. We securitised approximately $133 billion and $101 billion of residential mortgage loans in 2005 and 2004.'

In 2004, Lehman had an 8 per cent market share of originating non-agency mortgages for mortgage-backed securities (MBS), and a 12 per cent share of securitising these mortgages. Bear Stearns was the firm that specialised most in mortgage products. It was consistently rated the top securitiser of MBS securities from 2000 onwards.

Given the extreme gearing, and the lax standards that emerged in the mortgage markets of both America and Europe after 2005, it is absolutely no surprise that these the two companies were also the most spectacular investment banking failures. They led the field for so long, and were so wedded to MBS, it would have been amazing if they had survived the crisis.

Mortgage originators also grew fast. Countrywide's earnings before tax were $842 million in 2002 and nearly tripled the following year to $2.4 billion. From 2003, increasing competition from other companies and increasing costs – from compensation and rents plus 'other operating expenses' – meant the bottom line remained virtually static from 2003 till 2006 at around $2.5 billion. Profits struggled to improve even though net interest income doubled between 2003 and 2006 from $1.4 billion to $3 billion.

The servicers did not have the field to themselves for long. Other companies were quickly filling the space to take advantage of the riches available. Some were created by investment banks. In 2003, Bear Stearns bought Texas subprime originator EMC and its acquisition immediately contributed to the fixed-income department's profitability. The subsidiary quickly took on a balance sheet persona of its own. In 2000, EMC's principal holdings were $4.2 billion; by 2005 it had holdings of $69 billion. Lehman Brothers also began acquiring companies to feed it with mortgages.

Monoline bond insurers are specialised companies that use their financial strength to guarantee bonds, and in return they take a fee. One monoline company, Ambac, initially benefited from the expansion of asset-backed bond issues but quickly found increasing revenues depended on taking on increasingly risky underwriting. Revenues rose 46 per cent at Ambac between 2002 and 2004, but in the subsequent two years growth fell to 15 per cent, then 13.5 per cent. Insurers had to move to underwriting products that were much more highly structured – and also more risky, such as collateralised debt obligations (CDOs) – to maintain their revenues. As we now know, monolines were among the principal victims of the crisis, which exposed their weakened positions after years of declining revenues.

One of the consequences of the explosion in origination was that banks frequently lost money on lending mortgages, but made it back through creating and selling the securities or by holding them and relying on cheap funding. For instance, a two-year, fixed-rate mortgage in the US and the UK was frequently offered with an interest rate below the cost of two-year bank funding. Mortgage borrowers received lending on better terms than the banks who were lending to them. The bank would not mind if it was convinced it could finance itself at a lower rate in the short term, or sell the securities, or create a CDO. After nearly a decade of this, the amount of short-term wholesale funding in the banking system became unable to support the number of assets held on – and off – bank balance sheets in any sustained financial disturbance.

The Great Moderation

Throughout the period of explosive growth in mortgage lending, global financial markets displayed remarkable calmness. Economists and central bankers congratulated themselves on their contributions to what became known as the 'Great Moderation'; high, stable growth, low inflation, flat yield curves, contracting spreads, falling insurance costs and lower volatility. Almost every measure of investor appetite for risky assets showed investors were convinced by the Great Moderation story; spreading their investments into previously shunned areas. By 2005, even Africa, a continent usually shunned by mainstream investors, was feeling the benefit of investment flows from Western investors.

We're losing money, buy more bonds!

Under the surface, calm banks were feeling increasing pressure. The flat yield curve and low bond spreads caused margins in America and Europe to fall to the lowest point in 16 years. US bank margins would have been even lower except banks were slow to pass on interest rate rises to depositors. Banks became more reliant on increased securitisation fees and off-balance sheet funding from structured investment vehicles. Just at the time banks would normally aim to attract depositors with higher rates, which would shore up funding if the economy began to slow and defaults rise, financial innovation was taking banks away from depositors. This was to prove disastrous in mid-2007 when the wholesale market seized up.

If low funding costs helped banks to move into securitised portfolio management, the competition in banking also kept rates down and low rates offered to depositors became a way to remain competitive. The low rates reflected increased pressure that bank balance sheets were experiencing even in 2006 in the face of an unusually flat curve and intense competition.

> the low rates reflected increased pressure that bank balance sheets were experiencing

Originators responded to the competition by selling more subprime mortgages, to maintain profitability through volume. A large number of commercial banks chose to sell low-yielding, but high-quality, mortgage assets in 2006 to relieve funding pressures. Some also purchased non-securitised mortgage loans, which offered higher income than bonds. Some banks, such as Bank of America in late 2006, chose to limit the amount of securitisation of their new mortgage loans because of a lack of returns. Yet, rather than opting for a strategy of safety, Bank of America exchanged low-yielding, high-grade bonds for even riskier assets (loans) in an attempt to enhance returns without adding to its securitisation holdings. The gain in yield was small – calculated to be only 0.2 per cent on the amounts they exchanged. Pressure to maintain profits pushed US banks into making or acquiring loans more aggressively, even as the credit cycle was turning sour. From 2006 onwards, many mortgage originators, borrowers and banks were dealing in wildly optimistic expectations that the world would always be benign.

The Bank of England governor Mervyn King summed up the developments:[4]

> 'Investors, including banks, overlooked the fact that higher returns could be generated only by taking higher risks. As a result, money was lent on easier terms. That helped push up further asset prices that had already risen as real interest rates were falling. It also led to an explosion in the size of the financial sector as new instruments were created to satisfy the search for yield. As well as lending to households and businesses, banks lent to other banks which bought ever more exotic instruments created by the financial system itself. The effect was to replicate the original risky loans many times over.'

Originate and distribute, the case of UBS

Europe followed America, in America and in Europe. Home-grown investment banks – UBS, Deutsche Bank, Barclays – could enter the US mortgage market directly, and often benefit from a cheaper funding base back home. This was certainly the case for the Swiss bank UBS.

UBS, which I know well after working there for twelve years, had been concerned that its investment banking division was falling behind US competitors in fixed income. It had also been slow to

---

4 Mervyn King, speech to CBI dinner 20 January 2009.

develop brokerage to hedge funds, an area that had been dominated by Goldman Sachs and Morgan Stanley. A report from management consultants in 2005 on how to close the gap with these competitors led to an ambitious five-year plan aimed at closing the gap. Memos were sent round announcing the plan. The most important message was that the bank would take much more risk. All members of the fixed-income business were asked to seek ways in which the bank could deploy its capital in a more aggressive manner. This was a huge departure for what had been a conservative bank whose main business relied on long-standing wealth management. The bank also had experience of the damage caused by aggressive trading in the losses sustained on its investments in Long Term Capital Management.

Part of the new plan called for the establishment of an internal hedge fund, Dillon Read Capital Management (DRCM), set up to ensure ambitious staff were not lured away by high-paying funds. With its low-cost funding from huge deposits in Swiss francs, the bank assisted the start-up of the fund and also took from the investment bank important business areas in mortgage origination, commercial real estate and credit arbitrage. There had been no special aim to emphasise real estate within the DRCM and the transfer of the investment bank personnel was agreed relatively late in the day. At the time, the business case made sense because demand for mortgage funds was high. There were also few other areas available that offered attractive returns after years of increasingly congested investment in US markets.

As a separate initiative, the investment bank had identified securitised products as the main area in which it was deficient, compared with the three main competitors, together with an increase in the servicing of hedge funds, development of emerging markets and commodities. In all the expanding business areas the bank emphasised its conservative history; presentations included prominent reference to the company's 'superior credit rating and balance sheet'.

Losses were first noted within DCRM on subprime positions from 2006 mortgages. The fund had chosen the very last moment to enter the subprime market. Already there were worrying signs of the end. In fact, the mortgage analysts of UBS, regarded as the best in Wall Street, had already published a report asking '2006: is this the worst vintage ever?' A flood of mortgage products had entered the market that enticed borrowers to refinance by suggesting these were the last subprime mortgages available, while mortgage originators competed to sell more and more. Lenders began to increase the size of loans compared with the value of the properties. Documentation requirements were also relaxed considerably.

Subprime securities as 'central bank money'

At face value, one of the more surprising revelations of UBS's subprime holdings were those held in the portfolio used to fund the bank's balance sheet. This function typically invests only in the very best assets. From 2003 onwards, the portfolio managed by this group acquired increasing amounts of mortgage-backed bonds, including subprime. The decision to expand the mortgage-backed holdings was taken because these bonds were accepted by central banks as collateral. The bonds were also readily saleable. In other words, from the point of view of UBS, the mortgage-backed bonds were indistinguishable from 'central bank money', the most liquid and valuable medium of exchange. Indeed, the reason UBS held on to its subprime bonds for so long, despite losses, was that they were accepted by central banks.

> from the point of view of UBS, the mortgage-backed bonds were indistinguishable from 'central bank money'

The use of asset-backed bonds as collateral at central banks, particularly the Fed, was widespread. In the aftermath of the financial crisis, the central banks of the US and Europe became probably the largest repositories of these bonds, as private owners refused to have anything to do with them. UBS had made the decision to switch to asset-backed bonds because the credit rating downgrade of Japan – prompted by its interminable recession and banking crisis – had made the bank's holdings of

Japanese government bonds appear more risky. The holdings of subprime at the Swiss bank were a response to the global nature of the bank, and also to the effects of an earlier banking crisis in Japan.[5]

From February 2007, it became obvious that subprime mortgage-backed securities had become illiquid. Far from offering greater security, they offered none. Holders resorted to estimating expected cashflows and making assumptions about the likelihood of default. The assumptions often tended to be wildly optimistic, sometimes with management encouragement.

UBS, together with all the other affected banks, suffered from assuming recent history indicated normal conditions, whereas the calm economic environment of the Great Moderation was actually a historical aberration.

The problem of data was especially acute for subprime finance because there was no long-term history of such lending, especially through a testing recession. The behaviour of subprime during 2001 was taken as a benchmark even though it was clear that recession had been limited and was accompanied by a great deal of official support for housing, particularly that offered by the Fed's low interest rates.

Probably because of its late arrival on the scene, UBS became the greatest European casualty of over-enthusiasm for subprime; losing a total of $50 billion in writedowns in the 18 months that followed August 2007. The lessons from the downfall of an ambitious global bank are rooted in its conservatism – it took years to be persuaded to bolster its mortgage holdings – and its global presence. The focus on mortgage-backed securities, especially subprime securitisations, was driven by a desire to catch up with competitors. The bank's five-year plan of 2005 shows it aimed to increase its presence in commodities, emerging markets and mortgage securitisation on the advice of consultants. It was a move symptomatic of a crowded investment space where investors jostled for returns.

5 Details of UBS problems taken from 'Shareholder Report on UBS's Write-Downs', April 2008.

Once the financial crisis began, the writedowns at UBS spread beyond subprime securities to other holdings. It seemed that in each new quarter the portfolio of affected securities widened. From high-risk CDOs the mark-downs spread to better quality mortgages, then to bonds insured by monoline bond insurers. In the end, the losses on subprime at UBS amounted to only half the total writedowns.

UBS was just the most public humiliation among European banks. Others achieved less widespread publicity, but large losses, both in American and in European asset-backed securities, were common. And as the market losses widened, so the number of securities that were refused by other banks increased, leaving only central banks to accept them, unwillingly, to forestall a broader problem. Thus, central bank money was made to accept even more of the toxic investments that no-one else wanted. If the demand returns, then the central banks will be judged to have acted wisely. If the defaults rise, the losses will either cause more bank problems, or the central banks will have to absorb them.

The decision of UBS to increase its asset-backed portfolio because it was accepted at the Fed illustrates the widespread regulatory forbearance of such assets before the crisis. Leverage, risk models, product innovation, balance sheet expansion, off-balance sheet contingent liabilities were all known about and in most cases encouraged by regulators and central banks. There was no attempt to slow or reverse the trend to securitisation and increasing complexity. To have suggested such a course would have invited ridicule.

Commercial banks aim to make a profit in a competitive environment; if the only way they can make a profit is to engage in risky investments, then the alternative for some may be commercial eclipse. Commercial banks are expected to take risks to make money; regulators are expected to stop them, but none of them did.

It was an attitude summed up by Greenspan in the late 1990s: 'If we wish to foster financial innovation, we must be careful not to impose rules that inhibit it.'[6] The ECB, in its support for financial

---

6 Alan Greenspan, Fostering Financial Innovation: The Role of Government, 1997.

integration, followed a similar 'hands off' approach. The European Commission encouraged the new products. In 2005, European Commissioner Charlie McCreevy[7] lauded the benefits of financial innovation, quite rightly:

> 'Financial innovation can help to boost returns on savings. It can help to transform wealth into a stream of annuities. We have to put it to work. My job is to provide a European regulatory environment which sustains financial innovation; which allows fund managers to develop new investment propositions; which respond to investor needs. In ways that are sensible.'

It is only after the event that banks – and apparently regulators – can determine what innovations were sensible, and what concentration of innovation is sensible.

How to place 'value at risk'

> greater criticism should be reserved for the systems to measure overall risk within banks

One area that certainly needs radical surgery is the risk systems of banks. Many of the techniques used for 'slicing and dicing' risk into securities can be criticised. But greater criticism should be reserved for the systems to measure overall risk within banks. Risk systems were supposed to measure and control the balance sheets of banks through data analysis, variance calculations, measurements of correlation, and expected returns. These systems shared many of the characteristics of the securities that would cause problems; they were model-based and reliant on an assumption about the future that lay within certain constrained parameters. They also relied on the quality and the circumstances of the data used. Risk models measure the past moves of a portfolio and calculate the likelihood of losing money in future. They are called 'value at risk' (VaR) models. Risk systems based on VaR cost banks money to create and maintain, then proved not

7 Charlie McCreevy, Innovation in finance – and how Europe can be at the leading edge, 7th Annual Finance Dublin Conference Dublin, 28–29 March 2005.

only useless, but an incentive to dangerous behaviour. It is probable that the use of VaR systems was responsible for the loss of much more money than the total writedowns on CDOs.

VaR works by analysis of a history of securities' behaviour and comparing this with other securities. It then works out risk measures for the portfolio run by the bank that indicate the degree of risk being run. VaR attempts to show the probability of a given loss. Many people assume this indicates the maximum loss but that depends on what probability is used and what volatility assumptions are used. On bank trading floors, risk control was alternately a constant source of amusement and annoyance.

There are several dangerous aspects to this system. First, there may be a 99.5 per cent chance of not losing a large amount of money, but the small 0.5 per cent chance of losing an extremely large amount of money may have such severe consequences that it outweighs the remaining 99.5 per cent probability. And so it was for many banks. Their VaR systems suggested the sort of market behaviour that followed the subprime bust was possible only perhaps once in the history of the world. Such implausibly low odds of catastrophe illustrate the limited use of the models.

If the probabilities were wildly wrong, it is easy to see how this was so. VaR systems often used data with a history of five years. This is less history than a typical economic cycle and certainly a great deal less than the long expansionary period of the Great Moderation period, which ran from 1994 to 2007.

The terrorist attacks of September 2001 on the World Trade Center introduced enormous dislocation into the price histories of securities. The way that VaR systems operate concluded that the period that followed the attacks contained greater risk than the period before the attacks; a classic case of shutting the door after the horse has bolted.

There was a more fundamental problem in VaR that stemmed from the way that severe dislocations are seen – such as the 2001 attacks. Because the system used a set period of history, a time comes when the dislocating event drops out of the history. For some banks, including UBS, this occurred in October 2006, five years after the attacks. As the period after the attacks had been the most benign market conditions known, the removal of the attacks caused risk limits to jump overnight. In some cases, risk-taking was able to double. Bearing in mind the bull market in credit was approaching a time when it would have been sensible to reduce risk, it is highly likely that the application of VaR models contributed to the last mad period of investment in risky securities.

High pay policies

Banks' pay policies have attracted a lot of attention. The UBS report showed that rewards at banks took no account of the low cost of funds offered by the bank, nor of the long-term risks involved. Its employees could buy an asset that yielded only slightly more than the cost of funds and, if invested in large enough quantities, the dollar returns would determine a high reward for the employee. The bank assumed its access to cheap funding would survive financial market disturbance. Similar incentives proved the undoing for many others, including Lehman Brothers, Bear Sterns, Northern Rock and Depfa. The investments themselves would not have looked attractive without access to low-cost funds, so the added skill in many investments was largely irrelevant. As I showed earlier, the provision of these funds often originated in countries such as Switzerland and, more frequently, Japan, where interest rates had been kept at ultra-low levels for several years.

Incentives to engage in riskier securitisations were also high because they offered bigger fees and long-term investments provided upfront bonuses for employees. According to the UBS report, bonus payments 'for successful and senior IB Fixed Income traders, including those in the businesses holding subprime positions were significant. Essentially, bonuses were measured against gross revenue after personnel costs, with no formal account taken of the quality or sustainability of those earnings.'

Employees were given a free call option on shareholder and taxpayer capital. In the event, they were also given liberty to play with the system of trust that underpins payments. The alternative, losing high quality staff to more amenable competitors, was not acceptable and remains likely to stall any long-term change to the culture of bonuses.

According to figures published by the Securities Industry and Financial Markets Association, the pay costs of broker dealers at companies such as Goldman Sachs, Merrill Lynch and Morgan Stanley in 2003–08 amounted to $550 billion.[8] Add to that figure the cost of compensation in the banking sector plus mortgage originators and the losses estimated by the IMF for US banks ($1 trillion) through writedowns look roughly equal to the amount of money paid to the workers in the industry. Considering the disruption caused and the long-term damage likely to growth in the rest of the economy, it would have been better value to have paid the money direct to all the brokers and bankers and asked them not to come to work for six years.

the cost to the wider society has been colossal, in lost opportunity, trust and future growth

The cost to the wider society has been colossal, in lost opportunity, trust and future growth, running well above the cost of writedowns to buyers of 'toxic assets'. The cost of banking collapse is transferred to the wider society to protect the payment systems. The most transparent measure of society's cost is the increase in government debt in the countries affected. The US Federal deficit in 2009 is expected to be nearly $2 trillion in 2009 alone or 14 per cent of gross domestic product (GDP), with more debt ahead to ameliorate the damage to the economy. The UK is likely to see government debt expand from 42 per cent of GDP to 75 per cent over the next four years, a total of $1.2 trillion over that period. Spain's and Ireland's government debt will expand from 36 per cent and 21 per cent of GDP to over 70 per cent, or about $650 billion.

8 US securities industry financial results since 2001 available at: www.sifma.org/research/statistics/securities_industry_financial_results.html.

A still greater loss may be in the trust in a system that seemed to have helped transform the world for the better. A loss of trust in the financial system could undermine support for more obviously beneficial institutions, such as democratic government in less stable countries, and possibly even in the developed world. The political storm that shook Britain over parliamentarians' expense claims in the spring of 2009 would probably not have shown the venom it did without the backdrop of rising unemployment and falling purchasing power by the British public, both caused by the financial crisis.

Banks writedowns are a loss of Western wealth

The banking system of Europe and America lost up to $2.8 trillion according to the IMF. Greed, concentrated risk in poorly researched products, lack of appropriate data on subprime investors, leverage through financial products such as CDOs, poor judgement, misaligned incentives, competition, lax lending standards. All of these factors played a part.

There is another effect too. The losses were an explicit measure of the loss of competitiveness to Eastern economies, particularly China. Banks work as intermediaries – go-betweens between lenders and borrowers – but the losses of Western banks express, in some sense, the loss of the societies in which they are lodged. There are losses for reserve managers too, if they invested in subprime mortgage products. But most reserve managers did not put a high proportion of their investments in these types of securities; reserve managers have emerged relatively well from the crisis. At one level there has been a transfer of wealth, through the official organs of reserve management policy, from Western countries to those countries following high reserve accumulation policies.

There is further damage to Western wealth creation from the crisis through the probable lower rate of growth in the West that will follow the crisis, plus the lower levels of debt that will be tolerated, or desired, by the population. Both will limit future growth levels.

These effects occur just as many countries in the West face ageing problems in their societies and would like to deliver as much growth as possible. Just when society as a whole would ideally be requesting more credit to pay for pensions and healthcare for its elderly, the amounts used to save the banks will severely limit the spending plans of governments. On the other hand, the amounts to be spent on the ageing population are so colossal that the extent of spending on the banking system pales into insignificance. And perhaps that is one of the more bitter lessons we have to learn; that for all the disruption we have suffered in the financial crisis, it is nothing compared with the sacrifices to come.

De-rated: how ratings agencies and regulations failed

When one sets his heart on being highly esteemed, and achieves such rating, then he is automatically involved in fear of losing his status.

Lao Tzu

Banks cannot be excused for the lack of prudence they showed in their business practices from 2005 onwards. Their over-reliance on models based on benign assumptions, perverse incentives, lack of data, bad timing and misguided competition all added to the build-up of leverage that affected not just subprime but all lending in the US and Europe. Their partners in miscalculation were the credit rating agencies that conferred high ratings on the assets acquired by banks. The relationship between banks and the rating agencies was an unholy alliance designed to bolster the benefits of banks' 'originate and distribute' business model; their actions precipitated its destruction. Ratings are also a way to institutionalise trust in payments. When a bond is rated AAA it is assumed to be of unimpeachably soundness; because this has proved hopelessly wrong, trust in the entire payments system could be damaged; hence need for government capital, and ultimately nationalisation of banks, agencies and insurance companies. The system ceased to rely on private sector debt money, and instead was forced to demand the pledge of entire societies.

Rating agencies: uncontrolled private regulation

In testimony before the Senate Banking Committee on 8 February 2005, Kathleen Corbet, then president of Standard & Poor's said:

> 'Credit ratings provide reliable standards for issuers and investors around the world, facilitating efficient capital raising and the growth of new markets. Indeed, credit rating opinions have supported the development of deeper, broader and more cost effective global debt markets.'

Corbet's description of the services provided by credit rating agencies contains the seeds of much criticism of these companies after the credit crunch. While there is little doubt the agencies facilitated capital raising and the growth of new markets, this was of little use to investors if their advice was not reliable, and they stand charged with systematically failing to provide trustworthy standards.

The main agencies, Moody's Investor Services and Standard & Poor's, control about 80 per cent of the worldwide ratings market while the smaller Fitch Ratings had a market share of some 12 per cent. There are other agencies in America, and in China and India, but they pale next to the largest companies. The oligopoly of major agencies is not completely alone. Local companies exist, and in America the introduction of the 2006 Credit Rating Reform Act was, in part, an attempt to stimulate competition. Yet, the three major companies are so dominant they may distort even the results of their competition; it has been claimed that minor agencies give more favourable ratings to issuers than the 'big three', presumably because this is a way to expand their business.[1]

Rating agencies are different from regulatory bodies, which are paid for by the public, but in many ways they also perform a regulatory duty. The difference is that their business generates fees and their approval comes at a price. Critics have highlighted a seemingly inherent conflict of interest between agencies and their issuer clients. The companies' fees are generated by issuers. In

---

[1] Patrick Van Roy, 'Credit ratings and the standardised approach to credit risk in Basel II,' ECB working paper 517, August 2005.

return, the ratings provide standardised guidance to investors to help decide which issuers suit their investment criteria. In the aftermath of the 2001 dot-com crash, agencies were accused of placing the interests of the issuer over those of the investor. It was a charge that reappeared with much greater force after 2007. The inclusion of rating agencies into the regulatory environment has become more pervasive over the past five years. The further embedding of rating agencies has occurred despite the accusations of conflicted and misleading opinions.

> after the dot-com bust, the business of all rating agencies shifted towards credit derivatives

After the dot-com bust, the business of all rating agencies shifted towards credit derivatives, particularly collateralised debt obligations (CDOs), which depended for their marketability on attractive ratings. The agencies found a new role in facilitating such intermediation. It was suggested that their 'rating methodologies for collateralised debt obligations (CDOs) have created and sustained that multi-trillion dollar market', and that they acted 'more like "gate-openers" than gatekeepers.'[2] During the expansionary phase, almost any means of providing liquidity for markets was rewarded.

The ratings industry seems always to be predisposed to criticism. As an elite group, the number of agencies had been limited by the Securities and Exchange Commission (SEC). Unlike almost any industry, there is a hefty barrier to entry controlled by the SEC in the form of registration as a nationally recognised statistical rating organisation (NRSRO). Once registered, approval provides a staple of work without competitive appraisal of performance, as many investors are required by law or mandate to invest according to NRSRO ratings. They are therefore forced to accept the conclusion of approved rating agencies, whatever their quality.

In March 2005, *The Economist* ran an article called 'Who rates the

2 Amadou N. R. Sy, 'The systemic regulation of credit rating agencies and rated markets,' IMF working paper WP/09/129, June 2009.

raters?' which highlighted lack of competition in the ratings industry. 'The business functions as an oligopoly. Upstarts have a hard time breaking in because it takes years, even decades, to build a sufficient reputation.'

'Rent-seeking oligopoly' is a charge that most companies would seek to avoid, and I assume rating agencies would also dislike being thus charged. Yet to some it does appear that this is how they operate. There have been further charges that even after official recognition the ratings offered by agencies may be either of limited value or even damaging.

Ratings were notoriously slow to change, often occurring after a company had defaulted on its payments, or well after the market price of its bonds had declined. Multiple downgrades are not uncommon and often follow the market, which has frequently already made price adjustments to match a lower expectation of payment. The investment protection offered by ratings is therefore questionable. Scepticism about the value of ratings increases when different agencies offer different ratings for the same product. Disagreements between the three main agencies are noticeable, and while these may be the product of different methodologies used to assign ratings, there are also some apparently consistent biases. Some rating agencies consistently rate banks higher than other agencies, and others consistently rank some companies higher than others. Even before the growth in subprime, an issuer could shop around for marginal improvement in its ratings if it aided the sale of their bonds. With the introduction of ratings on complex securitisation vehicles and the inclusion of ratings into international capital regulations, pitfalls became much more pronounced.

Rating agencies grew out of the era of railroad expansion in the late nineteenth century – an era of expanding investor participation that demanded easily digestible analysis of bond issues. *The Economist* describes their beginning:[3] 'Starting in 1909, a dense book from John Moody would thud on to subscribers' desks in America, following days or even weeks in the post. The

---

3 Credit rating agencies, Who rates the raters? *The Economist*, 26 March 2005.

annual railroad-bond ratings were out. America's fledgling debt markets moved accordingly.'

Both Standard & Poor's and Moody's really came of age in the 1920s when the economic expansion was accompanied by a demand for standardisation of investment analysis. Their services were increasingly demanded through the market boom of the 1920s – especially for bond issues. The 1929 crash gave the first indication that the agencies might not be as valuable as they claimed. The Chicago, Rock Island and Pacific Railroad defaulted on its bonds in spite of obtaining the highest ratings from S&P, Moody's and Fitch. Largely as a result of the loss of confidence in ratings due to the defaults that followed the 1929 crash, the ratings business slipped into obscurity for decades.

Salvation came when the SEC decided, in the early 1970s, to use rating agencies to assess broker-dealers (investment banks). It was a seminal move for the agencies. Thereafter they received an increasing flow of regulatory work.

It was in the 1970s too that the agencies decided to charge issuers for their ratings. They were prompted to shift from subscription fees to issuer fees by the rise of securitisation, and grew with the business till its apotheosis in 2007. Their aim of providing guidance to investors – actually, initially just regulators – was always combined with a willingness to promote products. Where the investment of cash was concerned the agencies were always available to provide a rationale for investing.

During the 1990s the power and prosperity of the rating agencies grew, as public and private bond issues multiplied. By the mid-1990s, Moody's dominated the industry with ratings issued on 20,000 US issuers and 1,500 issuers from other countries. Moody's in particular embodied the information nexus the agencies represented. Pulitzer Prize winning *New York Times* writer Thomas Friedman in February 1996 highlighted the power of the agencies in a television interview:

'Free market principles [are] spreading all over the world, and markets being integrated more and more. And as that's happening, it's putting a lot of pressure on every country in the world to compete to attract capital. Under that pressure, there are winners and losers. There are people who have the knowledge, skills in order to tap into that market, and there are people who don't, who are left behind. And really what I found is that some of the most interesting conflicts in the world today are between winners and losers within countries.'

In this world, Moody's acquired an immense power, said Friedman:

> 'There are two superpowers in the world today in my opinion. There's the United States and there's Moody's Bond Rating Service. The United States can destroy you by dropping bombs, and Moody's can destroy you by downgrading your bonds. And believe me; it's not clear sometimes who's more powerful.'

Far from competing to attract capital in the decade after 1996, as Friedman forecast, there was competition to provide capital. Friedmand also misunderstood the power of the agencies. They hardly ever destroyed a company by downgrading its bonds. The bonds often default first, and only afterwards are downgraded.

Even so, the value of controlling information, as Google was to show a decade later, was for the agencies immense and their power grew with increasing numbers of securitisation issues. As tho business grew, so did their profits. Moody's operating margins had always been high, but from 2000 onwards they rose above 50 per cent. Standard & Poor's as a subsidiary of McGraw-Hill reported operating margins of 40–45 per cent. In 2005, Standard & Poor's reported much-improved results from the strong performance of structured finance and corporate finance ratings – representing about 40 per cent and 17 per cent of the growth in revenue respectively.

The agencies also continued to benefit from official regulation. One of the reasons for strong revenues in the fourth quarter of 2005 was due to the SEC introducing regulation AB (asset-backed) on 1 January 2006. To avoid the rules, many issues were brought forward, providing the agencies with a fillip for the end of the year.

Securitisation – and its increasingly exotic offspring – remained their main source of growth. Moody's reported in 2003: 'Structured finance is Moody's largest and fastest growing ratings business segment. Globally, rated structured finance issuance has grown at a compound annual rate of 24 per cent since 1996... We expect rapid growth in structured finance to continue for many years.' Three years later, Moody's annual report continued the theme:[4] by 2006, structured finance fees accounted for 44 per cent of its revenues.

Transactions and market liquidity had therefore become integral for the continued profitability of credit rating agencies. And as liquidity increased, so the agencies embedded themselves more and more deeply into the financial process. Issuers and investors passed responsibility for the role of assessing credit to the rating agencies, to facilitate the number of transactions. This suited the borrower, the originator and the investor. It also suited the credit rating agencies, whose virtual monopoly was reinforced. They charged fees accordingly and increased profitability.

As part of the role in assessing securitisations, the agencies developed complex models to structure and value products. These were then useful in constructing more complex products such as collateralised debt obligations. The models required input on numerous assumptions, each one a potential opportunity for over-optimism. It was noted that so-called arbitrage CDOs could only extract value if either the pricing in cash bonds was wildly inefficient, or assumptions used by rating agencies somehow 'created' the extra value – in other words the value of such products was probably illusory.

To increase efficiency in the origination process, rating agencies frequently gave their models to investment banks so the banks could construct products that matched the required ratings profile without direct agency intervention. This meant the industry that stood to gain the most from aggressive assumptions (investment banks) was also in control of assessing the inputs needed to obtain the highest ratings. The liquidity machine of rating agencies, investment banks and credit derivatives worked together to generate the greatest quantity of investable assets that could be

4 Moody's annual report 2003.

produced right in time for the burgeoning liquidity glut of
2005–07.

many of the highest-rated tranches never left the investment banks

Many asset-backed CDOs were sold to insurance companies or to
specialist funds often funded by investment banks. Yet, many of
the highest-rated tranches never left the investment banks. Instead,
the AAA portions of CDOs found a ready-made home on bank
balance sheets because they were so highly rated, and therefore
attracted little capital cushion. By creating instruments yielding
more than comparably-rated instruments, the capital adequacy
regulations could be satisfied and a nice profit generated for both
bank and rating agency.

A large part of the agencies' success was their steady inclusion
into first the US, then the international regulatory regime as
transactional finance overtook traditional credit provision. Issuers
increased their use of ratings from the agencies to enhance their
attractiveness to funds, who often define investment strategy with
reference to a category of rating. For instance, bond funds often
include their ratings parameters into the marketing material for
their funds in an effort to persuade investors that their strategy is
safe.

The greatest coup for rating agencies was their inclusion into the
international bank capital regulation known as Basel II. The first
Basel accord (signed in 1988) did not require ratings. The quality
of bank assets was assessed on the basis of a limited palette of risk
weightings against which an international bank was required to
hold a minimum level of capital. The growth of securitisation and
increase in capital flows prompted the much more sophisticated
Basel II. Signed in 2002, Basel II also included an endorsement of
agency ratings as a measure of the quality of the assets.

With agencies being intimately involved in the rating of
securitisations, their inclusion as an adjudicator of capital
adequacy was not surprising, but this should have generated
concerns about impartiality. Some did worry that the agencies
were gaining too much power. David Clementi of the Bank of

England recommended that banks opt to generate their own ratings instead of relying on outside agencies. In light of the 'enhancement' of ratings by banks using agencies' own models in CDOs, it was a bit much to expect the banks to decide voluntarily to be more rigorous in their rating assessment than the agencies, but the example does show how concerned some regulators were. Of course, the models were checked by regulators, but the parameters of assets such as CDOs were malleable enough to contain plenty of unsavoury assets without loss of AAA rating. Agencies increased their power with the explicit inclusion of ratings into the capital adequacy framework of Basel II.

The US Senate Banking Committee was also concerned that agencies offered more favourable ratings to attract business from Wall Street. Christopher Cox, chairman of the SEC, was called to the committee to testify on the matter.[5] As overseer of the agencies, he found himself under fire for failing to constrain them. He defended the companies, saying their over-optimistic ratings had stemmed not from flawed methodology or undue influence from investment banks, but because of an unexpected spike in delinquent loans, due to poor lending standards and fraud.

The same committee had heard Standard & Poor's president Kathleen Corbet two years earlier claim: 'Credit ratings provide reliable standards for issuers and investors around the world, facilitating efficient capital raising and the growth of new markets.' In those two years, the value of Moody's stock had risen from $43.12 to a peak of $73.7 in February 2007. But from September 2007, a different world appeared. The SEC and state attorneys general in New York and Ohio began to examine of how Standard & Poor's, Moody's and Fitch evaluated subprime-mortgage-backed securities.

On 29 August 2007, Standard & Poor's received a subpoena from the New York attorney general requesting information and documents relating to the company's ratings of securities backed

---

5 'The role and impact of credit rating agencies on the subprime credit markets,' US Senate Committee on Banking, Housing and Urban Affairs, 26 September 2007.

by residential real estate mortgages. In September 2007, the SEC began an examination of rating agencies' policies and procedures relating to conflict of interest with regard to ratings on RMBS and related CDOs. Other lawsuits charged not only that the agencies had over-rated mortgage bonds and CDOs, but that in so doing, they had deliberately under-rated other bonds. The Connecticut attorney general alleged that both Moody's and Standard & Poor's had given artificially low ratings to states, municipalities and other public bodies compared with better-paying alternatives. Moody's faced similar subpoenas and investigations.

The epitome of the agencies' power came with the peak in the housing market in late 2006. Their role in 'facilitating new markets' rose with the market liquidity. Required for securitisation, the agencies grew fat with the industry, and may have been fatally tainted by its collapse. Their influence ensured their role was explicitly included in the international bank capital regulations in Basel II in 2004. From the point of view of the two approaches to money, the rating agencies clearly promoted transactional finance over credit finance, despite their stated aim to assess credit worthiness. In fact, their role seemed to be to remove credit considerations from transactions to facilitate further transactions, and fees. This was, of course, in their interests and they prospered because of it.

Criticism of rating agencies peaks with every financial crisis; Asia, dot-com, Enron and again in the past two years. When financial market liquidity evaporated in September 2007, it was no surprise that questions about the behaviour of rating agencies re-emerged. This time, the problems were much more profound. Moody's and Standard & Poor's were forced within months to admit that their CDO models needed 'recalibration'. Downgrades of scores of issues followed. Some rated bonds fell as much as 16 notches in one downgrade – of course, after the prices of the bonds had already declined, meaning the rating was of little actual value to investors. I know of an investor who owns one asset-backed security that has been downgraded to CA (junk) by Moody's but retains an AAA rating from Standard & Poor's. Iceland was simultaneously rated AAA and A. These ratings are useless. Investors need to find a way to use their own resources, and the publicly disclosed information of the bond issuer to decide how they rate a bond, without relying on rating agencies.

Basel I and II: regulatory innovation

Another problem to rebound on banks was financial regulation designed to reduce the probability of a crisis, and to enhance trust internationally. Problems of international lending in the 1970s and 1980s led to a new layer of regulation in 1988 with the introduction of the first Basel accord, which attempted to standardise the use of risk capital across developed countries. The first accord has subsequently been replaced by the much more complex Basel II, described[6] 'as the 'most influential – and misunderstood – agreements in modern international finance'. The Basel accords set the framework for international finance. From the beginning the banking system saw them as a hurdle to overcome, or circumvent. Partly this stemmed from an ambiguous authority of the accords themselves, which were designed to standardise basic capital assessment among developed country banks with international operations. Soon the accords were treated as binding minimum requirements not just for developed country banks but for all banks regardless of their international exposure. By apparently defining what was not permissible, what had initially been standards for a relatively limited number of institutions became a seal of approval for any bank that could meet the standards, or credibly avoid them.

Transactional finance itself influenced the regulations that sprang up to guard the system. In the process, regulators themselves provided avenues through which their rules could be circumvented by defining what was acceptable. The regulations were designed to encourage transactions and liquidity in financial instruments. Accordingly, they placed great stress on the role of rating agencies and the historical assessment of securities' performance.

6 Bryan J. Balin, 'Basel I, Basel II, and emerging markets: a nontechnical analysis,' May 2008, Johns Hopkins University School of Advanced International Studies.

The end of the petrodollar boom and the collapse of Latin American sovereign debt in the early 1980s had a disastrous effect on Western bank capital. This, and the fact that different jurisdictions offered different, sometimes contradictory regulations, was the catalyst for the first international rules to emerge from the BIS in 1988. This first Basel accord merely established the minimum capital to be held by international (transnational) banks operating in G10 countries. By allocating different risk scores to different types of assets, and requiring banks hold a minimum of 8 per cent capital against the risk-adjusted assets, Basel I was a simple, empirical and relatively transparent method of standardising bank capital across the developed world. It also emphasised securities on bank balance sheets, rather than traditional loans.

The restrictions of Basel I were soon applied to almost all banks in the developed world, and to banks in the emerging economies – something the Basel committee had specifically excluded. Nevertheless, just like ratings from agencies, the easy to understand rules of Basel I encouraged its application across many countries. The rules were embraced by regulators and investors, although Japan delayed implementation of Basel I for five years because of the poor state of its banking system.

Banks became adept at avoiding the Basel rules. One incentive towards greater securitisation was that Basel I made no provision for the securitisation of loans. Banks could therefore create a security from a loan, retain the riskier part of the loan and sell the less risky, yet the capital charge did not change. Over time, risk concentration within banks increased.

Another way to circumvent the rules was to swap high-risk, long-dated debt for a string of short-dated paper from the same issuer – thereby avoiding the higher capital charge associated with the long-dated assets. Interest rate swaps allowed banks to create an instrument that matched the profile of a long-dated bond, but reflected a lower capital charge. Financial innovation made circumvention easy, indeed, trivial.

Furthermore, by ranking short-term debt as less risky than long-term debt, Basel I encouraged developed world banks to invest more 'hot money' in emerging markets. The Basel accords were thus a (modest) contributor to the Asian crisis of 1997–98.

the Basel accords were thus a (modest) contributor to the Asian crisis of 1997–98

By the late 1990s, it was recognised that the practice of international banking had changed so much since Basel I was introduced that new regulations were needed. The publicly announced intention was to regulate international banks within acceptable, transparent limits. Yet, the end result was a set of rules designed to assist the banks in creating securities – a set of rules to aid the efficient provision of transactional credit.

Rules were suggested that offered greater flexibility than the one-size-fits all approach of Basel I. There was much greater emphasis on risk sensitivity in bank capital and the application of risk management techniques, with an emphasis on supervision and market discipline. In 2004, the second set of Basel accords (Basel II) was introduced.

The rules included the option for banks to use their own internal risk assessment models, which almost all relied on a value-at-risk (VaR) assessment of assets. Value-at-risk has become the standard measure of risk. Statistical analysis and historical analysis is used on the price history of assets to make a judgement about how their volatility could affect the portfolio. The techniques seek to answer the question 'What is the worst expected loss during a specified time period with a certain confidence level?' The simplest route is to find the daily standard deviation of an asset during its lifetime and calculate the expected volatility over the horizon over which it is expected the asset will remain in the portfolio. All the techniques – including more sophisticated techniques – suffer from the fact that markets tend to spend long periods with low volatility, with occasional bursts of very high volatility. Often there just is not enough data to model the expected outcome. VaR is a good first guess, but is limited by the history it uses as input. VaR does not necessarily tell you anything about the kind of world that created 'the bad event'. Often it is assumed that risk is not cumulative, that if one asset goes down, another may behave less badly. In fact, during crises, different assets often behave the same way even though during normal times they show little correlation.

Basel II placed a confidence in VaR that many professionals found simplistic, even dangerous, long before the crisis of 2007. A prolonged period of low volatility would bias expected losses lower.

Criticism was also levelled at the way the models treated risk as if it was an external process. In reality, risk is embedded in the environment in which banks operate, and banks themselves can cause risk to rise or fall. From the outside the process looks random, but it is dependent on the activities of the participants. Model results, therefore, are inherently biased against the worst outcome.

Basel II also included a 'standard approach' to credit risk – the risk attached to a specific borrower – which relied on credit rating agency ratings of the borrower. Ratings from agencies were frequently questioned by the market, which would frequently price the bonds of one issuer higher than another with similar ratings. Agencies, as we have seen, were frequently fallible.

The problem with regulations

Regulations such as Basel 1 and II are comforts to regulators, who spend much time designing them to satisfy their desire for safety. Yet the Basel II rules contained a high level of self-regulation, which relieved national regulators from active – and probably controversial – assessment.

The rules were also an incentive to complacency in at least two other regards. First, if all banks adopt the same regulations, they will tend to standardise their risks around the regulations, opting to acquire similar assets to compete most effectively. A crisis could then be triggered by the application of VaR rules to similar portfolios across a number of banks – as it was when subprime bond declines spilled over into other assets. If banks all react the same way, assets initially not affected could collapse as banks sought to beat each other in selling.

This problem also affects another part of Basel II, namely the call for banks to be transparent about the assets they hold. A collection of transparent banks is of little help if the aggregate holdings of all banks could cause problems. Even knowing that their assets are similar to other banks may not lead to any change in behaviour, even though collectively they may be affected by the inherent risk. Transparency anyway does not necessarily reveal potential problems.

This is a perennial problem where regulation is empirically based; both Basel I and Basel II are a collection of measures that appear to address the configuration of banking systems at a particular time. The document outlining Basel II is 251 pages long, much of it technical and much of it prescriptive, yet there is no overarching philosophy that can adapt to changes in circumstance without a wholesale rewrite of the accords. For instance, the bankruptcy, or forced closure, of a major rating agency is no longer unthinkable, yet rating agencies are embedded into Basel II. Many of the credit derivative instruments that Basel II was designed to accommodate may never trade again after the debacle of the subprime writedowns. Accommodating nationally owned banks – or quasi-nationalised banks – is not addressed in Basel II, so several large international banks are now ambiguously positioned.

The presence of regulations provides a false sense of security. Based on empirical prescriptions that respond to particular circumstances, they are often both out of date and avoidable before they are implemented. Regulations are certainly circumvented. From the mid-1990s, an entire industry emerged devoted to moving assets off the balance sheets of banks, yet allowing the banks to retain the economic benefit of those assets. The benefits to the banks were enhanced returns from off-balance sheet, or contingent, investments that were not declarable to regulators. Citibank was a prime mover in the establishment of structured investment vehicles (SIVs). Once one bank began the process, competitive pressure ensured others followed. In fact, it is fair to say that a major impetus to financial innovation in the last decade was the incentive to circumvent the capital adequacy regulation embedded in the Basel accords.

Not surprisingly, many – if not most – aspects of the Basel II framework represented concessions to the dominance of American business, and its preference for securities rather than bank lending. The use of ratings from agencies covers most US companies, but much fewer elsewhere. The regulations themselves described a banking model devoted to structured finance and securitisation, an industry that originated in the US but which by 2004 was spreading across the globe, with the aid of the new rules.

Underlying the assumptions was the belief that expansion could be unlimited; that problems could be contained within individual banks. Systemic concerns were not considered. One of the consequences of embedding Basel rules into international banks was the adverse effect it would have during the systemic crisis of 2007 and later. Capital regulations are instantaneous; they measure a bank's capital against current prices – which in itself is an incentive to move towards transactional finance. If those prices all fell, then many banks would become impaired together. During good times banks hold too little capital, and during a crisis they are required to hold what may be too much. By making no allowance for fluctuations in the economic environment, regulation actually make crises more likely and more violent. This is the regulatory equivalent of the 'cash surplus' that liquid margined markets such as futures inject into underlying instruments. It can enhance a profitable position, but severely undermine a losing position.

The Basel accords, both I and II, reflected the banking system they sought to regulate. The first accord was needed to provide national regulators with comfort to acquiesce in international expansion in the 1990s. Basel II was designed around an expansion of credit trading and credit derivatives and it too sought to endorse the way banks operated. Regulators adapted their frameworks to the banking environment they found, rather than the other way round.

The politics of housing

Promises and pie-crust are made to be broken.

Jonathan Swift

Housing attracted feverish investment in Western economies from the mid-1990s. But why? What drove the Americans, British, Irish, Spanish and others to increase their debt to dangerous levels just so that they could own a home of their own? The obsession with housing extended across the media, into television schedules, buying preferences of consumers, and even the sort of higher education courses students chose to follow. In January 2006 there were 47 UK television shows dedicated to property, plus a further 31 shows on gardening that in many cases included some promotion of property. Where did this consensus on home promotion originate? And how did the politics of housing affect the market, particularly in America, the most important market? This is what we'll be looking at in this chapter.

An unproductive asset

Housing is important to everyone. It is the largest investment most people make, requiring the largest debt. A home is essential for everyone, whether you are renting or owning, and it is the basis for numerous support and development businesses such as construction, estate agents, landlords and DIY stores. Residential housing is also the main use of urban land. Politically, changes to housing stock have often accompanied the most far-reaching social change in a society. And at all times housing has been used to signify wealth. So whether we like it or not, housing is a political issue.

The primary function of housing started out as shelter; which, while essential, is almost entirely non-productive. If a house fulfils its role as a shelter it has achieved its main purpose; it does not make the owner or a nation wealthier, though it may act as a store of wealth. The creation of wealth relies on actions that add value to a process. Houses are repositories and do not, generally, add value. So, when house prices rise faster than the inflation of the rest of the economy, it is usually not because housing has become productive, but because there is greater confidence among buyers that their wealth has increased enough to pay more, and of course, this makes the sellers feel more wealthy too, because someone is prepared to pay more.

It is the combination of wealth and the lack of added value in housing that is probably responsible for the starring role that property seems to play in many financial crises: America in the 1920s; Japan in the 1980s; Thailand in the 1990s; America and Europe in the 2000s.

The latest boom – and crash – grew with the tension of wealth and added value, but was accompanied by an unusually marked ideological angle: housing, and house ownership, symbolised freedom and success, and the rejection of state interference. Housing markets and housing finance before and after the fall of the Berlin Wall became a political activity in a way that would not have been recognised by the preceding generation. Not surprisingly, many of the countries that experienced sustained housing booms were those in the vanguard against socialism; America and the UK in the 1980s, together with allies in the Anglo-sphere such as Australia and New Zealand and like-minded Western European allies such as Spain, plus the post-Communist Eastern bloc.

A unique housing model, with familiar results

America follows a unique model for housing finance; with mortgage lending directed through federal agencies, the Federal

Home Loan Mortgage Corporation (FHLMC or 'Freddie Mac') and the Federal National Mortgage Association (FNMA or 'Fannie Mae'), operating as quasi-official organs of state policy – at least since the Clinton presidency. When politics changed with the Bush administration, policies deliberately sought to undermine their power, and enhance a 'free market' solution, with the result that the quality of mortgage lending declined. The worst excesses therefore came after the political elite limited government agencies and encouraged the private sector.

In brief, subprime lending was lending to people who would not normally have been able to obtain a loan. As we'll see, this lending was often encouraged by social and political pressure, and was made palatable by higher fees.

they did not acknowledge the encouragement local politicians had given

While the subprime lending spree was a particularly American response to a political requirement, similar effects appeared elsewhere. When the financial crisis first broke in August 2007, the Spanish, German and British governments all protested that there was no subprime lending in their countries. Their banks should not be threatened, it was claimed, by the US problems. They failed to realise, at least initially, how lax lending standards had affected their own financial systems. And they did not acknowledge the encouragement local politicians had given. In Spain, Britain and Ireland, politicians also gained benefits from the housing boom.

The politics of home ownership

Government support for the housing boom – and subprime lending – in all cases was political. It is often altruistic in the sense of wishing to expand the perceived benefits of home ownership to previously excluded members of society, but it was also associated with power over resources, taxable revenues, so-called developer 'incentives' and votes.

We've seen that housing is an important policy issue at all times, but it took on an additional philosophical value with the election of Margaret Thatcher in the UK in 1979. Beginning in 1980, the UK government introduced its 'Right to Buy' policy, which gave secure tenants of local authority housing the right to buy their rented accommodation. The aim was to encourage individuals to take personal responsibility for their homes, and introduce incentives to contribute to improving their environment. Margaret Thatcher's most famous quote was given in 1987, long after the introduction of Right-to-Buy, but sums up the philosophy behind the policy:

> 'As you know there is no such thing as society. There are individual men and women and there are families. And no government can do anything except through people, and people must look after themselves first. It is our duty to look after ourselves and then, also, to look after our neighbours.'

Offering house ownership was a fundamental political act of individualism, and, despite the financial crisis, is likely to remain so.

Practical support for housing from governing parties in America and Britain stems from the link between house prices and consumption. A rise in house prices may widen the gap between moderate and high-priced houses, and therefore limit movement from a small house to a larger house, but a rise in house prices reliably encourages all owners to feel wealthier, and therefore to spend more. More prosperous electors are generally more amenable to existing governments. Politicians always had a strong incentive to encourage house price rises.

Yet, the housing market was always of unreliable assistance to politicians. Housing booms and busts are common in all advanced economies, so much so that any study of recent history around the globe suggests politicians would be foolish to rely on permanently rising prices. The public perception that falls in house prices are exceptional is false. Japan's house prices fell by a third after adjusting for inflation between 1990 and 2002 and it is not unusual; house prices in Italy and Canada followed a similar downward move for most of the same period. UK house prices fell much faster than those of Japan at the beginning of the 1990s.

Prices in the Netherlands fell much faster, and much further in real terms, in the late 1970s and early 1980s than in Japan. America itself had noticeable moves up and down through the 1990s. Since 1980 there has been only one constant; German house prices never go up.

House prices in most advanced countries rose and fell by half over the last thirty years; sometimes more than once. In some cases (Spain) the variation was much higher – 250 per cent. The politics of housing is, therefore, inherently unstable.

Not only the politics, but also the financing of housing is unstable. America, the UK, Spain, Australia, Canada, France and Italy all suffered large banking losses related to property lending in the early 1990s. Housing booms seem to act as an indicator of lending excess; if there are no productive investment opportunities left, invest in housing.

Clinton's third way; social inclusion and market economics

The housing boom and crash of the late 1980s and early 1990s grew out of the Thatcher–Reagan doctrine of individualism and established a consensus about the success of market economics that would remain unchallenged for nearly twenty years.

Victory for Bill Clinton in the US presidential election of 1992 brought in an administration committed to social inclusion as well as the market economy. In his inaugural address as president Clinton identified the challenges that would define both his terms:

> 'Today, a generation raised in the shadows of the Cold War assumes new responsibilities in a world warmed by the sunshine of freedom but threatened still by ancient hatreds and new plagues. Raised in unrivalled prosperity, we inherit an economy that is still the world's strongest, but is weakened by business failures, stagnant wages, increasing inequality, and deep divisions among our people.'

With these two sentences, Clinton defined overall US domestic and foreign policy for almost a decade, until September 2001. The themes of pre-eminence, evangelical free-enterprise and global leadership in Clinton's address reappeared throughout the 1990s, especially in Robert Rubin and Larry Summer's foreign trade policy. They also anchored housing policy to the aim of reducing inequality and spreading of prosperity to those who had been excluded. It was a patriotic mission.

Clinton's first election campaign is best remembered for his quip, 'It's the economy, stupid!' Housing was so important to the US economy he could have said 'It's housing, stupid!' By luck, the president entered the White House just as the economy was recovering from the recession of the early 1990s, and the housing market was bottoming out after the property bust that accompanied that recession.

Economic recovery further stimulated Clinton's housing policy. In 1994, the president initiated a plan called the 'National Homeownership Strategy', sub-titled 'Partners in the American Dream'. The strategy aimed to expand home ownership as widely as possible, which meant expanding it to include those parts of society that could not qualify for a mortgage and did not have enough money for a down payment. The administration flirted with the idea that buyers could use some of their personal pension money as a down payment.

The National Homeownership Strategy also encouraged lenders to offer interest rate costs lower than the market would normally charge for such high-risk borrowers.

> 'Other households do not have sufficient available income to
> make the monthly payments on mortgages financed at market
> interest rates for standard loan terms. Financing strategies,
> fuelled by the creativity and resources of the private and public
> sectors, should address both of these financial barriers to
> homeownership.'

In other words, 'Get creative about offering loans to people you would not normally want to lend to'. This initiative built on the Community Reinvestment Act of 1977, passed during the Carter presidency, which required mortgage providers to extend lending to borrowers and areas usually considered too risky. To be in the mortgage business from 1977 onwards required some exposure to subprime. So the progress of US mortgage lending in the past thirty years has been marked by systematic political interference under the banner of 'house ownership for all', whether the borrowers meet conventional credit criteria or not. We now know this was storing up problems.

Of course, the policies of both Clinton and Carter were part of an honourable tradition that sought to eliminate discrimination in lending. Services such as banking and insurance had been withheld or provided at higher cost to areas denoted by 'red lines', those deemed not creditworthy enough for normal services. 'Redlining' of districts had been a problem for minority communities from at least the 1930s. While the practice was illegal, it was very hard to stop if large numbers of low-credit families lived in close proximity. Banking is not well suited to implementing social policies, which are much better made by government agencies. Unfortunately, the mortgage agencies Freddie Mac and Fannie Mae straddled the banking and political spheres and seemed admirably suited to implementing the political agenda, beholden, as they were, to government for their survival.

The overlap of politics and bankers

The Clinton administration's decision 'creatively' to finance monthly payments was a more daring step forward in mandatory subprime lending than had been seen before. It was an important precursor for the subprime lending that followed because it committed the mortgage agencies to a policy of lending to 'unconventional' borrowers. Moreover, by demonstrating to politicians that they could lend to lower-credit borrowers, the agencies could market themselves as the only means of delivering this policy, of providing the American Dream to the poorer sections of society. In a good move for the agencies, they acquired a patriotic mantle they did not have before, and so placed themselves firmly at the heart of the economic policy of the nation.

the agencies gained commercial benefits from the implied backing of the US government

An important part of the Clinton administration's strategy was to mandate the mortgage agencies to adopt 'affordable housing goals', to lend to disadvantaged groups within society. The agencies gained commercial benefits from the implied backing of the US government, including lower cost of funding, tax relief, greater leverage than private sector banks, exemption from some banking regulations and a direct line of credit from the Treasury. These were conditions well beyond what was considered prudent for commercial banks. The exemptions and lower prudential controls allowed the private shareholders to reap a benefit estimated to be worth in total perhaps $10 billion a year or more.

In return for these benefits of state approval, Freddie Mac and Fannie Mae were required to provide liquid and stable secondary mortgage markets. This role they performed well for many years. Fannie Mae was one of the first institutions to issue mortgage-backed securities in the early 1970s and in earlier chapters we've seen the significance of securities. These securities led to a big increase in credit to house owners, and a new class of asset for investors – the mortgage-backed bond. While this has been tarnished by the financial crisis, it was such a useful innovation that it will undoubtedly return. Financial life in the US has come to rely on securitisation to function. It is not an option for banks to function without asset-backed and mortgage-backed securities because the practice has become so embedded into the system. Though Europe is not as reliant on asset-backed securities, its continued financial advance probably requires extending the use of these assets in future.

The agencies were also required to support secondary mortgages for moderate and low income families and provide access to mortgages across the entire nation, including areas not normally served by lenders. The agencies were therefore directed, in spite of being nominally private companies, to follow a political agenda; to alleviate lending discrimination.

Affordable housing goals, originally set in the Housing Act of 1990, included targets, set by Congress, to provide lending to less creditworthy borrowers, and the goals were raised over time. Lending to moderate or low income families was set at 42 per cent of all lending in 1997–2000. This was a very high level, but it did not stop politicians from raising the threshold every time the Act was revised by Congress. The threshold was raised to 50 per cent between 2001 and 2004, and expected to rise to 57 per cent by 2008. Another goal was to extend lending to special groups that did not fall into the low to moderate income bracket but who might otherwise find borrowing difficult. In the first period, this target was set at 14 per cent, rising to 20 per cent by 2001 with a target of 28 per cent by 2008. These two goals alone meant that by 2005 70 per cent per cent of agency lending from the largest mortgage lenders was to be directed at borrowers deemed less creditworthy than a conventional borrower. Not all the 'affordable housing' lending was risky, but by 2007, the damage was cumulative and affordable housing goals increasingly led the agencies into poor lending. By then, about a third of the companies' lending involved risky mortgages, compared with 14 per cent in 2005.

The concentration on affordable housing goals also meant conventional borrowers went elsewhere. So, the portfolio of assets held by the agencies deteriorated from the mid-1990s onwards, in line with the political pressure to provide lending.

Nor was the encouragement to lend to less robust borrowers limited to politicians; the Federal Reserve endorsed the wider remit, at least until Bush took office. In 2000, Fed governor Edward Gramlich addressed an audience of affordable housing specialists and said:[1]

> 'As a result of the good economy, various technological changes, and innovative financial products, credit to low-income and minority borrowers has exploded in recent years... Between 1993 and 1998, conventional home-purchase mortgage lending to low-income borrowers increased nearly 75 per cent, compared

[1] Edward M. Gramlich, at the Fair Housing Council of New York, Syracuse, New York, 14 April 2000.

with a 52 per cent rise for upper-income borrowers.
Conventional mortgages to African-Americans increased 95 per
cent over this period and to Hispanics 78 per cent, compared
with a 40 per cent increase in all conventional mortgage
borrowing. A significant portion of this expansion of low-income
lending appears to be in the so-called subprime lending market.'

At the time (2000) increased subprime lending was clearly cause
for celebration. The speech reveals a worrying overlap of central
banking, social engineering and political encouragement to lax
lending standards.

The previous support, and cajoling, of Congress and Fed did not
aid the mortgage agencies during their demise in 2008. The same
people that had set the affordable housing goals were later to
criticise lenders for their lax standards. Sometimes, they even
criticised lax lending standards while complaining that the
agencies had failed to meet the affordable housing goals. In
September 2008, James Lockhart, director of the Federal Housing
Finance Agency, reported to the Senate Banking Committee that
the agencies missed the government-mandated affordable housing
goals in 2007 and 'the miss will be larger in 2008'. At the same
hearings, Lockhart also complained that Freddie and Fannie in
2006 and 2007 purchased and guaranteed 'many more low-
documentation, low verification and non-standard mortgages than
they ever had, despite regulators' warnings'. Mr Lockhart could
have added that the affordability goals led to a big incentive to the
creation of the 'private label' mortgage products, which were to
cause so many problems later. There was a contradiction in home-
lending that even the regulator seemed unable to recognise.

Not surprisingly, the agencies were embedded in the Washington
lobbying process. They employed large numbers of professionals
to fend off criticism of their commercial advantages that appeared
periodically from some members of the Senate. Their relationship
with the Democratic Party was so strong that senior executives
moved from the mortgage agencies into the administration. The
administration also provided staff in the other direction.
Sometimes it worked both ways for the same person. Franklin
Raines became Fannie Mae's vice-chairman in 1991, a post he held

until he left in 1996 to join the Clinton administration as the director of the Office of Management and Budget (OMB). He rejoined Fannie Mae in 1999 as chief executive, the 'first black man to head a Fortune 500 company'.

Raines' move from Fannie Mae to OMB was no political coincidence. The OMB is the largest office within the executive branch of the US administration. Its role is to direct and monitor the performance of a large range of government programmes as well as to draw up the annual government budget. It is a powerful political position. The move from OMB back to Fannie Mae by Raines is an illustration of how important the agencies were in the domestic policies of Bill Clinton. It is also an indication of how important to the political process the agencies themselves had become.

Beyond domestic politics

Nor was it just domestic politics that were affected by the behaviour of the agencies. The size of agency issuance in the secondary bond market ensured they played an important role in capital markets. In the late 1990s, the government ran a budget surplus and agency issuance far outstripped Treasury issuance. As a result, the agencies took on the role of government bond proxies. The intertwining of political relationships and constant comparison with Treasury bonds imbued the agencies' debt with the cachet of government debt, without any official support being offered.

For investors such as Chinese reserve managers, there was increasingly little to differentiate between the Treasury bond market and the agency bond market, which offered slightly higher returns. Both were apparently guaranteed by the most powerful government in the world and embedded in government policy. It was unthinkable that the agencies would be allowed to default on their own debt or the repackaged mortgage debt they offered, so any sensible investor, even one as risk averse as reserve managers, was better off buying agency as well as Treasury bonds. From 2003, reserve managers, and especially China, divided their US bond purchases between pure government debt and agency debt. To an outsider, as well as to the political elite within America, the agencies appeared as a privatised arm of government policy.

A change of politics; a change of subprime

The Bush administration initially pursued a similar, if uneasy, symbiotic relationship with Freddie Mac and Fannie Mae. The agencies were regarded as deeply Democratic institutions, but useful for the introduction of the Bush doctrine of an 'ownership society'.

Bush's second inauguration in 2004 spoke of giving 'every American a stake in the promise and future of our country... and build an ownership society'. The Bush policy of 'ownership' merely reactivated a policy that had, in practice, been in place for years. The policy had been used to rescue the economy in 2001, by promoting housing finance as an agent to support consumption.

If the ideals of home ownership sat well with Republican ideology, the institutions of the semi-official mortgage agencies did not. The agencies were increasingly seen as quasi-monopolists whose allegiances were tainted by close ties to the defeated Democrats and impeded private sector providers of lending. Nevertheless, for most of the first term, the Bush administration was happy to consort with the enemy, and use the agencies to fund expanded mortgage lending.

A clear change towards the agencies emerged in 2003 when Freddie Mac and Fannie Mae were investigated by the Office of Federal Housing Enterprise Oversight (OFHEO) and found to have systematically under-reported the volatility of their earnings. Freddie Mac had understated profits in an effort to make its earnings appear more predictable, and bolster its share price. Six months later, regulators found Fannie Mae had also engaged in a 'pervasive misapplication of accounting rules'. Regulators wrote that Fannie Mae 'maintained a corporate culture that emphasized stable earnings at the expense of accurate financial disclosures'.[2]

2 Report slams Fannie Mae, David S. Hilzenrath, 23 September 2004, *Washington Post*.

The previous Democratic allegiance of the agencies now definitely counted against them. The similarity of the charges against the two agencies also indicated a degree of cartel-like behaviour. This was the other side of the intense political pressure placed on the companies; they worked together to extract the greatest economic advantage.

The companies attempted to fight the criticism of their accounting practices. Fannie's chairman Franklin Raines dismissed the criticism, but the establishment had turned against them. The Securities and Exchange Commission's chief accountant said the Fannie Mae was not even 'on the page' of allowable accounting interpretation.

> investors have been fooled, homebuyers have been cheated, and taxpayers are at risk

Congress had been forcefully and regularly reminded of the risks in the agencies by Richard H. Baker, a Republican congressman from Louisiana. Baker's response to the Fannie report was typical of his frequent scathing comments of both companies: 'Investors have been fooled, homebuyers have been cheated, and taxpayers are at risk. Fool us once, shame on you. Fool us twice, shame on us.'

It was an opportunity for Republicans to limit the influence of the agencies and promote the true private sector. Both Fed chairman Alan Greenspan (a Republican) and the Treasury secretary, John Snow, called for tougher supervision of the companies, and a reduction in the size of their balance sheets – which would mean other companies having to step in to provide mortgages, including mortgages to those unable to qualify for conventional borrowing. In a speech in February 2004, Greenspan insisted that 'most of the concerns associated with systemic risks (in the American financial system) flow from the size of the balance sheets that these GSEs (government-sponsored enterprises Freddie Mac and Fannie Mae) maintain'.[3] After a decade of Democratic-influenced and agency-

3 Testimony of Alan Greenspan before the Committee on Banking, Housing, and Urban Affairs, US Senate, 24 February 2004.

led mortgage policy, it was time to sample the Republican option, based on regional mortgage brokers originating loans and sending them to Wall Street for packaging into securities. This, of course, meant the expansion of subprime as well as the expansion of normal lending.

So the Bush administration – and Greenspan – wished to remove the agencies' central role in housing finance and replace it with the purely private sector alternative. Greenspan specifically referred to such a plan in his February testimony the Senate Banking Committee:[4]

> 'Fannie and Freddie can borrow at a subsidised rate, they have been able to pay higher prices to originators for their mortgages than can potential competitors and to gradually but inexorably take over the market for conforming mortgages. This process has provided Fannie and Freddie with a powerful vehicle and incentive for achieving extremely rapid growth of their balance sheets. The resultant scale gives Fannie and Freddie additional advantages that potential private-sector competitors cannot overcome... The current system depends on the risk managers at Fannie and Freddie to do everything just right, rather than depending on a market-based system supported by the risk assessments and management capabilities of many participants with different views and different strategies for hedging risks. Our financial system would be more robust if we relied on a market-based system that spreads interest rate risks, rather than on the current system, which concentrates such risk with the GSEs.'

In December 2004, both Freddie and Fannie agreed to manage 'total balance sheet asset size by reducing the portfolio principally through normal mortgage liquidations, in order to limit overall minimum capital requirements'.[5] The agencies' reduction of their balance sheets also reduced the agency bonds available to investors, mainly through not replacing bonds as they were redeemed. Of course, it also limited the provision of mortgages backed by the agencies.

4 Testimony of Alan Greenspan before the Committee on Banking, Housing, and Urban Affairs, US Senate, 24 February 2004.
5 Statement by Fannie Mae, Update on Capital Plan and Accounting Issues, 23 February 2005.

As expected, the need to continue production of mortgages meant the space had to be filled by non-agency lending and securitisation. The private sector saw that the highest fees and the greatest returns for investors (at the time) lay in the lower end of the credit spectrum – in subprime. In one year (2004) subprime originated from the private sector rather than the agencies rose from 7 per cent to nearly 20 per cent of total outstanding mortgage-backed securities.

Other 'non-conforming' loan types also rose sharply after the limits placed on Fannie and Freddie. Alt-A (a mortgage with better quality borrowers than subprime, but less good than prime) rose from less than 3 per cent to 8.5 per cent. The share of the market taken by both categories rose again the following year. The agencies' market share of mortgage bonds fell in both 2005 and 2006. Non-agency mortgage issuance rose from 21.5 per cent of the market in 2003 to 55.3 per cent of the market in 2005. Chinese reserve managers were among the many investors who were forced to include at least some of the private sector mortgage bonds into their portfolio after a fall in the issuance of agency bonds.

Reserve managers, including the Chinese, by this time so dominated the agency and Treasury market that other investors were more-or-less forced into buying subprime mortgages, or accede to very low returns. The Bush administration's restrictions on the agencies had forced investors – though not banks – to invest in private sector subprime mortgages.

We've seen that Bush and Greenspan supported the move to private sector mortgage providers because they thought it would reduce the risk to taxpayers. In fact, the move added to the momentum of credit competition that led to catastrophe in 2007. In the end, Freddie and Fannie were not saved because by then the entire mortgage system was compromised. In mid-2008, both companies were placed into 'conservatorship' – direct government responsibility, with capital injections from the taxpayer required to save them from bankruptcy. The agencies could not escape from their forced mandate into 'affordable housing', together with its less creditworthy lending. Their highly leveraged, relatively low capitalised business model was unable to survive the hostile conditions that accompanied the credit crunch.

The politics of housing destroyed the very policies it had set out to bolster. Rather than encouraging less well-off Americans into patriotic support for their communities, thousands were forced into, or volunteered for, default on their mortgages. Some were fraudulent and had benefited from a policy of inclusion. Many others had accepted the home-ownership policy endorsed by Washington at face value and been ousted from their homes, while banks and the mortgage agencies received billions in bail-outs. A policy designed to be socially inclusive led to one of the more divisive episodes of recent US history.

As 2008 progressed, reserve managers reversed their policy of buying agency debt. When the government effectively nationalised Fannie and Freddie in June 2008, reserve managers had already begun to sell agency bonds, rather than buy them, even though the implicit state guarantee, which successive administrations had been at pains to avoid making explicit, was now shown to be binding. In place of agency bonds, reserve managers turned particularly to ultra-low yielding – but highly liquid – Treasury Bills. Just as money changes its character in a financial crisis, emphasising the importance of 'central bank money' at the expense of all other types, so the focus of investors switches towards the centre of the system, with Treasury bonds and bills offering the safest investment of all.

European political distortions in lending

Did any other countries follow Washington's model of residential mortgage production? There are no agencies similar to Freddie Mac and Fannie Mae in the UK. There were no such institutions in France, Germany or Spain. However, politics remains integral to property loans in these countries too. Depfa from Germany and Dexia in France ran similar – but even less robust – business models to Freddie and Fannie and, not surprisingly, both companies ran into problems in 2008.

Just as the US agencies built up a bond market comparable, or larger than, the US Treasury market, so European Depfa and Dexia built up the second-largest bond market in Europe through issuing bonds backed by public sector loans. Originating in Germany, the covered bond market – or *Pfandbriefe* – was designed by the Prussian state in the eighteenth century. Rather similar to asset-backed securities, they possessed more collateral so the bonds were deemed to be very safe and had never defaulted. Once again, that did not help the performance of the bonds when crisis struck.

Both European companies built their businesses as specialist financiers of public sector projects, so they gained a similar high profile and implicit guaranteed status to the US agencies – though in the usual European fashion it was less scrutinised. Just as the credit crunch proved the business model of Freddie and Fannie was woefully short of capital, so Depfa and Dexia failed in the aftermath of Lehman Brothers' demise.

There were specifically European problems for Depfa and Dexia. After the single currency began in 1999, both turned their attention from public sector finance towards asset management. Backed by their status as financiers of the public sector, they could rely on a low cost of funding. After European monetary union, some government bonds, such as Italy's, persistently offered returns that were higher than the cost of funding of both companies. It paid them, therefore, to buy Italian bonds and hold them to maturity. Depfa in particular was among the largest buyers of Italian debt. As their buying acted to 'converge' Italian yields towards Germany, so they were forced to buy longer and longer maturity debt, out to thirty years, which offered slightly more yield. Thus the two companies acted as the private sector conduits of the political aims of the architects of monetary union. In the process, they transferred long-dated Italian state debt into the ownership of Germans – who owned Depfa. Thus financial integration of the monetary union was effectively privatised.

The business model of both Depfa and Dexia depended on them maintaining low financing costs relative to the income from the bonds. Accounting norms allowed the companies to mark their holding on a hold-to-maturity basis. When money markets froze from August 2007, the funding levels of the companies rose, reducing the annuity they were paid on their portfolio. Given the very long-dated nature of their business, the rise in funding cost would have been manageable. However, both were undone when Lehman Brothers collapsed, forcing them to replace some of their interest rate swaps. In accounting terms, this forced a mark-to-market of the existing positions, which by this time were heavily loss-making. Within three weeks of the demise of Lehman, both Depfa and Dexia were forced to appeal for government help.

If these companies were the continent's Freddie and Fannie, then financial integration was to Europe what 'affordable housing' and the 'ownership society' had been to the administrations of Bill Clinton and George W. Bush. Financial integration encouraged Spanish banks to collect mortgages on their balance sheets for issuance to German investors in similar covered bonds to the German *Pfandbriefe*. It also encouraged Austrian and Italian banks to engage in risky lending to Central and Eastern European countries. This was politics without parties, but driven by background support from governments, the European Commission and the European Central Bank.

Eurocrats and euro-lending

The increase in cross-border lending represented by Depfa and Dexia was part of a conscious plan by Eurocrats to deepen the financial markets within the single currency. Housing finance supported by cross-border lending was an important part of this plan. Measured by the volume of lending made until mid-2007 it was wildly successful, though certainly it came with major risks.

In November 1998, just before the single currency was launched, a member of the executive board of the ECB, Tommaso Padoa-Schioppa, spoke about the benefits of the single currency in the provision of housing finance, and discussed his vision for an integrated currency area that would emulate the market-based, liquid mortgage markets of America:

> 'From the perspective of the euro area, attempting to establish a more integrated housing finance market is a desirable objective since it would bring benefits to consumers in terms of both a

wider range of products on offer and reduced costs stemming from increased competition among lenders and lending practices. Whether the EU housing finance market will actually become more integrated under the influence of the euro will depend, to a certain extent, on the attitude of the institutions concerned. These institutions are expected, wherever and to the extent possible, to make use of the opportunity offered by the introduction of the euro to expand beyond their own home markets. Further integration will, of course, also depend on the degree to which remaining fiscal and regulatory differences across countries are eliminated. The sooner these differences can be reduced by the competent authorities, the faster the euro will have a perceptible impact. Second, it should be acknowledged that the introduction of the euro will trigger substantial changes in the European capital markets by fostering an increased width and depth of these markets. In general, financial institutions operating in the mortgage sector are expected further to increase their recourse to the capital market since it represents a possibility for more efficient funding. This also demands that those financial institutions which have not resorted to capital market funding so far, are invited to exploit this opportunity. Indeed, the issuance of securities as a form of funding mortgage lending might even become a necessity, if saving shifts increasingly away from bank deposits.'

This was a laudable aim, except that the enthusiasm with which the cross-border lending progressed between countries such as Germany and Spain, and the increased reliance on 'capital market funding', were both prime triggers in the financial crisis of 2007. To be fair to Padoa-Shioppa, he recognised the risks, even in 1998:

'Finally, it should be pointed out that the changes in the financial landscape triggered by the introduction of the euro will bring numerous strategic challenges and risks for credit and financial institutions. The forecast increase in competition is also likely to affect the funding side and to reduce the share of cheap retail deposits. Therefore, all institutions should be aware of, and prepared to adapt to, changes in market conditions, fiercer competition and increasing demand for low-cost service. This will also apply to institutions operating in the mortgage sector. Against this background, it is important that the adjustment takes place smoothly, without any adverse effects on the stability of the financial system.'

cross-border lending and housing finance leapt ahead in the next nine years

While cross-border lending and housing finance leapt ahead in the next nine years, almost no progress was made in the area of European financial stability. Memoranda of understanding between the financial regulators of European countries gave the impression of progress without leading to anything more substantive. The euro area, led by the ECB, advanced its long-term experiment in financial integration, promoting securitisation, cross-border lending and novel financing methods without a proper regulatory safety net.

The politics of tax

The politics of housing permeated UK governments too. It is often assumed that the exit from the European Exchange Rate (ERM) mechanism in 1992 was the event that destroyed the John Major government. Most Britons did not care too much about the so-called humiliation of ejection and the following devaluation, particularly as it allowed crippling interest rates to be reduced. What did bother Britons was the fall in house prices that accompanied their participation in the ERM. House prices began to fall in 1990 and did not bottom out until 1995.

When Tony Blair was elected in 1997, house prices had begun to move higher, though this was not widely recognised. The claim of the incoming government that 'things can only get better' was perhaps founded on an unstated promise that middle-class concern for house prices would be central to their administration – together with 'education, education, education'.

The Labour governments of Blair and later Gordon Brown were lucky to gain the upswing of a profoundly bullish housing market, backed by the expansion of securitised mortgage funding and international capital flows. Housing not only provided them with a backdrop of optimism with which to win successive elections, it also provided the Treasury with an increasing stream of revenue. In Labour's first budget, higher rates of stamp duty were introduced. Subsequent rises in the higher rates plus house price inflation meant the politicians became increasingly dependent on the housing market for revenue. In the last year before Labour came to office in 1997, stamp duty on houses raised £675 million. Ten years later, the Treasury raised £6.5 billion. This figure is estimated to be roughly double the amount that would have been collected had the allowances been kept in line with house price inflation. The political opprobrium heaped on bankers by British politicians in the aftermath of the credit crunch is understandable given the direct benefits the government received, for the financial crisis had turned off a big source of tax income.

The indirect benefits were more substantial. Brown was regularly described as the best British chancellor ever, for his stewardship of an economy with low consumer inflation and consistent growth. In fact, the consistency of that growth, as in the US, Spain and Ireland, was based on continuing house price rises. This allowed foreign credit that had backed British securitisations to be recycled within the economy as consumer credit, liberated through home equity loans and second mortgages.

Is it the same everywhere? Why some countries boom

Political involvement in housing is perhaps a perennial issue, and the damage caused by distortion of incentives will not be curbed even with the largest international housing market crash in history. What *is* unique about the housing and mortgage boom of the past decade are the similarities across countries and across continents. The US, UK, Spain, Ireland, Sweden, Denmark, Belgium and Australia – and to a lesser extent Italy, the Netherlands, France, China and South Korea along with South American countries such as Argentina and Brazil – experienced similar housing booms, and busts, which suggests an unprecedented global co-ordination of real estate markets.

It is peculiar that a widespread boom could happen across such different legal systems, regulatory controls and social systems. It suggests that the common factor was not only lax lending practices but included other pervasive developments, such as globalisation, financial innovation, international banking and the level of real interest rates.

There is certainly a similarity in the fall in real interest rates between 2001 and 2005 for all the countries mentioned, but this similarity is shared with countries that conspicuously did not experience a property boom – Germany, Switzerland and Japan. Moreover, the fall in real mortgage rates never stayed below zero for any noticeable period for any country except Ireland.[6] Why did the countries that experienced the booms show such similar developments, while some others were left out?

Part of the answer lies in the strong performance of real estate generally – not just residential property. Commercial property in all the countries with residential booms showed strong returns; often well above the returns gained from the stock market between 2002 and 2006. France returned 300 per cent and the UK returned 236 per cent over the period. Even Japan, with no residential real estate boom, showed strong gains; commercial real estate returned 262 per cent, compared with US returns of 216 per cent. What was common to these countries was the prevalence of real estate investment trusts (REITs) – pools of publicly traded property assets which often contained a high degree of leverage. The gearing both aided the financing of the investments, and also, of course, magnified the returns. Legislation supporting REITs has been introduced in most developed countries in the past seven years, suggesting the added interest in property was at least assisted by new investment vehicles.

There is something different about the residential housing booms. In particular, most of the booms occurred in countries reliant on international lending. Current account deficits seemingly were created specifically to boost the housing markets of Spain, the UK, Ireland, the US and Australia. Central and Eastern European countries all had current account deficits at the same time as housing booms. France too showed signs of a strong housing

---

6 Christopher Mayer and R. Glenn Hubbard, *House Prices, Interest Rates and the Mortgage Market Meltdown*, 2008.

market only after its current account surplus had fallen below 1 per cent in 2003, and accelerated again once the current account had moved into deficit in 2005. Conversely, those developed countries that showed large current account surpluses – Japan, Germany and Switzerland – showed no signs of residential housing boom.

Borrowers in the US, UK, Spain, Ireland and, latterly, France were all so intent on raising the prices of their houses they were forced to borrow from foreign, surplus countries.

But why housing?

This explanation does not satisfy the question of why surplus country lenders kept the flow going year after year despite the clear risks in someone else's housing market. We need to accept that foreign lenders were willing participants in the boom. In fact, we can almost certainly go further and say that the house price boom would not have occurred in the US, the UK, Ireland and Spain without willing foreign lenders. Those countries that missed out on the boom contributed to it elsewhere. Without current account imbalances there probably would not have been a housing boom, and therefore no housing bust.

There is no doubt that financial innovation such as securitisation aided the transfer of lending from surplus countries to deficit countries. It transformed inconvenient mortgage loans into attractive securities, offering high ratings and relatively high returns. The surpluses generated by Germany, Switzerland and Japan could readily be recycled into portfolios either held by banks or sold on to retail investors.

The transfer of lending from surplus countries to deficit countries also tracked a lack of earnings growth in the countries donating their savings to foreigners. Real wages in Japan were almost stagnant from 1997 till 2007 even though companies boosted their profits. The ageing of the population encouraged Japanese companies to retain most of their profits for investment into automation as a precaution against future loss of workers. Until 2008 real wages in Germany had been broadly static since reunification. Switzerland too has experienced low real wage growth for most of the past ten years.

Low real wages meant low consumption in all of these countries – and as consumption is such a large part of overall growth, it also meant low growth. A circular pressure on wages and consumption was initiated, which emphasised the need to export. The lack of consumption meant less attractive investment opportunities at home, which enhanced the investment offers from foreigners. Those open to lending therefore received the lion's share of surplus country savings.

China was also a large surplus country. It differed from Germany and Japan in that Beijing used state-directed savings instead of private sector savings to lend overseas – mostly to America to keep the currency in check. In Germany, Switzerland and Japan it was companies that withheld wage increases from their workers. In China, it was the government's currency policy that withheld from workers the returns from their export success. In all cases, the results were used not to enhance the living standards of their citizens, but those of other countries, particularly the US – albeit temporarily.

The mercantilist beliefs behind German, Swiss, Japanese and Chinese trade policy did not help their businesses in the end either. All these countries were hit by the fall in world trade that came with the recession of 2008–09. The fall in economic activity in the surplus countries actually exceeded the economic decline in most deficit countries. Also, the banking systems of Germany and Switzerland were both jammed with foreign underperforming loans, the counterpart to the previous lending – prudence really did not pay. Depfa, UBS and the German Landesbanks were the victims of imprudent lending by entire countries, not just imprudent lending by individual banks.

the quantity of foreign lending had to find an outlet, and housing was chosen

Housing booms in the US, Spain, the UK and elsewhere were characterised by receptiveness to foreign investment. The quantity of foreign lending had to find an outlet, and housing was chosen;

partly because the returns of apparently high-grade bonds issued in support of the lending offered much better returns than comparable bonds from other sources.

Housing was also chosen because there was no alternative for the quantities of investment needed. China, in particular, found its surpluses growing so fast it could not buy enough Treasury bonds. Already the dominant buyer at Treasury bond auctions by 2003, the trade surplus with America drew China into buying agencies simply through its own 'crowding out' effect. And once it had switched to agency purchases, China dominated that too. By June 2008, China owned 48 per cent of all foreign-owned asset-backed securities issued by the agencies and 23 per cent of all other foreign-owned agency debt. As recently as June 2004, China owned just 8 per cent of foreign-owned asset-backed agency bonds. Moreover, the entry of China seems to have caused other foreign holders to shift their investments from agencies towards non-agency mortgage-backed securities – crowding out other investors into riskier assets.

Blinded by ratings

We now know these non-agency bonds are much riskier than agency bonds; but this was not necessarily known during the great credit bubble of 2003 to 2007. The ratings of most prime and subprime mortgage bonds were given AAA ratings by agencies such as Moody's, Standard & Poor's and Fitch. We've heard of all this before and in the last chapter we learned how rating agencies operated, and their relevance in supporting the investment in housing securitisations was crucial. Once again, without their approval, investors – including the banks who would eventually succumb to the credit crunch – would have had no incentive to invest in these products.

The conspiracy of housing finance

We've seen that all members of a truly free society should have an interest in the quality of the housing of all their members. The conspiracy of the past decade is that this concern either distorted domestic priorities in allocating loans to people who would not otherwise have had them or distorted international investment.

Almost without exception, the media have portrayed housing as a local issue, both in the expansionary phase of the boom, and in its bust. The problems of local borrowers and the difficulties among local banks garnered almost all the headlines. This is not surprising; there is a local component to the crisis, and there will be local suffering to provide headlines from the after-effects of the boom.

The most important effects, however, are spread globally and the conspiracy of housing is shown not just in the political dealings of institutions such as the US mortgage agencies, but in the construction of international capital flows. Without a booming housing and securitisation market in which to invest their trade surplus, the Chinese would have had to resort to other investment avenues. This might have meant buying equities, or direct purchases of companies or real estate. The quantities involved would probably have created difficulties for the Chinese, as their attempts to buy local American companies have shown.

The same international capital forces had a similar effect before the Asian crisis of 1997. There, too, an increase in current account deficits, created in part by very high foreign lending into the countries, had to find an outlet. There, too, it was property, both commercial and residential, that provided the investment vehicle.

Property seems to act as the investment of last resort for a financial system overflowing with liquidity. Perhaps this is natural. While property produces no wealth, it is a precondition for an acceptable lifestyle. Politicians can always find a reason to expand the benefits of affordable housing finance to members of society cut off from normal credit, and so they should. Faced with a determined inflow of money – as occurred in America and Spain as well as Thailand in the mid-1990s – it seemed an attractive option to direct it towards those people who had previously often been excluded from mortgage-lending. The conspiracy is that far from benefiting from the added international lending, many, if not most, of the low and moderate income Americans who obtained a mortgage as a result have subsequently lost their homes, and probably also lost faith in the American Dream that government initiatives were designed to support. In Europe, the enthusiasm shown by the ECB for cross-border lending might have jeopardised the project through the promotion of the colossal Spanish and Irish housing bubbles.

It is worth quoting Thatcher on the Asian crises in light of what happened in America itself:

> 'Examination of what actually happened in Russia and the Far East shows that in all the most important cases there were very good reasons for investors to take fright, ones which relate to a multitude of shortcomings in the policies of governments of those countries. Lack of transparency, cronyism and corruption, corporatism, exchange rates pegged at unrealistic levels – these and other home-grown factors contributed to the collapse. Those weaknesses were exposed, but they were not caused, by the "contagion"... They were classically problems of government failure. They were not essentially problems of market failure.'

Much the same conclusion, including the role of cronyism, lack of transparency and pegged exchange rates, could be made about the American, British, Irish and Spanish housing collapses.

It's not all bad: the costs and benefits of financial crises

Inside of a ring or out, ain't nothing wrong with going down. It's staying down that's wrong.

Muhammad Ali

Robert Zoellick of the World Bank has warned that financial crisis will lead to 'a risk of a great human and social crisis, with major political implications'.[1] Unfortunately, the news will continue to be grim for some time.

Recessions caused by financial crises are typically more acute than normal recessions, and last longer. Problems in loans in normal recessions appear well after the economic downturn has begun, and in some cases signal that it is near an end. Financial crises, on the other hand, start with credit problems; the rejection of credit then leads to a recession in the wider economy. If problems in credit are large enough to cause a crisis, it means access to credit in the wider economy will be difficult for good companies as well as bad. So a financial crisis may damage or destroy companies that would otherwise contribute to the long-term wealth of a country. Industries and skills may disappear forever.

Estimates of the cost of the current crisis exceed $4 trillion; equivalent to a tenth of world GDP, a reflection of the international scale of the problem. Banks alone are expected to lose $2.8 trillion. Earlier banking crises provoked as much disbelief with far lower sums. A financial catastrophe of this size is beyond the capacity of

1 Robert Zoellick, interview with El Pais newspaper, 25 May 2009.

almost anyone to grasp. The evidence from some countries is alarming; Spanish unemployment rising to nearly 20 per cent, its industrial production down a quarter in a year. The fall in world trade on which Japan and Germany depend has driven both countries, neither of which took part in the housing boom directly, into deep recession. Furthermore, crimes against property usually increase in recessions.

Costs are not limited to the economic system. Governments almost always come to the aid of banks, taking on huge debts in the process. A shift in debt from the banking sector to government requires adjustments to the priorities of governments, and the population at large, for which few of us are prepared. The cost of repairing banks is so large it diverts resources that might otherwise have been spent on medicine, or education, or infrastructure, or defence. The social costs too are often higher than the initial bill for fixing the banking system; if industries disappear, unemployment can be higher for longer, and some workers may never get a job again.

Change is as likely to be political as financial. Contractual trust, which is the basis of currency, and a foundation of society, is damaged. Political costs in the aftermath of a financial crisis are the natural consequence of the importance of money and banking across society. In the US presidential election of 2008, the Republican Party suffered ignominious defeat. The political class as a whole has been attacked in the UK. Polls suggest French president Nicolas Sarkozy has fallen from favour because of the crisis, even though the country has avoided most of the problems.

The costs are also social in a wider sense; in the 1930s, the emancipation of black Americans went into reverse in some southern states. Discrimination rose in the South, sometimes savagely. The political class was powerless to stop racism, which became embedded in local and state politics. It would take another thirty years to make meaningful strides towards civil rights for African Americans.

Yet despite the trauma in many cases, post-crisis life continues with trends that were evident before the bust, though priorities may be reshaped. If this is acute enough, of course, it can lead to radical change in the institutions of government. But mostly, the aftermath of financial crises seems to be a strange blend of the familiar and the new. The 'unsustainable' boom has run its course, brought catastrophe and its consequences. Yet there is usually no long-term appetite to reject the past completely, although immediate reactions may suggest otherwise. Debts have to be paid, or repudiated. Regulations are changed, with mixed and usually unforeseen consequences. Political alignments are usually reshaped, often only temporarily.

> like many ecosystems, relative stability is followed in the economy by 'mass extinctions'

Like many ecosystems, relative stability is followed in the economy by 'mass extinctions' that allow newer, more nimble institutions to take a more important place in the system. But for the most part life goes on. As there is a link between the long period of low inflation and the high growth between 1992 and 2007, the level of disruption caused by the banking crisis may be higher this time. It may also be more severe because of its global nature. But many financial crises are highly disruptive for society for a relatively short time – unless crisis itself is part of the 'normal' behaviour of the society, like Argentina, or Japan. After four years – and we have had two already – long-term adjustment begins, and recovery is usually obvious.

If crises heighten existing characteristics and directions, rather than lead to a wholesale restructuring of society, that may be both comforting to many, and also disturbing for those who see the problems embedded in the 'old ways'. There is no guarantee that the problem that caused the crisis will be fixed in the aftermath, or fixed effectively. The social and business structures that emerge out of the wreckage of the earlier arrangements often carry similar characteristics. The same elites may reappear and attempt to rebuild the old way of doing things. Often, the reactions to one crisis set the pathway to the next.

Yet, continuation may be needed to assist our adjustment, and social trends in place before the crisis often continue, and grow more important. This is particularly true of technological changes. Some technologies, particularly communications, might have contributed to the crisis, yet the history of the past two centuries shows they later emerge as the most important industries of the post-crisis world.

Continuity may encourage benefits as well as costs; or at least, the conditions that caused the crisis may also deliver benefits in the long run. The banking crisis in the early 1990s in Scandinavia helped redirect national energies to focus on high technology, particularly mobile telephony, networking and software; a trend that was already in progress before the bust of 1990. And, as perhaps everyone knows, with Nokia, Finland developed as one of the world leaders in mobile phones. All the Scandinavian countries have been keen to integrate the internet into their society and all of them are among the highest users of online services in the world.

Crises are not just a continuation of normal life, but a marker of change. The political mainstream may become rearranged. New parties emerge, old ones die. The influence of new means of communication, which frequently accompany financial booms and crises, offers the population political participation not previously available.

Finally, in a reverse of the normal way of looking at costs and benefits, benefits may arrive before the costs – globalisation, expansion of the world trade system, cheap electronic goods, mobile telephony, utility computing for everyone. If the banking crisis is caused in part by an advance in communication technology and the ideas and political realignment that accompanied it, then we may already have experienced some of the benefits before the crash, including the gains from international trade. Should we resist the temptation to condemn the benefits because of the costs? Certainly, the retreat into national isolation that has been a feature of a number of countries in the past two years must be tempered, and hopefully reversed – for good economic reasons.

The unsustainable has run its course

After twenty years of acting as the 'consumer of last resort' for the world, the American public does not have the savings to consume strongly – and may not for several years. Job losses may prolong the increase in saving. Unemployment in the US is already at the highest level since 1983, and likely to rise a great deal more. The number of people who have left the workforce because they were discouraged from lack of available work has risen. This has long-term implications for the way the US economy works.

We know what to expect. There have been enough financial crises since 1971; an average of eleven countries a year are affected either by banking or currency crises, an unprecedented rash of crises. Throughout the twenties and the Great Depression there were at most only five countries afflicted at a time. Developed countries have been largely spared; more than ten of the recent average annual crises occurred in developing nations. Scandinavia and Japan provide the only reliable indications of how developed countries react.

Dear old Stockholm – and Helsinki

From the mid-1980s until 1990, Norway, Sweden and Finland experienced a financial boom with many of the characteristics of the recent boom in the US and Europe. Deregulation of the financial system had provided competition to local banks, encouraging lending to commercial and residential housing. The boom turned to bust with the global downturn of 1990. Whereas the UK and US experienced problems with banks, the Scandinavian countries suffered wholesale collapse.

The Soviet Union from the mid-1980s began to reform, based on perestroika (restructure) and glasnost (openness). Optimism about the end of the division of Europe lifted already high economic confidence in the Scandinavian countries. The Scandinavian countries were among the first to benefit from the thawing of relations between East and West.

In 1989, presidents George Bush senior of the US and Mikhail Gorbachev of the Soviet Union declared the Cold War was over. Defence spending in Sweden had been falling as a share of GDP, and the displaced capacity was directed by the government into civilian manufacturing. The term 'peace dividend' was coined in 1990 and was eagerly embraced in Scandinavia. Bank lending, already strong, grew stronger still. Commercial and residential house prices rose sharply, together with indebtedness.

Things did not follow a straight path to the new world order, imagined by the West. The Soviet Union collapsed in 1991 and with it the largest export customer for Finland. Finnish trade with Russia fell 70 per cent in 1991. Banks, already wildly overextended to property, suffered badly. Sweden was less exposed to the Soviet Union, but was exposed to the downturn in Finland. The openness of the three Scandinavian countries and the degree of over-leverage meant the bursting of their property bubble was accompanied by a banking (and insurance company) crisis. The three followed similar strategies: creating a 'bad bank' and nationalising many of their lenders.

Economic performance suffered a shocking collapse. Unemployment rose abruptly. All three countries had low rates of unemployment till the financial boom of 1987–90, which saw unemployment rates fall to almost zero (Sweden fell to 1.1 per cent unemployment rate in June 1989, Finland also bottomed out at 2.1 per cent in the same month. Norway reached a low of 1.7 per cent at the end of 1986).

From 1991 onwards, the three countries saw a massive contraction in economic growth and a large rise in the jobless population. Swedish unemployment rose to 9.4 per cent in August 1993. Finland, with a smaller economy than Sweden and close trade links to the disintegrating Soviet Union, suffered much more from the financial crisis of the early 1990s. Between 1990 and 1993, Finnish GDP contracted 13 per cent and in 1994 unemployment rose from 3.5 per cent to 20 per cent. Neither Sweden nor Finland returned to the low levels of unemployment they had been used to before the crisis. Norway managed to contain the jobless rate to a peak of 6.2 per cent. Partly because the country was aided by the benefits of a large boost from the oil industry, employment eventually returned to about 3 per cent. This did not happen in Sweden or Finland for many years.

> the Scandinavian experience is held up as a model response to a banking crisis

The Scandinavian experience is held up as a model response to a banking crisis. The speed with which the authorities reacted and the efforts to clear the banks of bad debts have been studied by the Federal Reserve, the US government and others as a lesson in how best to deal with a financial collapse. Sweden and Finland were 'good financial crises', with swift nationalisation, transparent accounting of the problems and the establishment of special funds to deal with the problem assets. Within five years, the scars of the disaster had healed, and growth rates were again rising more strongly than their larger neighbours – particularly Germany.

They run, chanting revolution

While it might have been a 'good financial crisis' in retrospect, the Scandinavian experience undermined the dominant Social Democratic party in Sweden. It allowed other political thought to enter the political discourse for the first time since the Second World War and liberal and free-market philosophy emerged as an alternative to the previous orthodoxy. Welfare policy, the cornerstone of Swedish politics since the end of the Second World War, was constrained for the first time. Neutrality, the centrepiece of defence policy, was also shelved. Both policy changes were likely to have occurred without the collapse of the Swedish banks, but events hastened the demise of these cherished institutions.

American political change has already begun after the recent crisis, relatively quietly. Barak Obama may represent a radical change in the history of African Americans, but his politics represent continuity thrust into extraordinary circumstances. A mark of the continuity of political trust is the continuation of party political criticism. Republicans, despite the extent of financial damage to their country, continue to provide a distinctly party political critique of the administration.

Change looks more disruptive in the UK, where the entire political class has been attacked. The government of Gordon Brown first looked as if it was able to use the financial emergency to remodel itself as a protector of national interest. The bounce in popularity was brief, and by early 2009 the political disarray was so pervasive that effective government was all but suspended. And it looks as if there will be a change in the contractual trust between voters and politicians.

Interestingly, it seems the political class most damaged in the aftermath of the crisis is not the executive itself, but the legislature, the Houses of Parliament, which continues a trend towards a presidential style government that has emerged informally since the election of Margaret Thatcher in 1979. While the recent criticism of Parliament – especially for financial sins such as wrongful expenses claims – was heightened by the near-collapse of the British banking system in late 2008, the long-term trend has been away from constituency representation for some time.

Some British politicians recognise the link between the financial crisis and their plight. David Cameron, leader of the opposition Conservative party, summarised the trust lost by politicians and explicitly linked it to the financial crisis:[2]

> 'Of course the immediate trigger of the anger over expenses is the realisation of what some MPs have actually been doing with taxpayers' money. But the fundamental cause is, I believe, something different. It is, in fact, the same thing that made people so angry about the bankers who got rich while they were bringing the economy to its knees… when it comes to the things we ask from politics, government and the state – there is a sense of power and control draining away; having to take what you're given, with someone else pulling the strings. And then when people see MPs caught cheating but still clinging on… bankers reaping their bonuses despite breaking the economy… and bureaucrats whose incompetence is never punished… they see a world that is built to benefit powerful elites, and they feel a terrible but impotent anger.'

2 David Cameron, 'Fixing Broken Politics', 26 May 2009.

The early 1990s brought political change even to the long-standing political structure of Sweden. In July 1991, prime minister Ingvar Carlsson led Sweden to apply to join the EU. The stability of the economic bloc was a strong inducement to join – an appeal to something more solid.

Carlsson's overtures to the EU were never enough to save the government. The 1991 elections in Sweden brought the Moderaterna (liberal-right) government of Carl Bildt to power, who blamed the policies of Social Democrats for the economic collapse. He received enough support for the wholesale disruption of the Swedish model. Monopolies were dismantled, tariffs reduced. Under pressure from international financiers, including hedge funds, the krona was floated. Unemployment rose from already high levels. Swedish economist and politician Carl Hamilton suggested the recession that accompanied Bildt's dismantling of the Social Democratic model was as bad as the financial crisis itself; it was 'a human and economic waste without parallel in the entire history of Sweden'.

Negotiations to join the EU began in February 1993 and the referendum on entry the next year gained much more support than reported in earlier years. Isolation and neutrality were much less appealing in the aftermath of the Cold War and the bursting of the financial bubble. The Social Democratic government 'had lost its confidence that it could manage the national economy. It turned away from full employment and adopted price stability as the main concern of economic policy. At this stage, membership (of the EU) suddenly became attractive as a solution for the continuation of capital accumulation after the failure of both Keynesianism and the "third way".'[3]

It is not clear what America or Britain can join to deflect domestic crisis, and unlike crises of the past, the current one challenges liberal capitalism, rather than pushes political leaders towards it. The Swedish decision was a clear turn away from the uniquely Scandinavian identity that had informed policy. It was also a sign of international integration. The Swedish government ministries

---

3 Andreas Bieler, 'Globalisation and enlargement of the European Union', 2000.

that led the decision to join the EU were those linked to international trade, such as the foreign ministry. Those ministries that had to deal with the domestic problems of the financial crisis – such as the labour ministry – were not consulted. In the aftermath of the recent financial crisis, the consensus on market-oriented politics has been damaged without any viable option being in place; there is no political route to offer salvation. The 'third way' of politics is too recently associated with Clinton and Blair and old-style socialism has proven its flaws too painfully for anyone seriously to consider returning to the state-run model.

Old relationships are sure to be challenged. In the early 1990s, neither the Finns nor the Norwegians were consulted before the Swedish application to join the EU was made. The leaders of both countries 'were taken aback by the move. President [Mauno] Koivisto [of Finland] has even noted that he felt Sweden, in order to gain a head start on its eastern neighbour, would have preferred Finland not to apply... in challenging the continued salience of Swedish neutrality, the collapse of the Cold War order facilitated a Swedish application.'[4] The Swedish decision to open discussions with the EU marked a break in the tradition of sharing discussions with other Scandinavian countries, reflecting the dominance of new internationalism, as compared with the previous regionalism.

Finland had its own economic reasons for joining the single currency – principally the loss of its trading partner in the fall of the Soviet Union. The country joined the EU on 1 January 1995, along with Sweden and Austria. The deeper Finnish recession that followed the financial crisis encouraged more commitment than in Sweden to the full integration of the continent. The country was a founding member of the European single currency four years later, while Sweden continued with its own currency. So the Scandinavian financial crisis unpicked nearly a hundred years of political alignment in both Sweden and Finland within four years.

Despite the political refocus, the Scandinavian crisis did show that quick response from an alert government could curtail the worst of the damage. But the damage could still be extensive, and the

4 David Arter, *Scandinavian Politics Today*, Manchester University Press, 1999.

politicians running the country at the time would still suffer. It also showed that strategic change with immensely important long-term implications (joining the EU and the single currency) could be taken very quickly. It changed the way the Scandinavians saw themselves forever, oriented their economies to the West more firmly and set them on a course to a high-technology future. No longer would Finland be thought of only as a wood pulp producer.

Yet while it encouraged such large changes, the crisis failed to change some fundamental aspects of society, despite throwing up huge challenges. The unique welfare system, perhaps the defining social feature of Scandinavia, remains largely intact in all Nordic countries, with most of the population returning to support the model that had seemed so broken in the aftermath of the crisis. It is debatable whether this was because the Scandinavians are predisposed to this system, or whether they were lucky that world growth provided enough of a cushion.

Not so relaxed: recovery in Thailand

Other countries have suffered more than Scandinavia, with less good fortune in the rebound from crisis. The Asian Tiger recovery from the crisis of 1997–98 was marked by the ghost of the past, both political and economic. Thailand in particular found adjustment difficult. The economy shrank nearly 11 per cent in 1998, and when growth returned it was at lower rates. Thai unemployment rose by three times the pre-crisis level.

> the Asian Tiger recovery... was marked by the ghost of the past, both political and economic

In some ways, Thailand followed the same policies in recovery as it followed in the lead-up to the crisis. Thailand's reliance on manufacturing increased from 39 per cent of output in 1995 to 42 per cent in 2002, while both services and agriculture continued to shrink.[5] Thailand experienced a sharp adjustment between

5 John Benson and Ying Zhu, *Unemployment in Asia*, Routledge, 2005.

domestic growth and exports, reflecting the adjustment to the current account deficit. Exports grew from 40 per cent of GDP in 1995 to 73 per cent by 2007. International trade therefore aided Thai recovery in the same way it aided Scandinavian countries. Thailand also followed a more typical export-led model of development, similar to that followed by Japan and Korea in the years after the Second World War. The re-focus on exports has been followed by Indonesia, Malaysia and China.

Thai politics has always been volatile, when it is not held in check by a military strong man. Just as Scandinavian financial catastrophe brought wholesale challenges to the political consensus, the emergence of political participation after the Asian crisis was seen as a solution to problems brought about by the devaluation of the baht, particularly the corruption that was exposed during and after the crisis. Political participation rather than relying on existing political institutions was seen as a way forward. The economic costs, therefore, were accompanied by political costs for the incumbent elite.

Thai economist Pasuk Phongpaichit says:

> 'The parliamentary system had simply been co-opted into the bureaucratic state. The battle was still between the people and the state, the people and paternalist domination, the people and *rabop upatham*, the patronage system which now encompassed not only bureaucrats but elected representatives... With this declining faith in "democracy" as the route to a better political future, and in parliamentary institutions as a mechanism of change, the idea of "civil society" has been seized upon to play the [role] as the repository of hope.'

The political reform movement gained momentum and in October 1997, after the devaluation, Thailand enacted the sixteenth constitution together with a broad range of reforms, including the establishment of an electoral commission, a decision that was hastened by the emergence of the crisis.

But, just as in Sweden, the old guard fought back. The focus on a single party government led to the near-dominance of the Thai Rak Thai (TRT) party led by Thaksin Shinawatra. In 2001, the party 'ran the most expensive and populist election campaign ever in

Thailand'. It offered $23,000 to each village and suggested farmers could postpone their debt repayments for several years. The success of TRT was built on the slowness of recovery following the Asian crisis.

Thai politics was authoritarian during the Cold War. Politicians seemed to recognise a need to develop civil institutions after the Asian crisis and that it was inappropriate for military involvement in politics. This did not stop a *coup d'état* from ousting Thaksin in 2006.

Despite the integration of Thailand into the wider world through exports, it has not been followed by a similar move in politics. Even in 2008, the old tendency towards authoritarianism was at work, with protests against the government causing the forced removal of the prime minister in December 2008.

Political reform in Indonesia seems to have achieved much greater strides than Thailand, partly because it began with fewer advantages. The Asian crisis precipitated the end of the Suharto regime in May 1998, after three decades of dictatorial rule. Real reform began in 1999 and democratic reforms have been meaningful. The People's Consultative Assembly (MPR) and the People's Representative Council (the House of Representatives) gained much wider powers to challenge the executive, which they have exercised. Candidates for political office engage directly with voters in ways that were alien just over a decade ago. The media too has become lively with political debate, although violence against journalists remains a problem.

For several years in the wake of the Asian crisis, Indonesia appeared threatened by Islamic terror. The Bali bombings in 2002 seemed to show the country running away from tolerance, led by the Jemaah Islamiyah. But the group has lost influence and strength, partly due to police operations against senior members of the organisation, partly because the population has little sympathy with the aims of the organisation.

Indonesia's comparative advance and Thailand's comparative political regression were both a reaction to the initial political instability brought about by the crisis of 1997.

Japan: what recovery?

The costs of financial crisis for Japan, of course, are endless. The country has yet to recover from the bust of its bubble economy collapse in 1990. The first 'lost decade' is likely to turn into a lost twenty years, maybe longer. Its growth rate remains anaemic and is not likely to recover because of a falling population. Not surprisingly, the country's regional power has been eclipsed by China.

Compared with the West, Japan's unemployed receive little in welfare payments, and a system to retrain, re-educate, house and look after the unemployed was almost non-existent before the 1990s. While manufacturing jobs declined by 2.2 million between 1998 and 2004, those registered for 'social welfare' rose by only 700,000 to 5.1 million.

The number of homeless people rose from less than 1,000 in the mid-1980s to 25,000 by mid-2002. The homeless erected small cities of tents around the main cities, made from blue tarpaulins taken from building sites. Osaka Castle Park and the ancient capital Kyoto both saw makeshift communities grow up, known generically as 'blue homes'. They contained a high number of ex-construction workers.

Despite Japan's problems, political and economic change looks as far away as ever. The Liberal Democratic Party has ruled the country since the end of the Second World War apart from a short time in the early 1990s. The success of technocratic government in the 1950s and 1960s continues to leave a mark. The reign of the LDP was a legacy of the Cold War, which ended at a similar date as the bubble economy collapse in 1990. As a creation of post-war politics, the LDP has lost its raison d'être, and undermined the economic prosperity that accompanied it. Japan's role as an Eastern pole of US foreign policy is largely symbolic. Yet the LDP continues to hold power.

Slowly, Japanese public opinion has become more critical. Politicians have changed too. Prime minister Junichiro Koizumi privatised the vast savings of the Post Office, which had been used for decades to finance local projects to buy votes for the LDP, and the style of Koizumi himself was a radical departure from faceless politicians of the past. But this is really only a minor adjustment considering the extent of the damage done to Japan's standing since 1990. The real process of adjustment has not made much headway yet in Japan.

Japan seems determined to show how not to do it

If Sweden and Finland are held up as examples of how best to deal with a financial crisis in a modern economy, Japan seems determined to show how not to do it. Some of the criticism has become less strident since the West experienced its own problems. It has become obvious that radical change is much harder to initiate than it first appears. While the West preached to Japan that it must allow banks to close during the 1990s, the same countries making these suggestions (principally America) have conspicuously failed to move swiftly to close any of their own failing banks.

Recovery in both Scandinavia and Asia required world growth to help their economies. This background of global growth will be missing for America and Europe over the next two years, meaning the boost from exports is likely to be much weaker. Recovery will probably have to come from within the countries themselves. This may make the period of recovery much longer than it was for either Scandinavia or even Thailand.

Costs of crisis compound problems – the demographic decline of Japan is perhaps the biggest difficulty facing the nation. Falling population erodes the vitality needed to reform. Unfortunately, the demographic profiles of Germany and Italy are almost certain to follow the same pattern of decline of Japan. Indonesia's expanding population may have been a factor in its relative success in adapting to a post-crisis world; a rising number of mouths to feed means rising demand. America is better placed in population growth than any other Western country, so its recovery may be partly down to old-fashioned population growth.

Where's the good in bubbles and busts?

With the undoubted costs – financial, social and political – that follow busts and financial panics you may think it churlish to look for gains. How can something so destructive produce benefits?

This episode is not over, so we cannot be sure of the benefits that will emerge this time, but there is plenty of evidence of gains from past crises. The 'railway mania' of 1844 and 1845 collapsed in 1846. In its wake it:

> 'left as a legacy a vast mass of railway securities, many of which were held by investors far distant from the area of operation. Thus, as investor confidence returned in the early 1850s, railway securities again came to play the major role in linking trading in the London and provincial markets. This was further enhanced by a series of alliances and amalgamations which created a small number of highly capitalised railway companies whose securities offered a secure and predictable rate of return. They appealed to investors from all parts of the country.'

So, modern capitalism was born out of crisis.[6]

Despite the pain of the current episode, modern capitalism has produced a panoply of benefits that populations would be unwise to reject; large-scale enterprises that are much more productive, and much less environmentally damaging, than local small-scale manufacturing, insurance for all manner of eventualities, travel, challenges to existing elites and distribution of benefits across society and the globe. Often the advances and benefits follow from financial crises.

The advances in nineteenth century communications technology had certainly contributed to the banking panics of the 1840s, 1860s and 1890s (railways, telegraph, newspapers). The advances also brought social mobility, world news, instant communications and alleviation of distress. They were associated with later social advances and medical advances.

Financial crises are also often followed by a period in which

6 *The London Stock Exchange*, R.C. Mitchie, 1999, Oxford University Press.

technological advances, frequently associated with the preceding bubble, become embedded in society. Railways, telegraph and newspapers all expanded their reach after nineteenth century crises, as well as contributing to the preceding bubble.

Democracy itself has been extended by financial crises. After a particularly spectacular banking panic in 1866, a crisis that began with the collapse of the discount house Overend and Gurney and spread to many international banks, the British government under Disraeli introduced the 1867 Reform Bill. The act that followed enfranchised all male householders in Britain for the first time, doubling the franchise to one million men. The bill had been developing for many years, and had been suggested by Disraeli himself several years previously, but the bank crisis of 1866, and the public discontent that followed, prompted the actual introduction and passage of this important democratic advance.

The 1930s are usually written off as an economic wasteland, culminating in the outbreak of the Second World War. In fact, after 1934, growth improved until 1937, when the 'Roosevelt recession' hit. Unemployment remained high, but the condition of the unemployed did improve – it had to. National income and personal disposable income rose sharply from 1934 onwards, starting roughly three years after the banking crisis. Inflation remained subdued till the outbreak of war. America was more prosperous – as a whole – at the end of the decade than at the beginning, despite difficulties along the way. The same can be said about Britain, which was suffering added problems from challenges to its imperial dominance, in Europe and in the most important colony of all, India. But even in Britain, the condition of the working class improved through the decade.

Change in the US came with shifts in the role of government with the election in 1932 of Franklin D. Roosevelt. In the shadow of the Great Depression, the Democrat Roosevelt drew on support from the poor, unionised workers, ethnic minorities, urban elites and the Southern white population to gain a mandate for social change. For some, especially the black population, social change would take a long time coming and depression set back their progress. For others, it provided a levelling effect.

In his inaugural address in 1933, Roosevelt laid out a programme for change that rejected the political elite – and the bankers – of the past:

> 'Recognition of the falsity of material wealth as the standard of success goes hand in hand with the abandonment of the false belief that public office and high political position are to be valued only by the standards of pride of place and personal profit; and there must be an end to a conduct in banking and in business which too often has given to a sacred trust the likeness of callous and selfish wrongdoing... in our progress toward a resumption of work we require two safeguards against a return of the evils of the old order; there must be a strict supervision of all banking and credits and investments; there must be an end to speculation with other people's money, and there must be provision for an adequate but sound currency.'

This sounds familiar.

Roosevelt introduced a social security system. He also created the basis of a financial system that has lasted almost to the present day. The mortgage agencies were created in the 1930s, as was the SEC and the Federal Deposit Insurance Corporation (FDIC), and the Glass–Steagall Act was introduced. All these were significant advances. Most importantly for many people, Roosevelt also ended prohibition. Private sector development was not idle either. The Empire State Building, the Chrysler Building and Rockefeller Center were all completed in the 1930s.

Radio contributed to the boom in the 1920s, spreading the influence of instalment loans and share ownership as much as newspapers. Newspapers, telegraph and railways preceded a series of financial crises in the nineteenth century, yet survived the busts to become the most important communications media for the next fifty years. Radio was itself the cause of a rise in advertising of all manner of goods and services in the 1920s. During the depression that followed, the radio became the preferred means of communicating the news and took on a national unifying role in the US and the UK. The first Christmas message broadcast by a British monarch took place in 1932, not long after the Great Crash, and embodied a new ethos of collective effort.[7] Our own crisis grew from the communications technology revolution, and yet its benefits will probably grow for many years in the future.

Radio was a beneficiary of the depression, spreading much further as a result of the 1930s financial crisis. By the middle of the decade almost every household in America and Britain possessed a wireless. In fact, the continued success of radio was a direct result of the depression, with the cost savings of radio sets compared with other forms of entertainment encouraging many new purchases.

In 1930 the wealthiest areas had the highest and the poorest areas had the lowest concentration of radio ownership.[8]

> 'By 1936, despite the depression, all areas of the United States had made great strides in radio ownership. By then, 74 per cent of the nation's home contained a radio, and all areas of the country had seen their rates grow by at least 10 per cent... Growth in radio ownership between 1930 and 1936 was highest in the South... Radio was as close to depression-proof as any industry in the economy.'

The south, of course, was the poorest part of the country.

The benefits of radio were in entertainment, but it also brought wider access to national news, sport, a certain amount of education and, above all, music. All these benefits were free, after the initial purchase. American record companies produced 100 million records in the mid-1920s. By the early 1930s, only six million were being sold; the cost advantage of radio almost killed the record market. Radio advertising revenues continued to grow throughout the 1930s. The higher proportion of the population

---

7 King George V's Christmas message, 1932 included the lines 'take it as a good omen that Wireless should have reached its present perfection at a time when the Empire has been linked in closer union. For it offers us immense possibilities to make that union closer still. It may be that our future may lay upon us more than one stern test. Our past will have taught us how to meet it unshaken. For the present, the work to which we are all equally bound is to arrive at a reasoned tranquility within our borders; to regain prosperity without self-seeking; and to carry with us those whom the burden of past years has disheartened or overborne.'

8 Douglas B. Craig, *Fireside Politics*, Hopkins, 2005.

with access to radio brought support for the medium from business. The spread of radio raised interest in jazz, as well as classical music, during the 1930s.

The banking crash in Scandinavia in 1990 introduced many benefits; some rather surprising. One remarkable outcome was that the nationalised banks were eventually sold back to the private sector for a profit – meaning that what had looked like a cost to the taxpayer was greatly reduced. The initial cost was put at 2 per cent of GDP for Norway, and as high as 9 per cent of GDP for Finland. The end cost was much lower – for Finland it was 5.3 per cent of GDP, for Sweden only 0.2 per cent of GDP and for Norway a net gain of 0.4 per cent of GDP.

the crisis also introduced tax changes and improvements in efficiency

The crisis also introduced tax changes and improvements in efficiency, especially in Finland, that led to long-term gains. By the early twenty-first century, Finland had moved from the least developed Nordic country to the most developed. It was ranked number one in the World Economic Forum competitive index repeatedly. It was the top ranked country for higher education in the OECD. Finland achieved the highest score in information technology and the knowledge economy in 1995 and 2006.[9]

The main cause for all these accolades was the extraordinary success of Nokia, which grew from a local conglomerate to international industry leader following the crash of the early 1990s. The banking collapse caused Nokia to focus on its telecommunications business and sell off its domestic businesses, such as rubber and cables. Within four years it had become the largest mobile phone manufacturer in the world. It became the leading instigator of the digital GSM technology, which allowed roaming and SMS messaging for the first time on a large scale. Nokia, and GSM, laid the foundations for the worldwide boom in

9 Carl J. Dahlman, Jorma Routti, Pekka Yla Anttila, 'Finland as a knowledge economy', World Bank Institute, 2006.

mobile telephones; without the Scandinavian banking crisis, the competitive advances made by Nokia might not have occurred, or would have been delayed.

Finland itself was transformed, from a country largely dependent on natural resources – especially wood – into one of the high-technology centres of the globe. From 1996, the Finnish economy grew at an annual rate of 5.1 per cent – very high for a developed economy – driven by Nokia and the associated information technology sector. Similarly, Thailand concentrated its export energies on the high-technology sector in the aftermath of the Asian crisis, to its lasting benefit.

A complex of crises: 1970 to 2009

The current financial crisis is undoubtedly the most costly yet. It dwarfs the cost of the last American banking crisis, involving Savings and Loans banks in the late 1980s, even when adjusted for inflation. Yet, every financial crisis in a developed country seems to be the worst ever. Episodes are unlikely to be described as 'crises' unless they are the worst ever – in their time. Anything less can be dealt with using tools tried and honed in previous episodes.

Part of the reason for the shock of today's crisis is because the developed West is among the countries affected. The West, in particular, has become unused to financial disruption first hand. Compared with the rest of the world, the West has not had a fair share of financial disasters.

Our impression is that such crises are relatively rare: 'Black Swan' events that occur only once a generation. So rare that they catch regulators, central bankers, politicians and commercial bankers by surprise.

But this is not true. The IMF database on banking, currency and sovereign debt crises shows that between 1971 and 2008, there was just two years (1974 and 2006) when there was not a financial crisis of some sort in at least one country. For most of that time there were financial crises in several countries at one time.

The impression of the rarity of crises leads to other misconceptions. The Great Crash of 1929 did not end a decade of carefree partying. The banking crisis of the early 1930s that immediately preceded the depression was far from unique. The early 1920s were affected by a large number of panics, across a range of countries. In fact, between 1900 and 1971 the greatest number of countries affected by banking crises occurred in 1922, not the 1930s, caused by delayed after-effects of the Great War. Countries afflicted included the Netherlands, Italy, Sweden, Denmark and Norway. The Nordic countries suffered crises lasting half of the 1920s.

Rather than a single cataclysmic event following the crash, it is more accurate to think of a periodic series of crises through the 1920s, culminating in a final and more damaging crisis in the early 1930s. None of the earlier crises affected America, so it ignored the disruption elsewhere.

Similarly, the banking crises of the nineteenth century clustered around various dates, peaking in the 1840s, followed by a lull, then another series of crises between 1860 and 1880, with the final panics of the century in the 1890s. The crisis of today is actually the culmination of a rolling financial crisis that began in the mid-1970s; perhaps it is not even the culmination.

The current series closely matched the introduction of neo-liberal market policies, spreading from Britain and the US across the world. And as they spread, so the number of countries affected by crises rose. Some would point to this association between financial crisis and market systems and assume they would not have happened had neo-liberalism been thwarted. The French and some German politicians seem to hold this idea, and are not afraid to voice it.

A more challenging notion is that financial crises are an integral part of a system that brought greater freedom and greater wealth to more people than could have been possible otherwise. The assessment of costs and benefits must therefore assess how the social costs of neo-liberalism stack up against the undoubted benefits it has brought.

These benefits include the transformation of communications and computing power, the expansion of world trade, the fall of the communist bloc in Europe, the inclusion of Eastern Europe in the European Union. Perhaps the greatest achievement has been bringing China into the world trade system. The wealth this has brought to millions of previously impoverished Chinese is so immense it outweighs many, perhaps over time even all, of the negative aspects of neo-liberalism. Without these ideas, paramount leader Deng Xiaoping would probably not have declared in 1978 that 'to be rich is glorious'. China has a long way to go when it comes to freedom for individuals. But there is no doubt it is a much healthier and freer society than it was; though with some lapses, such as the Tiananmen Square massacre.

It is difficult to argue against the obvious links between the Japanese, Asian and Western crises that marked a decade of disruptive finance from 1990 onwards, and which led directly to the current crisis.

The transfer of crises from one region to another required a globalised world, employing sophisticated communications, investment and trade; these benefits were required to create the crisis we have. There is no-one in the West who has not benefited from these trade and technological developments, either through cheaper electronic goods, or cheaper clothes, or the resulting freeing of cash to spend on travel, or leisure.

All our new technologies of communication – from telegraph and telephone to the internet – offered novel means of transcending time and space. It is no coincidence that transcendence of time and space is also the purpose of banks. Banks distribute credit across time and space, and manage the considerable risks associated with that. New communication technologies expand horizons and both stimulate and require expanded credit to fund the exploitation of these new horizons. When we consider the costs of the provision of credit in the past decade, we should perhaps also remember that without these costs, there might have been no longer-term benefits either.

The internet: too early to tell

What kind of future can we expect? For the moment it looks unrelentingly grim. In the UK, unemployment is rising, government debt is rocketing, mainstream parties have lost public confidence and even parliament has been tainted by the abuse by MPs of expenses; a scandal that is unlikely to have had such an impact without the distress of the financial crisis. Worryingly, extremist parties are making electoral inroads.

Perhaps of greater concern is that the world has become globalised. Britain and the US cannot rely on the growth of other countries while they rebuild their economies; these were the economies, particularly America, which generated the growth for the entire world. Transformation through exports, which was the route followed by the Asian victims, Finland, Sweden and attempted by Japan, looks destined to fail.

> Finland proved it was possible to create new markets and shape them to its own advantage

At least it may fail if the only exports were those relying on existing markets. Finland proved it was possible to create new markets and shape them to its own advantage.

Information technology and globalisation formed the direct background of not one but two bubbles, the dot-com bubble of 1999–2001 and the housing bubble of 2003–2006, and was one of the causes of the crises in Japan, Thailand and Scandinavia. In between the end of 2001 and the end of the housing bubble, the internet had undergone the sort of growth that even its fanatical supporters in the late 1990s would have found surprising. In the process, it nearly wiped out the recorded music industry, challenged the film and software industries and created new economies in the virtual world *Second Life*. Social networking websites and blogging were embryonic and Google was just emerging from its birth as the experiment of two students.

A bubble may be rational and the disruption of the bust itself may be part of the long-term adjustment to technology, trade or social conditions. When Greenspan looked at the internet he looked at it in classical terms of improving efficiency, speeding processes, oiling the wheels of commerce and global trade. It is all these things, yet the economics of the internet fail when measured only by economic efficiency. Social sites do not work because they are efficient. Rather they become efficient – meaning profitable – through their social success. The metrics of measuring many of the newer successful online businesses are entirely different from those used to measure old industries.

If this sounds like a return of the dot-com optimism, then it is tempered with a demand for the bottom line, and informed by the fickleness of success in the still-new medium. There are perhaps only three lasting online brands so far; Amazon, eBay and Google. Their success is not driven by marketing in the conventional sense, but by use and word of mouth. At heart, all three are a modest collection of algorithms operating over a large number of servers. All three are based on marketplaces. Of the three, by far the most powerful is Google, whose marketplace is pure information. Without Google, that information would not be found, or, in many cases, would not exist at all, an attribute not shared by the other two companies.

I remain optimistic that economic recovery is tied to and likely to emerge from the connectedness we have created in the internet. The need to control, understand and manipulate that connectedness will lead to opportunities we did not think we needed. Communications technologies take many decades to fulfil their potential.

Many of the benefits of communication technologies are also unexpected. No-one could have predicted that the printing press would have a direct influence on the discovery of America through the huge popularity of printed editions of Ptolemy's *Geography*. It is likely that some New World remains to be discovered and the crises of the past twenty years are a symptom of the journey towards it.

What lessons for the future?

Life is uncertain. Eat dessert first.

Ernestine Ulmer

What can we learn from the wreck of our financial system? Policymakers across the world are determined there will be no repetition of the crisis and there has been much talk of rebuilding the architecture of global finance. The G20 has met in London, and will meet again intent on formulating permanent answers; some have already been proposed. Are there lessons that can be permanently learnt?

There are some bad signs from the start. The term 'architecture of global finance' shows a misunderstanding of how international finance works. It sounds good, but is as lacking in accuracy as a description as the 'science of boxing'. Unlike architecture, rules have always been circumvented, and the building blocks – credit and investment – are malleable. Architecture suggests a permanence of structure that just does not exist in the inherently unstable arrangements of finance. Any solution needs to recognise the instability – and contradictions – at the heart of finance, and there are few signs of that. A solution to financial crises would need to balance Menger's money (the money that we use for transactions and which powers market growth) and debt money. We have struggled with this dichotomy for so long without success we may as well give up. A single country, controlled by a central bank and economically sovereign, may achieve a balance between transactions and debt for some time – though that is not certain. But our world is no longer composed of isolated individual countries but interdependent states whose sovereignty is subsidiary to their importance as participants in a trading system. Those that introduce restrictions must recognise that they come with a price; lower growth, less opportunity, perhaps even less individual responsibility.

I began this book claiming it would help us with answers. We have seen that the problems are as much geo-political as regulatory. The solution must be geo-political too. The entry of emerging economies into the global economy (particularly China) cannot and should not be undone, but there has to be a more balanced arrangement by which the wealth of the world is distributed, and for the first time in history, it is clear that the risks in distribution are as much a threat to the developed world as to the less developed world. Technological changes that accompanied the expansion of trade and the growth of transactional finance should not be reversed. There are too many benefits that accompany both the entry of emerging economies and the rise of a networked world. The initial response – particularly from continental European politicians – is to go back to a safer time when our current problems did not exist. This is unrealistic, and if implemented, dangerous. It would risk shutting down the trading system exactly when we need it most. Luckily, the changes probably cannot be reversed, but they can be impeded, and that would be bad enough.

Europe in the 1930s shows how dangerous it is to subvert the international trading system in favour of perceived national interest. I am more hopeful that the lesson from the early twenty-first century is that it is impossible to subvert the international trading system in a similar move towards autarky and political disaster. The robustness of the system may be challenged, but for now Europe, America, Asia, South America, Russia and Australasia are tied into a system that has become more important than any single nation, and looks likely to continue in its main features. In June 1997, Robert Rubin talked about the 'centrality of economics to foreign policy... It is no exaggeration when we say that our economic well-being is enormously and irreversibly linked to the rest of the world'. Ten years later, the well-being of the US, and everyone else, has been shown to be irreversibly linked not to a single economy, but to every economy. America used to be the largest economy by far, and the most important. As an academic measurement it still is the largest economy. But the most important economy by far now encompasses the globe as a whole. The tying of America to the globe, and vice versa, was no accident but a policy objective, framed by Rubin and Larry Summers. It has played out probably beyond their public or private estimations.

the expanding global network has enriched millions of poor people

The expanding global network has enriched millions of poor people and enhanced the lives of both rich and emerging economies. The US led the way, but what does such integration mean for the future of that country? This is one of the most important questions for all of us. For not only was America the single largest economy, it was also the greatest military power. In many cases it remains the standard-setter for policy in many areas of public and private life. Once the undisputed mechanism of its economic might, US financial capitalism now lies damaged. While its military might is unchallenged, its leadership has been undermined and the primacy of its economic philosophy has been unhinged.

Yet there are reasons to think the future will be very similar to the past. America's deep and liquid markets, and the dominance of its political economy, sustained the dollar as the overwhelming favourite reserve currency. The benefits of such ascendancy have turned to costs and the dollar's dominance encouraged the imbalances that led to crisis. Some are now openly questioning the purpose of a dollar reserve. In the aftermath, China, Russia and Brazil have all identified the power of the dollar as a problem in itself – seemingly ignorant of their own role in promoting its ascendency. Several have announced they will in future switch their reserves into other currencies, and even into some kind of proto-global currency used by the International Monetary Fund. Yet, this will not solve the confusion of money. Investment of reserves is by definition a creation of a debt from the issuer. Is it reasonable to assume the IMF will be any better at containing unforeseen consequences of debt creation on a massive scale than was the US Treasury, or mortgage agencies? Is it reasonable to assume the IMF can issue as much debt as investors seem to want?

No doubt reserve managers can find investments for their holdings outside the dollar, but the colossal size of global reserves limits the number of places they can invest. They need large markets, liquid currencies and ready access. This probably restricts their scope to the largest US bond markets and perhaps the better quality Europeans. So, the dollar will, by dint of no alternative, remain the most important reserve currency.

Whose reserves are they anyway?

Better still would be a recognition that the money stashed in foreign reserves is no longer necessary for protection from devaluation and that the money really belongs to the people of those countries. The initial reason for accumulating such vast reserves was to avoid speculative attack, to build international confidence in stability; the subsequent reason was to protect exporters from the consequences of rising exchange rates.

Neither of these reasons is sufficient to justify withholding the profits of the people. For the trillions of dollars in reserves amount to trillions taken from the people who earned them. The workers of China, Brazil, Russia earned these reserves and their earnings should not, it seems to me, be any longer used as instruments of government whim. Far better for earnings from exports to be spent on improving roads, schools, building standards, hospitals and welfare of the population. Perhaps create a national pension fund based on both domestic and international investments. Better still, offer the money directly back to workers through higher earnings or improved conditions.

The future of America

What of America's future itself? The Obama administration has shown the country will not turn away from capitalism, but will adapt it, just as Franklin D. Roosevelt adapted capitalism to the circumstances of the Great Depression. Larry Summers, once more in the centre of policymaking with the Obama administration, said in June 2009:[1] 'Our objective is not to supplant or replace markets. Rather, the objective is to save them from their own excesses and improve our market-based system going forward.' Improvements, I think we can be sure, mean more regulation, but not a turning away from the core principles that dominate America's way of business: innovation, profit and individual aspiration. Those commitments will apply as much to finance as to any other industry. US bankers will find their personal greed may not be quite so circumscribed as many feared. There are, however, likely to be fewer bankers overall, at least for several years.

There are also likely to be fewer boasts about the virtues of its economic system. It is probable that Americans themselves will spend a considerable time adjusting to their straitened circumstances, even when the recession ends. Lower growth, lower consumption and higher savings rates look likely for a considerable time, possibly the next decade. This will affect everyone, with less employment, fewer new businesses, probably less innovation and certainly less fun.

Yet even with a background of lower growth, it is important not be too pessimistic. The dollar retains its status as a reserve currency, and is likely to continue as the main reserve currency for many years to come, despite its lead role in the credit crunch. Exporters require a destination for their goods and America is the natural buyer. The combination of the dollar's reserve status and largely unchanged trade patterns is likely to cause capital inflows into America to resume. A more likely surprise is not that this crisis undermines the old global economic arrangements but that it confirms old arrangements, under different constraints.

It is certainly in the interests of exporters to continue in 'the way we were'. Countries that rely on consumption to propel their growth, such as the US and the UK, can rebalance their economies simply by slowing domestic consumption, devaluing their

---

1 Larry Summers, 'Reflections on economic policy in time of crisis', the Council on Foreign Relations, New York, 12 June 2009.

currencies and increasing exports. For those that rely on exports, a fall in world growth damages their exports, but they cannot stimulate consumption to compensate. This is why the German economy has shrunk more than that of the UK and why Japanese industrial production has collapsed much more than American. The exporters themselves, who largely missed out on the consumption boom, were shown to be the most vulnerable to the crisis. It is another lesson in why it is better to pass on to the workers the fruits of their labour, so they can consume as they wish. If the exporters cannot produce growth, it is incumbent on America and the rest of the consuming countries to once again shoulder the burden of supporting world growth, possibly at a lower pace, possibly grudgingly. It is in everyone's interest that the same circumstances that led to the global crisis are allowed to continue, or at least wind down over perhaps a decade or more. The leadership of America is still the key to the well-being of all of us.

A long-term faith in the new

The US political establishment showed remarkable foresight about the challenges of the financial future at the end of the Cold War. This was obvious from the statements – and policies – of Rubin and Summers. The challenges of globalisation and technology run like a vein through speeches of the country's politicians and central bankers. A 1990 Senate report wrote: 'Innovation in technology and in financial instruments could contribute to sustained liquidity and expansion; but it is also possible that innovation could out-pace the capability of market participants to comprehend and control its effects.'[2] The conclusion of the report was that any threat to the US financial system came from foreign, not domestic, markets; from less well regulated countries upsetting American investments, not from America itself being part of the dislocation. Under a section titled 'American leadership' the report said, 'it seems reasonable to conclude that the United States now has, in the aggregate, the largest and most liquid securities and

2 United States Congress. Office of Technology Assessment, 'Trading around the clock', 1990.

futures market in the world...' The analysis was correct, and remains so. What the Senate failed to realise was it was exactly these attributes of liquidity and size that led, seventeen years later, to the financial damage of its own country. Success, and advanced markets, were the culprits. Yet there is no credible alternative to these markets for most investors, who lack the skills or patience to seek out illiquid or hard-to-value investments. Liquidity will continue to exert an important pull and the dominance of US markets will continue for many years. America remains needed.

Nor has America ever lost the ability to identify important themes, including trends in technology and (among its political class at least) globalisation. America's dominance in the past century is partly due to its seemingly endless capacity to reinvent itself. If something does not work, those who failed dust themselves down and attempt to find something that does work. It shows a remarkable, possibly unique, confidence in a better future. This quality will, I am sure, surface again, even under straitened circumstances.

The belief in the benevolent future extended to America's central bank. Greenspan always regarded technology with awe, despite the experience of the dot-com bust. In a passage we have already quoted, he also seemed aware of potential risks, though not able to see what these might be:[3]

> 'Technology continues to bring rapid change and, hence, considerable uncertainty, to the global marketplace. Monetary policy, supervision and regulation activities, and payments system operation will need to be calibrated to respond to the influences of that technological change.'

The country may have to rely on its ability to identify and adjust to trends that will dictate social change as much in the future as in the past. Yet, as by far the most important influence on information technology – particularly in social applications of that technology online – America retains control of the global 'means of production'. It is a power that its rivals envy, but cannot hope to

---

3 Closing remarks at a symposium sponsored by the Federal Reserve Bank of Kansas City, Jackson Hole, Wyoming, 27 August 2005.

supplant yet. It is also a power that plays to the strength of American culture – openness, transparency and public discussion – attributes still lacking or underdeveloped in many, perhaps most, other countries.

Despite signs to the contrary, it is in the interests of international banks to promote this culture. Their entire business is derived and expanded through use of information technology. The crisis that circulated around the globe for so long and finally reached the US in 2007 relies on both American and banks' recovery to alleviate the stress elsewhere. There is scope for leadership in information from both America and banks.

> the crisis has brought forward a shift to emerging economies by six years

That said, for the first time in recorded history, in 2009 the US, Canada and Europe are expected to generate less than half the world's growth. This was expected to happen in 2015; the crisis has brought forward a shift to emerging economies by six years. Economies such as Brazil and China are expected to continue to grow faster than the developed world for the foreseeable future, meaning the share of world growth produced by mature, democratic, liberal states will continue to decline. This has implications for the way geo-politics will be formulated. Already, China and Russia have indicated they want a greater share of decisions at institutions such as the IMF. The crisis was caused by a transfer of power to the large emerging countries via accumulation of reserves, and has hastened their further increase in power. Conspiracy theorists may see political designs in this accretion of power; I think it is just an inevitability. Looking at the way China invested its reserves suggests it has a lot to learn about investment, both in its own country and in its foreign ventures.

A never-ending crisis

So, continuation of most of the geo-political structures dominated by the US is likely for a long time. Americans dominate the institutional framework. In any case, our crisis itself is a continuation of a much longer disruption that has lasted for at least nineteen years. A never-ending crisis is unlikely to end present arrangements if it has been an integral part of them for nearly two decades. At the beginning of this book we saw that the ancient Greek stem for the English crisis, κρινω, meant to judge or to choose. Our delusion is that our own financial crisis differs from common experience. It certainly differs from our recent common experience in the West, but similar problems have been a feature for the globe for the past twenty years. During that time they have visited Europe and America at least twice, South-East Asia once and never left Japan. The shock of our financial crisis is that it is us rather than someone else who suffers. Of course, there will be changes, but do not expect arrangements in regulation, or the orientation of the financial framework, to change much. And for the sake of all of us, do not expect the economic leadership of America to diminish for long.

Challenges to central banks and exporters

On the other hand, there are likely to be some changes in the financial landscape particularly to the way that previously untouchable central banks are perceived. Public support for the independence of central banks may be challenged. Central bank independence is already under pressure from the vast assistance the Fed, the ECB, the BoJ and the Bank of England provide to their economies. They are already bound into the political process in ways they cannot have imagined two years ago.

Financial stability, which had taken a back seat at central banks since the end of the 1970s, has re-emerged as a requirement for central bankers. Inflation now looks the lesser evil, and despite confident assertions that inflation remains their main target, it is likely that at least as much effort will be devoted to maintaining growth and framing financial rules. In any case, judged by overall performance in the past ten years it is not clear that independent central banks are any more reliable at containing crises – and perhaps even inflation – than their non-independent predecessors. For politicians who must suffer the voter's judgement after crises, the luxury of independent central banks may look too costly.

Unaccountable central bankers are likely also to face many more calls to justify their decisions. This seems particularly true of the Fed and the Bank of England, but equally the pivotal role of the ECB in containing problems in the euro area raises questions. Its controversial liquidity and bond purchase policies ensure it will attract much more critical attention than it did before.

> without any conscious design the euro area has acquired a central leading institution

In fact, in Europe, the financial crisis has already caused a shift in the political balance, with the ECB taking a central role not provided by any state apparatus. The bank has become more important to the future of the single currency and the economies of the single currency than any member state, including Germany. It also holds the economic keys for countries that adjoin the euro area. This is enormous political power, masquerading as monetary policy. Without any conscious design the euro area has acquired a central leading institution that can command obedience throughout the area and to which as many as half the member states owe uncritical support for the aid it provided to their banking systems. That support will be needed for a considerable time, giving the ECB an extended period in which to consolidate its power.

The ECB adeptly crafted an ad-hoc response to the crisis and it should be congratulated for its success. But it had no option; individual countries in the single currency did not have the time or willingness to take the lead and the bank was forced to take a lead. The single currency is composed of a set of relationships that only the ECB has been able to support to date.

Without an overarching political framework, the ECB has had to step into the political arena, despite its qualms. In the long term, this power may be unsustainable. A state should not be run by a central bank. The only way forward is for the member states to pool their political power, and such pooling is inevitable. The cost of the current crisis is likely to be socialised across the region, which demands greater political integration. As the country likely to be presented with the largest bill, Germany will be justified in asking for the leading role in any political solution.

A new role for hedge funds

Hedge funds too are likely to experience change, and probably in ways many would consider an unlikely direction. Few shed tears over the hedge funds that have fallen over the past two years, and there are moves by Europeans in particular to limit their activity. Yet, unlike banks in many countries, hedge funds have received no government assistance, and never will. Those that have made it through the difficulties of the past twelve months or so are more experienced, more stable and often with higher quality personnel than many banks. These pools of capital will remain a force in finance. Their role as harbingers of bad news will certainly remain unwelcome to many, but they also act as early warnings on unsustainable risks. Those that have colluded with the political class – such as Long Term Capital – have been shown to be the funds that are most at risk. Bloody-mindedness is the future for hedge funds, not acquiescence.

Those funds that remain will inhabit a landscape markedly different from that which preceded 2007, but which they are well equipped to navigate. All the big funds are politically savvy and fully capable of playing one jurisdiction off against another for the privilege of hosting these supposed beasts of the markets. In many circumstances, an economy benefits from their presence. Of course, many will also disappear (or may have already done so), because their business model was built purely on liquidity, which will not return in its old form. But for those that are left, the rewards are likely to be high for several years yet, without taking much leverage, so dislocated are the prices of investments in some areas.

There are other reasons to expect hedge funds – or other funds like them – to retain an important role. These funds represent a migration of financial power from banks to smaller institutions. It is a process intimately connected to improvements in technology and it is almost impossible to halt. The cull of hedge funds that occurred in the eighteen months after August 2007 has not killed the sector, but opened opportunities for survivors. With few pure investment banks, these mobile pools of capital will not only remain important, they may assume more roles previously reserved for banks: mergers and acquisitions, advice to issuers and investors, interpretation of investment trends. It is possible to see hedge funds expanding their role considerably. Larry Summers said: 'The financial system did not perform its intended function as a bearer and distributor of risk, but instead proved to be a creator of risk.' Why not admit that risk is an ever-present feature of the financial landscape and that creation of risk is a cost of advancement? This would allow those that seek risk – the hedge funds – to assume what others do not want.

Hedge funds represent, in some ways, the democratisation of financial risk that has permeated most of our lives. Finance has become ubiquitous in ways that would have been surprising even a decade ago. We have got used to the idea of being personally responsible for our own pensions, trading derivatives, even become experts in the safety of our own bank. The emergence of companies such as IG Index has brought sophisticated financial products to anyone with access to a computer – which is almost everyone in the West.

more participation is becoming mandatory, and not just in social network websites

It has been said that banks are like representative democracy; we appoint legislators to vote on our behalf on issues we do not have the expertise or time to consider. In the same way bankers aggregate our savings and decide who will borrow them. We do not vote for bankers, but they do, in a way, work for us. But representation is a model we can use technology to improve upon. More participation is becoming mandatory, and not just in social network websites. The process has begun in banking, and is necessary in our politics too, if it is to retain our interest. If individual investors can replicate for their own pension the sort of trades used by LTCM just a decade ago – and they can – there is no question we can be responsible enough to decide government policy through direct engagement.

What kind of regulatory change?

The Financial Stability Forum is an international organisation that includes almost all the central banks and financial regulators of major economies, plus important emerging economies such as Argentina, India, China, Russia and Brazil. In the immediate aftermath of the near-collapse of Western banking in late 2008, the forum drafted proposals to strengthen the financial system through more rigorous application of capital adequacy of banks, liquidity management and improved regulatory supervision. It also proposed making risk more transparent, addressing the conflicts in rating agencies and improving the response of the authorities to risk.

All are worthy goals. Many are not new, and there remains the problem that responses are empirical, not comprehensive – they address particular issues, which means that individual suggestions look sensible, but as a whole they are either not new or may even conflict. For instance, there is recognition that capital in banks is pro-cyclical – it is too high in good times and too low in crises. Accordingly, the forum recommends that capital should 'increase during strong economic conditions and can be drawn down during periods of economic and financial stress'. This is how capital adequacy has attempted to work for many years. Nothing radical or even different in this recommendation.

The current capital framework is riddled with anomalies, and I do not suppose the new framework will be any more coherent, though it may take years to uncover those anomalies that are most dangerous. The Basel II accord divided up capital according to ratings and apparent liquidity, just as suggested by the forum, but both measures have been highly misleading. The ECB treats German and Dutch government bonds as equal to Greek or Maltese government bonds. It is an equivalence that does not yet seem justified.

In another section, the forum recommends that it is important to 'limit the costs of incipient financial stress' through the use of flexible capital buffers. Flexibility is hard to implement when competitors do not seem to require such flexibility; and flexibility in a downturn will probably be viewed by competitors and shareholders alike as a sign of weakness. It may also be viewed as weakness by regulators themselves. Banks would have a huge incentive not to use such flexibility.

> ad hoc solutions do not command much respect from the banking industry

Ad hoc solutions do not command much respect from the banking industry, or even agreement among nations. There is little chance that even the modest suggestions made so far will be implemented fully, or if implemented, will be observed.

National competition will always trump collective agreement. Already, it is clear that the European Union cannot provide a united position on what sort of regulation it would like to see applied within its area. Britain objects to the application of rules across the EU that may impede the development of financial services on which its economy depends. If there is disagreement among medium-sized European countries sharing most of the same institutions, there is unlikely to be agreement across more important divides, such as between Europe and the US, or China and the US.

Besides, in the near term each government is more concerned with the fall-out of the financial crisis on its own economy. Already the impetus for pan-global regulation has been overtaken by country-specific adjustments to deal with specific problems. Nor is this likely to change. When Lord Turner of the UK's Financial Services Authority identified the consequences of 'global finance without global government' it was a neat observation, but one that did not come with any useful prescription. Global finance retains its precedence over global government. After the crisis many governments are even more directly dependent on foreign capital for their finances than before. I have witnessed the pleas of the US Treasury before foreign reserve managers not to abandon the Treasury market. The power of international finance is now perhaps as great as at any time during the boom years, and the dependence of government finances on that power is certainly evident.

Too many crises and yet not enough

There has been no shortage of financial crises in recent years. Some I have not even considered, such as the European Exchange Rate Mechanism crisis of 1992 and the Eastern European currency crisis in the mid-1990s. The period after the mid-1970s has produced the greatest cluster of financial crises at least for a century. In reality, our era has probably seen the greatest concentration of financial disruption in history. There have been two peaks in this thirty-year period; 1983 when 31 countries were affected, and 1994 when 36 countries were affected. Even the massive disruption of the current crisis does not come close to these numbers. According to my calculations, seventeen countries are currently affected – though that could rise quickly. Some say this is a demonstration of the great failure of capitalism and the high number of problems proves the system is unable to provide general well-being. The level of misery and difficulty in afflicted countries warrants our compassion – particularly if, as in Thailand, it was partly caused by the agents of integration such as the IMF.

There is another, much more positive, way of looking at this extraordinary rise in financial disruption. The explosion of currency, banking and government finance crises since the mid-1970s has followed the access to more widespread information sources of all sorts, including sources of credit. In many ways, the rise in afflicted countries is a 'barometer of freedom' rather than a signal of general distress.

When I was young my parents allowed me to use a Post Office passbook, which recorded my pocket money and from which I could withdraw money whenever I wished. The passbook would not, however, offer credit. For my parents it was the safest way to introduce a form of bank account to me. For an overdraft I had to wait until I was an adult and could assess the risks involved. With a passbook, my money appeared safe because I was always in credit and the Post Office seemed a bastion of security. I was not aware that I was owed money by the Post Office, merely that it was looking after my pennies for me. The money was never, as far as I was concerned, the Post Office's liability, just my asset. The

Post Office was large, safe and would never run into trouble. US Treasury and later mortgage agency markets were treated as the world's Post Office passbook for more than a decade; seemingly offering safe and deep markets from which money could be withdrawn instantly. There seems to have been little consideration on the part of the foreign investors that there was a debt on the other side of their asset. Nor that their preponderance in these markets forced other investors to seek other debts as investment, debts that were backed by less conscientious debtors.

The explosion of crises shows I was not the only one who increased my financial responsibility since the 1970s. The rash of dislocation that has afflicted the world may or may not be over. Crises indicate risk, and risk indicates a willingness to advance and seek greater opportunities. The irony of the past five years is not risky investments we have to worry about, but that risk-aversion on a sufficient scale can force others into taking unwarranted risks. It has been a concentration of avoidance of risk by reserve managers that precipitated many of our current problems.

The cost of cleaning up the crisis may be evident in higher government debt, or lower government spending, higher taxes or all three, for a generation. We in the West are just part of a long line of borrowers and investors who have been fooled by international capital flows and it will cost us as it has cost the Thais, the Swedes, the Finns, Mexicans and Argentines. It is possible we have not reached the end of the current series. If we are able to look back in another thirty years our Western crisis may simply be an interlude of perpetual financial instability. Who knows, a third or even fourth financial crisis may even have afflicted Japan by then?

There are geo-political costs none of us can ignore. The US has been shown not to be the land of limitless opportunities. Foreign Treasury investors have, ironically, done relatively well out of the crisis, so reserve managers seem to have gained something. But the Treasury market may be a long-term loser if foreigners shun the market as they threaten to do. A bigger loser still may be the moral authority of America itself. In the past ten years it has gone from a point of unambiguous global dominance at the end of 1997 to having to ask for foreign aid through its government bond market. Along the way its moral authority was challenged by Iraq. The allies who fought most publicly alongside America in Iraq – and Afghanistan – were often also the countries that suffered most in the first wave of crisis: the UK, Spain, Denmark, Iceland, the Netherlands, Poland, the Czech Republic, Japan and South Korea. The major common feature of this 'coalition of the willing' turned out to be their propensity for rising household debt.

The American Dream was shown to be a mirage, or unattainable for many poorer Americans, through policies that set out to foist house ownership on the poor whether they wanted it or not. The extent of this crisis may mean it is much harder for entire countries, as well as individuals, to contemplate a better future. The benefits from financial crises we looked at (Scandinavian exports, high-tech and adaptability) in the past have depended on growth elsewhere. Almost every country in the West and many others are likely to suffer subdued growth for a prolonged period. There may be no engine of recovery to help with the adjustment, and so frame the benefits. There is likely to be some growth in Asian countries, but will there be the same desire for Western goods?

governments were the only agencies with enough ready access to credit

Governments were the only agencies with enough ready access to credit to be able to assist the banking sectors of America, the UK, Spain, the Netherlands, Germany and France. The entry of governments at the time was essential, but it leaves a difficult legacy. Government interference in the economy may impede, rather than aid adjustment – look at the support for Opel cars in Germany, which would not normally have received such government largesse.

Economic advance depends on research and development and experimentation, things that governments are notoriously poor at implementing. Also, the rescue of the banks has left a legacy of enormous and still rising government debt. The liabilities of the private sector (mortgage-backed securities, commercial lending and consumer loans) that caused problems for banks have been replaced with government debt. During a crisis this government debt is actually demanded by investors as they seek securities as close to 'central bank money' as possible. Government debt is a claim on the tax receipts of future populations; it is most credible as a claim, but it may also be debilitating for the taxpayers of the future, who would otherwise invest in more productive areas.

I suspect the current rash of crises is not over. We in the West are just part of a long line of borrowers and investors who have been fooled yet again by the strange tricks that international capital plays on financial markets. When we look back in another thirty years, if the advances in individual responsibility continue as they have in the past thirty, the consequences will be a steady stream of financial mistakes, another series of fools.

And strangely, on balance, this fooling should be welcomed. For the danger lies not in the crises themselves, but in our willingness to believe we can avoid them, or that we should avoid them altogether. The damage from the current crisis was due, in large part, to confidence that such disruption was no longer possible. The Great Moderation of low inflation, high growth, low unemployment and expanding international trade fooled us into forgetting a basic contradiction at the heart of monetary systems: that they are a medium of exchange but built upon our debts.

Perhaps a better suggestion would be to make every individual, or every company, a part owner of a bank, or act as a bank. The technology is available. Central banks need not be changed too much to accommodate the much wider provision of collateralised credit. The past twenty years have progressively offered individuals and companies the tools of finance previously limited to banks. We are, compared with the early 1980s, all bankers now. Why not move forward with a trend that seems unstoppable anyway? Regulation would be problematic, but perhaps no more so than car registration. The educational aspects alone of widening the banking base would probably be worth it.

Expanding the definition of banks would have other tangible benefits. The greatest problem of the current crisis is that it exposed how similar were many of the banks that got into trouble; similar in their business models, their exposures and their risks. A systemic banking crisis would not happen without an alignment of interests. It would also not happen if individuals were more attuned to the risks that permanently beset finance, and which have been a constant theme in this book. We need frequent reminding of the fragility of money. The problem may be not that there are too many banking crises, but that there are too few. The obvious fragility of money, which can disappear at a moment's notice, does not stay with us long enough.

So, is it all bad news? Not at all. Here are some benefits.

If our lives were unsustainably unbalanced they needed adjustment. Recessions are part of capitalism and generally they have been periods of high creativity. The less nimble are removed, or restructured. New markets are discovered, or emerge spontaneously; costs are cut, allowing for future pay rises to become more certain.

There are, for instance, benefits to the now inevitable restructure of General Motors. In ten years' time, if the right quality adjustments are made, and the innovations of Japanese manufacturers are reincorporated, it is possible the company will still be producing cars, and perhaps even making a profit.

The disappearance of old companies has benefits too; it allows the survivors to expand their market share and become more profitable, at least until new competitors emerge. There are still far too many car makers in the world, and a restructured GM is not going to solve the problems of the industry. Some large retailers, on the other hand, have disappeared, in the UK, US and even Germany – a country not known for its retail industry. For those that remain, the benefits of survival are already apparent, and they will be equally apparent to the lenders to these companies. Once the truly vulnerable have gone, there is a more rational assessment of the long-term viability of these survivors.

One industry that will also benefit from the opportunities of survivorship is the banking industry, whether it suffers future regulation or not. It is in the interests of governments to ensure their assistance works, and that their banking systems show long-term stability. Profitability is necessary for banks, and for the governments that have saved them. There may be fewer bankers around, but it will probably be a good time to be in the banking business. Banks, after all, know more about the problems than anyone else, including governments and regulators.

There are less obvious benefits too; recognition of necessity. For ten years or more it has been obvious that Western governments cannot afford the pension promises they made to future retirees. With government deficits expanding, it will be impossible to maintain the fiction that these pensions can be paid for much longer. Without reform, the costs of the ageing population will dwarf the cost – and perhaps dwarf the disruption – caused by the financial crisis. The fiscal illusions of many Western governments have been destroyed by the financial crisis – revenues based on property taxes, stamp duty and rising asset prices were simply unsustainable. Some fiscal arrangements need to be rebuilt. And in their rebuilding the future must be addressed. The priorities of countries need to be spelled out. Is it reasonable to assume that everyone can retire at 55, or 60, or 62? Or is it more sensible to consider raising the retirement age to 70, or abolishing it altogether?

There are benefits from the effect the crisis has had on the assumptions of the West. Not long ago – before the millennium – it was assumed the liberal capitalist democracy was the pinnacle, and final design, of government and human society. Something similar dominated the thinking of Robert Rubin and Larry Summers in the Clinton administration. No longer can we consider there is the 'end of history' that was implied in this assumption. If our institutions are to survive, they need work; there is nothing inevitable about liberal democracy, or capitalism, and if we value these institutions they need defending, and promoting. A crisis can offer salvation for modes of government, as well as challenges.

There are obvious benefits for non-Western countries. The relative wealth now controlled by China and to a lesser extent Russia has increased. Both have gained relative global power through the crisis, compared with a relative weakening of America. This may not please Westerners, who have lost, perhaps permanently, their privileged position of control. But it also reveals the competition that abounds in a globalised world. Even in 'developed' countries we cannot take for granted our own wealth; someone always wants to share it with us. Together we can make that wealth larger, for both developed and emerging economies. We cannot assume in the West that we are owed a higher standard of living just because we have become used to it.

> this may not please Westerners, who have lost, perhaps permanently, their privileged position of control

There is more to gain, too, from the continued growth of China, Brazil and India. The crisis has forced all three to reconsider how they spend their national wealth, and in particular how they invest reserves. A shift to domestic investment in these countries will benefit their citizens, who are the rightful owners of the money invested in reserves. Just as a rebalancing of the Western priorities is beneficial, so it is with a rebalancing of reserve managers' priorities.

Nor should we overlook the benefits that have accrued to workers in emerging economies. If the imbalances that did so much to create the financial crisis stemmed from reserve managers in these countries, it was also a sign of growing individual wealth of populations. Even with the financial crisis, the average worker in Europe, America and China is better off than ten years ago. It may not need financial crises to produce this net gain for everyone, but it does seem to be part of the process.

There are less tangible, but equally important benefits in revisiting the question of what is meant by financial trust, and how intimately it intersects with social trust. There are similar benefits from asking what we mean by money, and how it can grow and shrink so rapidly.

There are benefits to any challenge to orthodoxy, and our understanding of the operation of financial markets had become orthodox, and ossified. All participants knew that the dominant efficient market hypothesis was far from representative of human behaviour in a marketplace. We know humans are less rational, or more charitably, have different, equally valid but opposing reasons for their behaviour. How else to explain the seemingly illogical investment decisions of reserve managers, and the frankly dangerous investment decisions of Japanese households?

Disruption contains an intrinsic value too. What about the reaction of reserve managers? Could the disruption they have caused and experienced also turn into a benefit? Their love-affair with the dollar is not likely to end soon. The dollar attracts 80 per cent of all reserve manager flows because America possesses the most liquid debt markets in the world. It is inconceivable – to me – that reserve managers can turn away from high liquidity; it is a key component of their portfolio strategy. Other currencies do not come close to the depth and/or transparency of American markets. So, in the medium term reserve managers may act to stabilise the crisis by continuing in their previous behaviour. This is certainly the way they have acted so far. In any case, they are so deeply invested in American debt that they cannot extract themselves easily.

Yet there were growing signs even before the crisis that recycling of reserves could take different forms. In particular, the rise of sovereign wealth funds was a way to channel the same excess dollars into a wider variety of investments than US debt markets. The sovereign wealth funds lost a lot of money in the crisis because they were exposed to riskier assets – including mortgage bonds, and tranches of CDOs, as well as equities. In just the same way that hedge funds are likely to survive and adjust, so sovereign wealth funds are not likely to disappear. Strategically, diversification into 'real assets' such as mines and food production as well as conventional equities is likely to continue. This will bring its gains, even to countries like the UK that have consciously avoided large-scale manufacturing, because they may stand out as competitive producers of high quality goods.

These are not the kind of benefits that most people recognise, but they are benefits nonetheless. And the opportunities of the world keep growing bigger as physical distance seems to grow smaller. The Chinese have a long view of history, and it was the first premier of communist China who, when asked in 1971 what he thought of the French Revolution, is reputed to have said: 'It's too early to tell.' It is too early to tell what benefits may accrue from the crisis. My guess is that international communications will be at the heart of the benefits that do emerge, just as they were at the heart of fooling us.

Index

AB (asset-backed) regulation 187
affordable housing goals 205–6
agency bonds 75, 80, 208–9, 211–13
Alpha 152
Alt-A mortgages 212
Amazon 118, 249
Ambac 169
American Dream 266
appearance of money 70–1
Asian crisis 46–67
　aftermath 62–3
　and Chinese policies 47, 55–6,
　　57–9
　currency pegs 47, 48
　and fiscal policies 60
　and hedge funds 53–5
　IMF response 59–61
　and Japan 101
　and property investment 49–50,
　　51, 56–7
　Thailand 15, 27, 30, 48–52
Asian Development Bank 60
Asian Monetary Fund 101
asset prices 29–30
asset swapping 89
auditors 30
Aurora Loan Services (ALS) 167
Australia 105
Austrian banks 88
avoidance innovation 133–4, 139

baht 48, 49, 52
Baker, Richard H. 210
balance sheets 139, 145
balance of trade 6
Bali bombings 237
Bangkok International Banking
　Facility (BIBF) 48–9, 50

Bangkok Land Public Company 56
Bank of America 171
Bank Charter Act 28, 152
Bank for International Settlements
　(BIS) 72, 84, 104
Bank of Japan (BoJ) policies 97–9,
　103–4, 127
banking crises
　England 28, 38, 241
　Japan 99–105
　Savings and Loans banks 245
　Scandinavia 5–6, 15, 228, 230–1,
　　234–5, 244
bankruptcies 15
banks 19–20, 26–8
　Austrian 88
　bonuses 178–9
　commercial banks 24
　competition between 161, 170
　creating money 26
　fixed-income trading 164–71
　fractional banking 23
　fund management arms 162
　funding costs 163
　German 51, 77, 88, 90, 221
　government support 26, 27, 158,
　　159, 226, 266–7
　investment banks 160
　lax lending standards 77–8, 200
　liquidity risk 166–7
　losses 158, 180–1, 225
　matching assets and liabilities
　　91–2
　offshore banking centres 84
　originate and distribute model
　　145, 160, 182
　payments system 160, 161
　reserve system 23–4

role 160
Spanish 215
Swiss 85
value at risk (VaR) models 176–8,
    194–5
central banks
barter 24
Basle capital adequacy rules 28,
    150, 166, 189, 191, 192–7, 262
Bear Stearns 143, 165, 167, 168
Berlin Wall 17, 69, 113
Bernanke, Ben 74–5, 120–1, 122
Beta 152
bid-offer spreads 35
Bildt, Carl 233
Black-Scholes option pricing model
    106, 134–5, 137, 138
Blair, Tony 217
bonds
    agency bonds 75, 80, 208–9,
        211–13
    crowding out 40
    fixed-income trading 164–71
    futures contracts 140
    government bonds 31
        Europe 90–1, 214
        Japan 174
        Treasuries 37, 38, 40, 78–80,
            213
    and Japanese corporations 99
    liquidity 140–1
    monoline bond insurers 169
    mortgage bonds 73, 75, 77, 79,
        80, 105, 148, 165, 168, 173,
        205, 214
    power-reverse dual currency
        bonds 83
    railway bonds 186
    spreads 72–3, 109, 110, 170
        bonds 82–3, 86, 105
    yield curve 79, 81, 89, 105, 121,
        163, 170
    yields 79, 80
bonuses 178–9
Bradford & Bingley 77, 78
Brown, Gordon 217
bubbles 8–9, 35, 37, 38, 240–5
Buiter, Willem 155
Bush administration 74
Bush, George senior 230

Cameron, David 65–6, 201, 224,
    232
capital account liberalisation 60–1
capital controls 49, 57
capital flows 3–4, 12, 27, 30, 46
    after the Asian crisis 76
    from Japan 47, 69, 81–2, 84, 86,
        104–5
    to emerging economies 48
capital withdrawals 53, 54–5
Carlsson, Ingvar 233
carry trade 81, 85
Carter administration 203–4
cash 37–8
Cayman Islands 84
central banks 22–4, 31, 127, 163,
    173
    Bank of Japan (BoJ) 97–9, 103–4,
        127
    Federal Reserve 39, 78
        rate cuts 109–13, 117, 119, 120,
            122, 124
    independence 258–9
    role 96–7
    ECB (European Central Bank)
channel capacity 32–3
Chicago Board Options Exchange
    134–5
Chicago Board of Trade 34
China
    agency bond purchases 75, 80,
        208–9, 212, 222
    and the Asian crisis 47, 55–6,
        57–9
    capital controls 57
    currency policy 57, 74, 221
    currency reserves 47, 55, 58, 59,
        71–4
    cutting Treasury holdings 78–9
    domestic investment 270
    economic growth 257
    exports 58
    human rights 247
    investment in America 58
Citibank 61, 152, 196
Clementi, David 189–90
Clinton administration 63, 202–6
Cold War 16–17, 44, 64, 65–6, 255
collaterised debt obligations (CDOs)
    73, 90, 147, 148–9, 184, 188–9

commercial banks 24
commodity markets 34
communications 35–7, 44, 153–4,
    228, 240, 247
Community Reinvestment Act
    (1977) 203–4
competition
    between banks 161, 170
    and financial innovation 132–3,
        143–4
    national competition 263
consumption 6, 69, 229, 254–5
    and the housing market 201
contingent claims 144
convergence 87–9, 90–1, 106–9,
    136–7
convertibility of money 21–2, 28
Corbet, Kathleen 183, 190
costs of the crisis 225–6, 265
counterparty risk 144
Countrywide 168
covered bond market 214
Cox, Christopher 190
credit creation 28–30, 160–1
    booms 43–4
    instability 29–30
credit default swaps 142, 148,
    149–50, 155
credit rating agencies 149, 182–92,
    196, 222
Credit Rating Reform Act (2006)
    183
credit risk transfer 135
crises 4–6, 11, 246
    banking crises
        England 28, 38, 241
        Japan 99–105
        Savings and Loans banks 245
        Scandinavia 5–6, 15, 228,
            230–1, 234–5, 244
    common features 15
    Eastern Europe currency crisis
        264
    financial crises 225, 245–6
cross-border eurozone lending
    76–7, 92, 126, 215–17
crowding out 40–1, 58, 78–81, 222
currency pegs 47, 48
currency reserves 39–40, 47, 69–74,
    253

China 47, 55, 58, 59, 71–4
    Indonesia 59
    Japan 71, 72
    Korea 59
    Malaysia 59
    Philippines 59
    reserve managers 39–40, 41, 56,
        68–9, 180
    Russia 71
    shift out of the dollar 75
    Thailand 59
Currency School 28
current account balance
    deficits 50, 60, 72, 75, 179,
        219–20
    Japan 85
    surpluses 220

debt 15, 22, 25–6
    fear of default 25, 27, 29, 43
    from recycled foreign reserves 70
    and growth 26–7
    lax lending standards 77–8, 200
    repayment from future wealth 26
defence spending 230
deflation 103, 104, 120–2
demographics 27, 239
Deng Xiaioping 247
Depfa 90, 213–15
deregulation 18–21, 27, 37, 150–1,
    229
derivatives 134–6
    collaterised debt obligations
        (CDOs) 73, 90, 147, 148–9,
        184, 188–9
    contingent claims 144
    costs of strategies 143
    counterparty risk 144
    futures markets 131, 139–40
    growth rates 148
    IMM (International Money
        Market) dates 142–3
    options 106, 129, 134–5, 137, 148
    OTC (over-the-counter) products
        141–2
    standardisation of contracts 155
    structured investment vehicles
        (SIVs) 150–2, 162, 170
    swaps 136, 138–9, 141–2, 148,
        149–50, 155

Desai, Padma 56
devaluations 48, 52, 53, 60, 254–5
Dexia 213–15
Dillon Read Capital Management 162, 172
disappearance of money 30–1, 33, 45, 51, 53
discounted cash flow 42
dollar 12, 17, 40, 47, 113–14, 252–3, 254
    currency pegs 47, 48
    strong dollar policy 63, 66
dot-com crash 8, 42, 103, 113–19, 165, 248
    ILoveYou virus 118–19
    millennium bug 116–18

Eastern Europe 27, 69–70, 91
    currency crisis 264
eBay 249
ECB (European Central Bank) 31, 79, 88, 92–3, 125–7, 175–6, 259–60
    acceptable collateral 163
    interest rate policy 125–6, 162–3
efficiency innovation 133–4, 135
Efficient Market Hypothesis 131–2
electronics industry 100
Ellington Capital Management 110
EMC 168–9
ERM (Exchange Rate Mechanism) 217, 264
Euribor swap market 89
Eurodollar market 131
European Bank of Reconstruction and Development 70
eurozone 87–91
    asset swapping 89
    convergence trades 87–9, 90–1
    cross-border lending 76–7, 92, 126, 215–17
    damage to the banking system 94
    Euribor swap market 89
    financial integration 92–3, 97
    government bonds 90–1, 214
    housing market 213–17
    launch of the single currency 71, 97
    losses of the banks 158
    monetary policy 88
    regulation 263
    synthetic credit derivatives 92–3
    yield curve 89
exchange traded funds 130
exporting countries 6, 255

Fannie Mae 47, 75, 80, 143, 165, 200, 204–13
    accounting practices 209–10
    conservatorship 212–13
fear of default 25, 27, 29, 43
Federal Reserve 39, 78
    rate cuts 109–13, 117, 119, 120, 122, 124
fiat money 21, 22
financial crises 225, 245–6
financial futures 131, 139–40
financial innovation 128–56, 175–6
    avoidance innovation 133–4, 139
    and competition 132–3, 143–4
    credit risk transfer 135
    efficiency innovation 133–4, 135
    Eurodollar market 131
    exchange traded funds 130
    future of 154–6
    need for 129–31
    and regulation 130–1, 145–6, 150
    regulatory arbitrage 151
    risk transfer 144
    securitisation 135, 144–8, 150, 161, 170, 171, 187–8, 220
    and technology 130, 132–3, 153–4
financial integration 92–3, 97
Financial Services Modernization Act 115
financial spread betting 153
financial stability 96, 258
Financial Stability Forum 262
Finland 5, 230–1, 244–5
    EU membership 234–5
    unemployment 230
First Bangkok City 61
fiscal policies 122, 217–18, 269
    and the Asian crisis 60
Fitch Ratings 183
fixed-income trading 164–71
floating currencies 48
foreclosures 154
foreign exchange 39–40

baht 48, 49, 52
  Chinese policies 57, 74, 221
  devaluations 48, 52, 53, 60, 254–5
  floating currencies 48
  yen 71, 72, 81, 82
fractional banking 23
Freddie Mac 47, 75, 80, 123, 143,
    165, 200, 204–13
  accounting practices 209–10
  conservatorship 212–13
Friedman, Thomas 186–7
functions of finance 128–9
fund management arms 162
funding costs of banks 163
future wealth 26–7
futures markets 131, 139–40

Galbraith, J.K. 6, 8, 129–30
General Motors 268–9
Germany
  banks 51, 77, 88, 90, 221
  Berlin Wall 17, 69, 113
  covered bond market 214
  demographics 239
  export reliance 255
  wages 220–1
Giovanni, Alberto 107–8
Glass-Steagall Act 115, 242
globalisation 3–4, 9, 37, 63, 248
  and Japan 99–101
gold 21–2
Goldman Sachs 167, 172
golf developments 50
Google 164, 187, 248, 249
Gorbachev, Mikhail 230
Gordian Knot 152
government bonds 31
  European 90–1, 214
  Japan 174
  Treasuries 37, 38, 40, 78–80, 213
government debt 179, 226
  Latin America 193
government support of banks 26,
    27, 158, 159, 226, 266–7
Gramlich, Edward 206
Gramm-Leach-Bliley Act 115
Great Crash (1929) 6–7, 15, 39, 246
Great Depression 229
Great Moderation 169–70, 174, 267
greed and risk 1–2, 7–8, 40

Greenspan, Alan 65, 81
  and the current account deficit
    75
  and the dot-com crash 113–14
  on Fannie Mae and Freddie Mac
    210–11
  and financial innovation 59,
    155–6, 175–6
  on house prices 123–4
  and the internet 249
  on regulatory capital arbitrage
    151
  on technology 256
  on technology and productivity
    116
Greenspan put 111–13

Hamilton, Carl 233
Hashimoto, Ryutaro 98
hedge funds 8, 43, 260–1
  and the Asian crisis 53–5
  bank owned 162
  borrowings 84–5
  carry trade 81, 85
  collapse 110
    Long Term Capital
        Management 108–10
Highbridge Capital 162
Hokkaido Takushoku Bank 101–2
homelessness 238
Housewives of Tokyo 82–3
Housing Act (1990) 206
Housing Loan Administration
    Corporation 101
housing market 198–224
  affordable housing goals 205–6
  boom and bust 77–8, 87, 105,
    120, 201–2, 219–22
  and consumption 201
  and current account deficits
    219–20
  and current account surpluses
    220
  distortions 222–3
  eurozone 213–17
  Japan 201–2
  politics of home ownership
    200–2
  Right to Buy policy 201
  role in financial crises 199

social inclusion 202–3
and taxation 217–18
United States 120, 122, 123, 124,
202–13

Iceland 191
IG Index 153, 261
ILoveYou virus 118–19
IMF (International Monetary Fund)
58, 252–3
response to the Asian crisis
59–61
IMM (International Money Market)
dates 142–3
independence of central banks
258–9
individualism 202
Indonesia
capital controls 49
currency meltdown 52
currency reserves 59
demographics 239
IMF loan conditions 61
political change 237
property investment 51
inflation 38–9, 80, 96, 115, 120
information access 154
information flows 44
infrastructure spending 69–70
interest rate swaps 138–9, 141–2
interest rates 38–9, 80, 96, 121,
162–3
ECB policy 125–6, 162–3
in Japan 82, 98, 103
Libor 163
rate rises 163
US rate cuts 109–13, 117, 119,
120, 122, 124
internet 9, 154, 248–9
invalid transactions 32
investment banks 160
investment opportunities 12, 13,
17, 40–1
investment returns 34, 37–8, 69
Ireland 179
(Shiller) 8–9
Italian bonds 214

Japan 11, 12, 15, 30, 55, 81–6
and the Asian crisis 101

Bank of Japan (BoJ) policies 97–9,
103–4, 127
banking crisis 99–105
bond finance 99
currency reserves 71, 72
current account balance 85
deflation 103, 104
demographics 239
electronics industry 100
export of capital 47, 69, 81–2, 84,
86, 104–5
and globalisation 99–101
government bonds 174
homelessness 238
house prices 201–2
Housewives of Tokyo 82–3
Housing Loan Administration
Corporation 101
interest rates 82, 98, 103, 101,
99–100
lost decade 97–9, 238
money supply 85, 104
political change 238–9
property market 100, 102, 219
quantitative easing 103–5
regulation 102–3
share prices 98
unemployment 238
bonds 82–3, 86, 105
wages 220
zombie loans 86–7
Jewish financiers 53
JPMorgan 162, 101, 99–100

Keynes, Maynard 25, 38
King, Mervyn 8, 171
Koivisto, Mauno 234
Koizumi, Junichiro 238–9
Korea
capital controls 49
currency reserves 59
foreigners buying up assets 60–1,
62
IMF loan conditions 62
property investment 51

Landesbanks 90, 126
Latin American government debt
193
Law of Large Numbers 154

Leach, Jim 63
Lehman Brothers 143, 159–60, 165, 167–8, 169
lending standards 77–8, 200
Levitt, Arthur 111
Libor 163
Lichtblau, John 66
liquidity 33–5, 41–3
  of bond markets 140–1
  capital controls 49
  capital withdrawals 53, 54–5
  central bank policies 127
  investment returns 34, 37–8
  market prices 42
  removal of liquidity 42–3, 45
  and the yield curve 121
liquidity risk 166–7
local authority borrowings 82
Lockhart, James 207
London Stock Exchange 34
Long Term Capital Management 87, 89, 102, 105–13, 136
  bail-out 110–13
  borrowings 106–7
  collapse 108–10
  trading strategies 106–7
losses of banks 158, 180–1, 225

McCreevy, Charles 176
McCulley, Paul 151
McDonough, William 113
Malaysia 53
  currency meltdown 52
  currency reserves 59
  property investment 51
margin calls 141
markets 34–5, 36–7
  bid-offer spreads 35
  supply and demand 42
Marshall Plan 64
matching assets and liabilities 91–2
medium of exchange 24–5, 31–2, 33, 159
Menger, Carl 24–5, 31–2, 33
Meriwether, John 106, 109
Merrill Lynch 167
Merton, Robert 89, 106, 128, 129, 135, 136–7, 143, 145–6
Mexico 27
Microsoft 118

Mieno, Yasushi 98
Mill, John Stuart 29
millennium bug 116–18
monetary policy
  eurozone 88
  Japan 85, 104
money 10–11, 17, 21–6
  appearance 70–1
  barter 24
  central bank money 22–4, 31, 163, 173
  convertibility 21–2, 28
  creating 26
  disappearance 30–1, 33, 45, 51, 53
  fiat money 21, 22
  medium of exchange 24–5, 31–2, 33, 159
  neo-classical view 25
  paper money 21
  purchasing power of individuals 29
  stock of money 29
  supply controls 28
  transactional money 32–3, 34
  and trust 22–3, 30, 157–8, 226
  velocity of money 29
monoline bond insurers 169
Moody's 183, 186–8, 190–1
Morgan Stanley 165–7, 172
mortgage bonds 43, 73, 75, 77, 79, 80, 105, 148, 165, 168, 173, 205
mortgage lending 24, 123–4, 146, 164–5, 169, 172, 199–200
  Alt-A mortgages 212
  subprime 40–1, 43, 78, 170–4, 200, 204–7, 212
Muang Thong Thani (MTT) scheme 56–7

National Homeownership Strategy 203
neo-classical view of money 25
new market entrants 9, 10
New Zealand 83, 105
Nishimura, Kiyohiko 83
Nokia 228, 244–5
Nordic banking crisis 5–6, 15, 228, 230–1, 234–5, 244
Northern Rock 77, 143

Norway 230–1
NRSRO ratings 184

Obama, Barak 231, 253–4
Obuchi, Keizo 102
off-balance sheet instruments 139, 144, 145
offshore banking centres 84
OFHEO 165
oil prices 66, 131
oil producing countries 72
options 106, 129, 134–5, 137, 148
  Black-Scholes option pricing model 140
originate and distribute model 145, 160, 182
Osaka Castle Park 238
OTC (over-the-counter) products 141–2
Overend and Gurney 241

Padoa-Schioppa, Tommaso 215–16
Papadia, Francesco 135
paper money 21
Paulson, Hank 160
pay policies 178–9
payments system 160, 161
peace dividend 230
Peel, Robert 28, 214
Philippines
  currency meltdown 52
  currency reserves 59
  property investment 51
Phongpaichit, Pasuk 236
Pitchford, John 50
Plunge Protection Team 111
politics 226
  of home ownership 200–2
  Indonesia 237
  Japan 238–9
  Sweden 231, 233
  Thailand 236–7
  third way 234
  United Kingdom 232
  United States 231
population changes 27, 239
power-reverse dual currency bonds 83
price trends 42
private sector investors 73

productivity 116, 119
purchasing power of individuals 29

quantitative easing 103–5

racism 226
radio ownership 242–4
railway mania 35, 186, 240
Raines, Franklin 207–8
rating agencies 149, 182–92, 196, 222
real estate investment
  and the Asian crisis 49–50, 51, 56–7
  Indonesia 51
  investment returns 219
  Japan 100, 102, 219
  Korea 51
  Malaysia 51
  Philippines 51
  REITs 219
  Thailand 51, 56–7
  and wealth creation 27
recessions 225
Reform Bill (1867) 241
regulation 16, 19–20, 262–3
  AB (asset-backed) regulation 187
  Basle rules 28, 150, 166, 189, 191, 192–7, 262
  eurozone 263
  and financial innovation 130–1, 145–6, 150
  Japan 102–3
regulatory arbitrage 151
REITs (real estate investment trusts) 219
relative value arbitrage 106
repayer of last resort 21–2
repurchase agreements (repos) 163–4
reserve managers 39–40, 41, 56, 68–9, 180
reserve system
  banks 23–4
Right to Buy policy 201
risk models 176–8
risk transfer 144
Robertson, Julian 54
Roosevelt, Franklin D. 241–2, 253–4

Rubin, Robert 63–5, 68, 94, 101, 111, 203, 251
Russia
  currency reserves 71
  debt default 102, 108

Sanyo Securities 101
savings 69, 74, 221, 229
Savings and Loans banks 245
Scandinavian banking crisis 5–6, 15, 228, 230–1, 234–5, 244
Scholes, Myron 106, 129, 150
SEC (Securities and Exchange Commission) 184, 187, 248
securitisation 84, 85, 90, 135, 144–8, 150, 161, 170, 171, 187–8, 220
Senate Banking Committee 190
September 11th 119–20, 177–8
share prices 98, 115, 118
Shiller, Robert J. 8–9, 42
Shinawatra, Thaksin 236
Sigma 152
Snow, John 210–11
social costs 226
social inclusion 202–3
social network banking 154
social networking websites 248
Soros, George 53, 54
sovereign wealth funds 271
Soviet Union 17, 229–30
Spain 51, 77, 126, 179
  banks 215
  unemployment 226
spreads 72–3, 109, 110, 170
stamp duty 218
Standard & Poor's 183, 186, 187, 190–1
standardisation of derivatives contracts 155
stock of money 29
structured investment vehicles (SIVs) 150–2, 162, 170
subprime lending 40–1, 43, 78, 170–4, 200, 204–7, 212
Summers, Larry 65–6, 68, 76, 203, 254, 261
swaps 136, 138–9, 141–2, 148, 149–50, 155
Sweden 230–1

defence spending 230
EU membership 233–4
politics 231, 233
unemployment 230
welfare policy 231
Switzerland 85, 221
synthetic credit derivatives 92–3

Takeda Pharmaceuticals 86
tally sticks 25
taxation 122, 217–18
TDK 86
technology 9, 10, 11, 13, 17, 35–6, 228
  and financial innovation 130, 132–3, 153–4
Templeton Funds 107
Thailand 235–7
  and the Asian crisis 15, 27, 30, 48–52
  recovery 235–6
  currency reserves 59
  foreign borrowings 50–1
  political change 236–7
  property investment 51, 56–7
Thatcher, Margaret 65–6, 201, 224, 232
third way 234
Tokio Marine 86
total return swaps 136
transactional finance 25
transactional money 32–3, 34
Treasury Bonds/Bills 37, 38, 40, 78–80, 213
Trichet, Jean-Claude 93
Trump, Donald 50
trust 22–3, 30, 157–8, 226
Tucker, Paul 155
Turner, Lord 147, 157–8, 263–4

UBS 162, 171–6
unemployment 15, 226, 230, 238
  United Kingdom 248
  United States 229, 241
United States 63–7, 251–8
  American Dream 266
  Bush administration 74
  Carter administration 203–4
  Clinton administration 63, 202–6

Index

Community Reinvestment Act (1977) 203–4
consumers 69, 229, 254–5
Credit Rating Reform Act (2006) 183
current account deficit 72, 75
Federal deficit 179
Financial Services Modernization Act 115
future of 253–7
Housing Act (1990) 206
housing boom 120, 122, 123, 124, 202–13
moral authority 266
Obama administration 253–4
political change 231
population growth 239
rate cuts 109–13, 117, 119, 120, 122, 124
Roosevelt recession 241
Savings and Loans banks 245
securities markets 255–6, 271
Senate Banking Committee 190
share prices 115, 118
strong dollar policy 63, 66
tax cuts 122
trade policies 63–4

unemployment 229, 241
USB 144

valid transactions 32
value at risk (VaR) models 176–8, 194–5
Veblen goods 41–2, 50
velocity of money 29
Volker, Paul 96

wages 220–1
Wall Street Crash (1929) 6–7, 15, 39, 246
welfare policies 226, 231
World Bank 49, 60
World Trade Center attacks 119–20, 177–8

Yamaichi Securities 101
yen 71, 72, 81, 82
yield curve 79, 81, 89, 105, 121, 163, 170
yields 79, 80
YouWalkAway.com 154

Zoellick, Robert 225
zombie loans 86–7